A THOROUGHLY UNHELPFUL HISTORY *of* AUSTRALIAN SPORT

Writer and broadcaster Titus O'Reily was born in Melbourne and raised by the Sisters of Collective Misery, a kindly but sombre order who placed an emphasis on sport above all other things, including religion. As a writer, Titus has carved out a reputation for inaccuracy and being difficult to work with. His unique take on sport has been hailed by some of the most respected figures in sport as 'awful', 'childish' and 'barely comprehensible'.

titusoreily.com

A THOROUGHLY UNHELPFUL HISTORY of AUSTRALIAN SPORT

TITUS O'REILY

MICHAEL JOSEPH
an imprint of
PENGUIN BOOKS

MICHAEL JOSEPH

UK | USA | Canada | Ireland | Australia
India | New Zealand | South Africa | China

Penguin Books is part of the Penguin Random House group of companies
whose addresses can be found at global.penguinrandomhouse.com.

Penguin
Random House
Australia

First published by Penguin Random House Australia Pty Ltd, 2017

10 9 8 7 6 5 4 3 2 1

Text copyright © Titus O'Reily, 2017

The moral right of the author has been asserted.

All rights reserved. Without limiting the rights under copyright reserved above, no part
of this publication may be reproduced, stored in or introduced into a retrieval system, or
transmitted, in any form or by any means (electronic, mechanical, photocopying, recording
or otherwise), without the prior written permission of both the copyright owner and the
above publisher of this book.

Cover design by Alex Ross © Penguin Random House Australia Pty Ltd
Cover illustration by Adolph Friedländer
Author photo by Jay Hynes
Text design by Louisa Maggio © Penguin Random House Australia Pty Ltd
Typeset in Sabon and Brandon Grotesque by Midland Typesetters, Australia
Colour separation by Splitting Image Colour Studio, Clayton, Victoria
Printed and bound in Australia by Griffin Press, an accredited ISO AS/NZS 14001
Environmental Management Systems printer.

National Library of Australia
Cataloguing-in-Publication data:

 O'Reily, Titus, author.
 A thoroughly unhelpful history of Australian sport / Titus O'Reily.
 9780143785217 (paperback)

 Sports – Australia – History.

penguin.com.au

CONTENTS

TWENTY-FOUR MILLION MAD PEOPLE

When you look at Australians today, you are seeing the most sports-obsessed people in the world. Twenty-four million people (barring some traitors to the cause) fixated on winning, following the exploits of athletes and placing the best ones on the highest pedestal. This obsession with sport is like some madness has taken hold; after all, why would the most obese nation on earth value athletic ability above all other traits?

The reason is that sport is the closest thing Australia has to a culture, to the point that even the few Australians who hate sport define themselves by their opposition to it. You know, it's the person at a barbecue who says, 'I'm not really into sport because it's just pointless,' and everyone just stares at them and then makes a mental note to never invite them to anything ever again.

While it's impossible to know how many Australians don't like sport, researchers put the number as high as twenty people.

So when you look at Australian sport today, you are seeing one of the most competitive sporting markets in the world. Given our population, there are more leagues, more participants, more spectators than anywhere else.

As Australia found its feet as a nation, it became clear that when it came to sporting ability, we were blessed like no other country. It's as if the very soil we grew our crops in, the water that fell from the sky and the sheep we hugged at night all contributed to breeding the perfect physical specimen. While those from our motherland suffered crippling vitamin D deficiencies, we Australians got a year's worth from the sun every hour, even when sitting inside. It made us the lithe, tanned Adonises you see around you everywhere today.

It was not long before it became obvious that while England had invented sports, we had mastered them, and then invented some new ones because we got bored.

As our nation grew, it was sport that defined us. Like a younger sibling, we were desperate to prove to the older countries that we mattered, that we had our own place in the world. When Australians started to win international sporting events, we looked at each other and said, 'This! This is what we are good at, this is our thing.' We may be a country isolated from the great civilisations of the world but we can run, jump, kick, swim and tackle better than the French, the Americans, the Chinese, the Brazilians and a lot better than the English.

In 1962, *Sports Illustrated* named Australia the most sports-obsessed country in the world. We were also named the second and third most obsessed. Sporting achievements have come to define this sunburnt country as a nation of athletes or, more accurately, a nation of people who watch athletes. Sporting success has always been the measure of our sense of worth, a commodity so fragile that it is always just a bad Olympics away from plummeting.

Sure, we appreciate the rather desperate attempts by scientists and artists to get our attention, but inventing the bionic ear, wi-fi, the black box flight recorder, penicillin and the Hills hoist doesn't come close to Don Bradman's career batting average, Rod Laver completing the Grand Slam twice or Brendon Fevola winning *I'm a Celebrity Get Me Out of Here.*

Perhaps the only Aussie invention that matches our top sporting moments was the wine cask, which supports our second-greatest love: drinking. Here, too, sport has had its influence. Many drinks are consumed in celebration of a victory and many more following a loss.[*]

In this sunburnt land, the athlete is king, free to do as they please and be forgiven afterwards. While other countries assign social standing based on family ties, wealth or intelligence, in Australia, being able to do something in the sporting arena places you higher than the prime minister or any captain of industry. Middle-aged business people will cross rooms to get their photo taken with twenty-year-old footballers and not even think that's weird.

Therefore, to understand Australia, you must understand its sporting history. The current sporting landscape is a heady mixture of the arrogance of Victoria, the narcissism of New South Wales, the isolation of Western Australia, the madness of the Northern Territory, the nothingness of Canberra, the shadiness of Queensland, the tedium of South Australia and the irrelevance of Tasmania.

People often complain that Australian history is boring, yet while we may not have a giant civil war like the United States, we do have the Bodyline series, arguably a more brutal and globally important event. We may not have had a revolution like France but we did have the Super League war and World Series Cricket, whose legacies cast longer shadows across the globe than the disagreements of 1789. Australia may not have had the Hundred Years' War but we did have the Essendon supplements saga, which went on just as long and certainly resulted in more tweets and Facebook posts.

---

[*] It's no surprise that the greatest ever achievement by an Australian involved a sportsman and drinking. In 1989, when the Australian cricket team flew to England to play for the Ashes, those on the plane were unaware they were about to witness greatness: David Boon downing fifty-two cans of beer. But perhaps the most amazing part of the feat was the fact that Boon was still sober and only stopped with the beer because he realised there were free spirits available on the plane.

The story of Australian sport is one of continued success punctuated by regular scandals, usually involving excessive alcohol consumption and an alarming amount of public urination. What began as a disorganised, amateur leisure pursuit has become a ruthless, billion-dollar industry, more important than politics, family and life itself.

From the earliest days on this continent, when Indigenous people played a wide variety of sports, to the British arriving and the nation's federation, sport has become increasingly organised and lucrative.

Once it was apparent that Australians would follow sport with an enthusiasm usually reserved for boy bands and cults, people worked out there was money to be made. Money has allowed some sports to grow into massive industries while others receive less attention than street theatre. Once sponsors, betting companies and TV networks realised the size of the audience that live sport could deliver, they poured money into the various codes like it was a scene from *The Wolf of Wall Street*.

WATCHING INSTEAD OF PLAYING

Almost two in three Australian adults are obese, despite their obsession with sport. Rather than playing sport, Australians seem to prefer watching it, and while watching it they see more fast food ads. Chicken nuggets may be the biggest threat to Australia's sporting dominance.

This influx of cold hard cash changed the very nature of sport. Money demands professionalism and the more money there is, the more professionalism is expected. Gone were the days when you could light up a smoke at quarter time, or play still slightly drunk from the night before. With big business now in bed with the various sporting codes, growing revenue became as important as the game itself.

A lot of positives have come from this, including better

stadiums, better broadcasting and a higher standard of play. But it hasn't been all good. It's introduced awful terms like 'stakeholders' and 'leadership groups' into the sporting vernacular and has led to an overabundance of marketers, management consultants and Pat Howard. It has split codes in two, created new leagues and made millionaires out of people who would normally have been PE teachers or personal trainers.

The march of professionalism, and sporting clubs operating as businesses first, has resulted in fans increasingly being seen as 'revenue streams' and the favouring of broadcasters and sponsors over the grassroots. In some ways this isn't surprising. If someone gave me a billion dollars every five years, I'd be paying a lot of attention to them too. On the other hand, those broadcasters and sponsors wouldn't be so interested in forking out Olympic swimming pools of cash if all those grassroots fans weren't following every moment.

It's a delicate balance for modern sport; pleasing fans as well as the corporations with piles of money is not always an easy tightrope to walk. To complicate things further, governments have also involved themselves in sport. While politics is a whole other lens to view sport through, it too comes back to money: where corporations want customers and revenue, governments want reflected glory and votes.

At a national level, governments and sport administrators are currently fighting about how to distribute taxpayer money. There's nothing better than taxpayer dollars; money you don't have to work for is always better, and in sport there's lots of it. The argument is only about where to put that money. Give it to the Olympic sports that have the best chance of winning us gold medals or to the sports the majority of Australians actually play?

Why are money, sport and politics so intertwined in Australia that they are impossible to separate? The reason is quite simple:

TOP FIVE REASONS PEOPLE DON'T LIKE SPORT

1. Hate life
2. Communist agent
3. Significant psychological disorder
4. Weren't loved as a child
5. Barrack for the Richmond Tigers

when it comes to sport, we Australians are mad. Completely, irrationally insane, with no sense of perspective.

Australians can handle the sporting scandals but we will not tolerate losing. Losing is something that, frankly, we're not interested in. It is essential to our sense of self, as important to us as wine is to the French, the sea is to the British and mentally ill people having access to guns is to the Americans.

Sure, some of the rubbish countries may accept losing, but being happy with being an average sporting nation makes you a traitor to the values of this wide brown land. Across gender, race, religion, sexuality, hair colour and star signs, we love playing and watching sport.

How did a nation of 24 million people end up with a culture that revolves around sport, from corporate CEOs to the lowest end of society, the reality TV stars? How has it attracted so much money and power? How did we get here? How did we all end up with this madness?

I'm glad you asked.

PART

I

THE VIEW FROM THE
TOP OF THE STAND

o provide a detailed history of Australian sport would require hundreds of books, each longer than a phone book.* I know you don't have time for that, you're already stressed about all the TV series you can't get through.

Think of this as the view from high up in the grandstand, the key bits to understanding why Australian sport is the way it is. It's not an attempt to give equal coverage to every sport, it's an attempt to show why some sports came to dominate the landscape and others** did not.

In this section, I'll take a whole lot of things you found tiresome at school and explain how they affected sport, and are therefore actually interesting. Take for example the gold rush, which becomes fascinating when you realise all those hairy, dirty men hanging out in mud helped spread sporting codes around the country as well as venereal disease. Other issues, like class (or lack thereof), are interesting when you see how they influenced the popularity of some sports. Even politics is no longer a subject you'd move suburbs to avoid talking about when you consider how political agendas shaped sport, including how your taxpayer dollars are probably funding a stadium for a team you hate.

Of course the sort of money and power involved in sport always makes for interesting reading, because the combination inevitably leads to corruption. And corruption is always fun to read about because it's a heady mix of brazen self-interest and spectacular stupidity.

Most importantly, you will come to appreciate how the common pursuit of beating the English in as many sports as possible united a young nation and drove it to become the greatest society humanity has ever seen.

---

* For younger readers: a phone book was a directory of everyone's phone numbers. Phone books were very thick and heavy, and useful for all sorts of things, like as a booster seat for kids or extracting a confession from a suspect.
** Such as table tennis, the sleeping giant of Australian sports.

FROM LITTLE THINGS

A novel approach some historians have taken recently is to mention that there were people in Australia before boatloads of white people showed up and set up shop. I suppose it did only last 50 000 odd years, but it would be nice if we knew a bit more about Australian sport in that pre-colonial era. A lot of what we do know comes from anecdotal evidence and, as anyone who listens to their friends' stories knows, anecdotal evidence is about as trustworthy as, well, your mates. Plus, a lot of this anecdotal evidence is from those white settlers, and they tended to present a rather unflattering portrait of Indigenous society. Luckily that's all changed these days.

What we do know is there seems to have been a lot of sport being played by the many groups located across the continent. Some, like the ball game marngrook from Victoria, involved large groups of people kicking a ball and, from available descriptions, it seemed to be chaotic, played in slightly different variants from group to group.

It's been claimed marngrook influenced the development of Australian Rules Football. Tom Wills, one of the sport's founders, is said to have witnessed marngrook when he was growing up in Western Victoria. There has been a lot of pushback against this theory in recent years, on the basis that there's no evidence. I say it's more fun to just believe that it is true. As we've all learnt in recent times, facts are overrated anyway.

Woggabaliri, another Indigenous sport, was documented in New South Wales and involved keeping a ball off the ground for as long as possible. While we don't know every type of sport played throughout the long pre-colonial period, it's clear sport was important in Indigenous culture and has remained so in the modern day. These sports seemed to be not unlike the various school sports played in England at the time: there were no agreed rules, they seemed to be made up as the game went along, and the matches were highly localised and played on a random basis.

As well as a love of sports, Indigenous people were the first Australians to experience another dominant cultural trait: not being thrilled that a bunch of migrants have shown up who don't want to adjust to the existing way of life.

LET'S TRY MAKING THIS ENGLAND

When the convicts arrived on Australian shores in 1788, they couldn't believe the English government had sent them to such a remote place. Except for the oldest continuous culture on the planet, it was completely empty.

Right there and then, the convicts gathered in a circle and vowed to develop a sporting nation that would one day rise up and defeat the English at the very sports they had invented. Some may say this story is apocryphal, and it almost certainly is, given I just made it up, but that doesn't make it any less true.

In the early days of the colony, Australia's newest residents were incredibly preoccupied with staying alive, some would say to an unhealthy degree. Hunger, disease and the work of displacing the Indigenous population all made conditions in the early days of the colony suboptimal for sporting pursuits. The few popular sports were 'killing something to eat', 'building a shelter', 'surviving dysentery' and 'wanting to go home'.

But hardship served a purpose. It bound the colonists together, especially the convicts, and created the great Aussie tradition of 'mateship', which is like friendship on steroids, something future athletes would become all too familiar with. This spirit of mateship has been identified as one of the keys to Australian sporting teams performing so well.* I suppose Australians thinking they have a superior sense of friendship could be seen as arrogant, but it's not. Australians are very modest. I reckon Australians are better at being modest than any other country, and by a very large margin.

Despite the challenges posed by not dying, the early Europeans did bring with them a love of organised sport. Lieutenant George Johnston, for example – reputedly first ashore at Port Jackson – was a keen breeder of racehorses, bringing to Australian shores that wonderful relationship between rich people and racehorses. It wasn't long before Australians could fix a horserace with the best of them.

Other sports were played to pass the time. Cockfighting was popular (now illegal to protect the animals) and two blokes belting each other always drew a crowd (still legal, with little interest shown in protecting the individuals). Shooting things, often animals, was also enjoyed by many, so much so they introduced foxes and rabbits for the sole purpose of shooting them. It's a decision the farmers of Australia and our native wildlife have appreciated ever since.

As the colony grew and starvation and death became slightly less of a worry, the colonists turned to their favourite hobby: making everything as similar to England as possible. Not only did this

---

* As well as sticking together on the field, mateship in sport often involves lying to cover for a teammate who's done something incredibly stupid. For example, Collingwood's Heath Shaw lied about teammate Alan Didak being in his car when Shaw crashed while three times over the legal alcohol limit.

mean mimicking the architecture of England, planting European trees and getting rid of the Indigenous population, it meant playing English sports.

The timing of the establishment of a convict colony in New South Wales and the subsequent waves of migration explain a lot about why some sports caught on in Australia and some didn't. It was all about what was happening in the mother country at the time.

In 1788, England had plenty of sporting activity going on. Cricket was already established, for example the Marylebone Cricket Club had just been formed in 1787, and horseracing was well underway with the Jockey Club at Newmarket established in 1751. Golf, that delightful combination of walking, bad fashion and frustration, was also becoming organised, with the now famous Royal and Ancient Golf Club of St Andrews underway from 1754.

'Football', on the other hand, was taking longer to get organised. It was little more than a loose term that described a wide variety of games played at English boarding schools. These were often just huge roving mauls, where grown men tried to move a ball around a giant piece of land through any means possible, often with no discernible aim. It seemed to be more of an excuse for mass hugging. There were variants of football games played at Cambridge, Eton and the Rugby School, to name just a few, and they all argued for the relative benefits of their own rules.

Attempts to codify all the versions had not even begun when Australia was colonised, and codes adopted by more than one school or area took even longer to sort out. It took the English until 1863 to establish what became the Football Association, which oversaw the codification of association football's (soccer's) rules, and Rugby Union's rules were only approved in 1871.

The arguments that defined these two football codes, and ultimately split them, came down to two main issues. The first was whether you could pick up the ball and run with it. There was a deep schism between the two codes over this, fought with religious zeal. The second issue is less well known, but became a major argument in the early formation of Australian Rules too. That issue was 'hacking', which meant kicking an opponent in the shins. Yes, being able to kick someone in the shins was seen as a God-given right by some, and a move by the Football Association to ban it in their original rules was met with outcry by the shin-kickers.

Francis Campbell, who played for the Blackheath club in London, argued outlawing hacking would 'do away with all the courage and pluck from the game, and I will be bound to bring over a lot of Frenchmen who would beat you with a week's practice'.

I can just imagine the reaction. Bringing the French into it was a deadly insult at the time. It probably still is in England, if Brexit is anything to go by. Now, I enjoy an occasional kick in the shins as much as the next person, but the fact it was considered a fun part of the game shows that people really were wired differently back then.

Those who preferred not to be kicked in the shins went off to form soccer and those who loved nothing more than kicking another man in the shins formed rugby. It seems odd that soccer is now the game where you are most likely to be kicked in the shins, to the point where you have to wear shin guards.

But you do have to admire these early footballers' passion. Consider also that the balls were made out of a pig's bladder, which, if infected, could result in nasty outcomes for players, like lung disease or death. You really had to love your sport:

'Where's Jeff?'

'Oh, he died after blowing up the ball last week.'

'Righto. Whose go is it this week?'

Luckily, by 1860 a rubber bladder had been invented, not the first time rubber was the solution to stopping the spread of disease.

The codification of these English sports came after the Australian colonists had begun to take sport a bit more seriously. By the 1850s there were enough people, sporting facilities and leisure time for organised sports in Australia. But with formalised football codes still a few decades away, there was a vacuum that needed to be filled. In South Australia and Victoria, for example, local rules were established, the 'Victorian Rules' being the most famous. It would have been very interesting if association football had been more advanced when Australia was colonised; the working class may have taken up soccer and Victorian Rules would never have gotten off the ground.

LET'S TAKE THIS TOO SERIOUSLY

In the early days of the colony, sports had to be relatively easy to play, because there weren't any facilities. Anything requiring a lot of organisation or equipment was out of the question. Boxing, for example, was done without gloves, but given the fact that the place was basically a prison, it was hard to discern what was competitive sport and what was run-of-the-mill prison violence. Either way it didn't stop people betting on it, a pursuit that Australians would take to with a passion pretty much unmatched across the globe.

The earliest sporting activities were often aligned with the local pub, which loaned out equipment and ran competitions in order to attract more customers. This was a practice that had been going on in England for years. It's no surprise then that some of the pivotal moments in Australian sport, especially the founding of associations, took place in a pub.*

Hyde Park in Sydney was a popular venue for sport, with cricket, horseracing, various types of football and even quoits** all played

---

* While almost all of Australia's sports and leagues were established in pubs, the first rugby union was established in a restaurant. The meeting, attended by twenty-one clubs, saw the formation of the Rugby Football Union (RFU). Three lawyers were appointed to draw up the first laws of the sport. In hindsight, lawyers meeting in a restaurant was the perfect start for Union.
** The sleeping giant of Australian sport.

there. The problem was it also provided a training field for soldiers' military drills and grazing for sheep, meaning it had a similar surface to that of ANZ Stadium today.

The soldiers also held sailing and rowing competitions. In fact, early cricket games and horseracing were all run by the military, which is not that surprising; handing cricket bats to convicts was probably seen as a bad idea.

As more free settlers arrived, sport became more of a priority. The British saw it as a way of reinforcing morals, of co-ordinating people in a way that had flow-on benefits for society and for the Empire, by creating sameness. Sport was to the British Empire what Hollywood and McDonald's are to the United States.*

One of the more popular sports at the time was hunting. Heading out to shoot dingoes and kangaroos was seen as an enormously enjoyable way to pass the time. While it's declined in popularity, and is now barely considered a sport, it's still practised by retired members of our Australian cricket team, who have done their bit to thin out Africa's herds.

From roughly the 1820s the growing colony's attempts to turn a jail into a society included the establishment of sporting clubs. The Sydney Turf Club was set up in 1825 and in 1833 Governor Bourke designated land on Botany Road, Randwick, for a racecourse, which was creatively called 'Randwick'.

The Currency Cricket Club, the Military Cricket Club and the Australian Cricket Club were all formed by 1826, followed by the Hobart Town Cricket Club in 1832 and the Melbourne Cricket Club in 1838. White people just love a club. They were aping the clubs of the home country, which provided a distraction from the harshness of daily life.

---

* The relevance of this point may depend on when you are reading this. There may no longer be a United States.

But while these were the beginnings of a sporting culture, it was the gold rushes and the associated population boom that popularised sport and made it the central component of Australian life. I suppose you need an outlet after all that digging without finding any gold, and there's only so much whiskey drinking and beard growing you can do.

TAKING SHAPE

The discovery of gold had a profound impact on Australia and shaped it in so many ways, they can't possibly all be recorded here.* People across the world began to think of Australia as less of a backwater with a prison and more of a backwater with a prison that also had lots of gold.

It started in the early 1850s when gold was found near Orange in New South Wales and in Clunes, Bendigo and Ballarat in Victoria. People came to make their fortune and, because there was no Border Force to torture everyone on Manus Island, they just poured in. Even the Chinese were allowed in, and of course were made to feel very welcome.

At the same time huge improvements were being made in communications, through international cables. All of a sudden, news of what was happening in the mother country arrived promptly. The rules of sports that were emerging in England were transmitted quickly, as were results.

Take this communications revolution, combine it with the emergence of clearly defined sporting codes in England and throw

---

*   I mean, I could list them all, but it would take a lot of work and just the thought of it makes me exhausted.

in all the pent-up energy that comes from a bunch of men living in close proximity without a lot of women around, and you have the rapid development of a sporting culture. It was the 'Ideas Boom' of sports, if the 'Ideas Boom' had been a real thing and not just a series of posters at bus stops.

Almost overnight the colonies had the population, and more importantly the money, to organise and develop sporting events and facilities. Australia went from a rural colonial outpost to a highly urbanised society with cities full of the latest infrastructure and real wealth, essential for underwriting sporting events.

In the 1850s and 60s, racetracks, ovals, parks, golf courses and facilities for indoor sports were set up. Sports also flourished at the new schools that were being established. People had money and more time to dedicate to sporting pursuits. As there was no interwebs or video games, there wasn't a lot to do in your down-time other than play sport or drink. Australians combined the two with gusto.

Athletics was a major winner out of the gold rushes. Professional sprinters came to the gold fields from overseas to compete for major prizes or 'gifts', often a gold nugget. Competitive running was then delightfully known as 'pedestrianism' and attracted huge crowds. The most famous of these events is the Stawell Gift.* Founded in 1878, it's still run every Easter Monday on a grass track in Stawell, in western Victoria.

These races on the goldfields led to the establishment of numerous athletic clubs. These clubs helped underpin the success Australians went on to have at the Olympics, providing ongoing competition outside of Olympic years.

---

* In 2010, the Stawell Gift was accidentally run over 123.2 metres – 3.2 metres more than intended – due to an old-fashioned measuring error. This was twelve years after an episode of the ABC comedy *The Games* aired in which the 100-metre athletics track in the main Olympic stadium was found to be only 94 metres long. When it comes to sports, satire often merely suggests stuff-ups real administrators then implement.

The greatest sporting legacy of the gold rushes was the cementing of the newly established 'Victorian Rules', first in Victoria and later in Western Australia, during their gold rush in the 1880s. Codified in 1859, the game's emergence was perfectly timed for it to spread and be financially supported by the gold rush, given the massive movement of both people and capital.

Much of the important sporting infrastructure was built around this time. The Sydney Cricket Ground and the Melbourne Cricket Ground, the most spiritual places in Australia, both opened in 1854. Working in Australia's favour was that it had plenty of land, so these grounds were built close to where people lived, making them part of the community. This was often harder to do in Europe, what with all its people, history and culture getting in the way.

CLASS LINES

It's common knowledge that rich people don't particularly care for poor people. Britain had spent centuries building a society where rich people could interact with the poor as little as possible. Yet in Australia, such is the desire to win that even the lowliest of upbringings will be overlooked by the wealthy if someone possesses above average sporting ability.

There were some class differences in sport early on, though, some of which remain to this day. One early flashpoint was a law passed in the British parliament in 1835 that also applied in the colonies. It banned certain blood sports, like cockfighting and dogfighting – good, clean sports favoured by the working class. There was outrage. 'Political correctness gone mad' and 'blood nanny state' were the cries of the masses.

The thinking behind the legislation was nothing to do with animal cruelty; this was England in the nineteenth century, almost no one cared about that. But cockfighting and dogfighting were seen as pursuits that encouraged drinking and gambling, and took place in grubby venues where poor people gathered. Fox hunting, on the other hand, was not banned. This was the sport of the upper class and it was believed to encourage people to be outdoors and get physical exercise. Back then the rich tended to make the laws, almost always to their own benefit, which would never happen in our day and age.

In Australia other sports managed to avoid class divisions, considered ways to build communities and keep the populace content. Horseracing was popular with everyone – the rich liked it because they could own racehorses and the working class liked it because they could lose money betting on the rich people's horses.

In cricket and Australian Rules the small population forced people of all classes to band together to make up the numbers. This led to a more egalitarian approach on the field and, as time progressed, it became an advantage, as we found sporting success against the motherland in cricket. In fact, those born in the colonies started to see things like different dressing rooms for amateurs and professionals as weird and something to be mocked.

Rugby, yet to split into Union and League, was a more egalitarian sport in Australia despite its British public-school origins. Early debates around payment, however, would be the fault line on which it would later split in two. In Australia League became the game of the working class in New South Wales and Queensland, consigning Union to the elite.

At the time of the split, the working-class rugby players only wanted to be compensated for missing work to play and for travel expenses. Instead, the wealthy players and administrators lectured them about the joys of amateurism and accused them of being greedy. This amateur-versus-professional debate caused issues in many sports, but for rugby it would have by far the most profound results, with League finding greater success. Rugby Union boxed itself in by spurning the working class, but it was an expensive box

NATIONAL TEAM NAMES

Wallabies: Australia's Rugby Union side. Originally, it was suggested calling them the 'Rabbits', which would have been fitting given they've been New Zealand's bunnies ever since.

Kangaroos: Australia's Rugby League team, named after they toured Britain with a real kangaroo, as you do.

Dropbears: Australia's national quidditch team. Yes, people play the sport from *Harry Potter*, and Australia won the World Cup in 2016, beating the US 150*–130. This proves that Australia is an amazing sporting nation even in made-up sports.

Diamonds: In 2008, Netball Australia announced that the national team would have a name for the first time: the 'Diamonds'. Apparently it took a twelve-month branding process to come up with it. Twelve months! Note to self, start a branding business.

with lots of other wonderfully rich people in it so they settled into their chesterfields and enjoyed it.

Other sports like tennis and golf started off more elite but, as equipment became more affordable and councils built public courts and courses, they opened up to the great unwashed. Then there is polo, which is just elitist and uses that as a selling point to people who aren't the elite but want to appear upper-class by watching it.

The key to becoming a major sport in Australia was to be accepted by the working and middle classes. Only then could a sport achieve the level of interest required to provide suffi-cient players and paying spectators. The rapid early growth Australian Rules was down to it attracting the support of every-one, regardless of background or circumstance, something it can still lay claim to.

MARKING THEIR TERRITORY

With Australia's economy and population at critical mass by the middle of the nineteenth century, popular sports began to consolidate their positions through the codification of rules, the building of sports grounds and the marking out of territory.

Australians really embraced cricket from very early on. The southern continent had the perfect climate for standing around outside all day at the height of summer.

In the 1860s, Australia started to play England in cricket. It was one-sided in the beginning, with England usually winning easily. Many Australians still considered themselves to be English but there was an emerging sense that Australia was its own place, its people happier, better-looking and more athletically gifted. Cricket matches between England and the best cricketers from New South Wales and Victoria started many people thinking of themselves as 'Australian' and helped to pave the way for federation.

Initially, the English teams came to play in Australia. But in 1868 a team of Indigenous cricketers went on a tour of England. It was unlike the tours of today. They played forty-seven games in total, winning fourteen, losing fourteen and drawing nineteen. It was an impressive result given the long sea voyage, the months away from home and the fact the English crowds saw them as a novelty rather than people.

It was during England's 1876/77 tour of Australia that a combined colonies team first defeated the English in a 'test'. It was a huge achievement. At the time, England had a population of 20 million compared to Australia's 2 million, although the census site had crashed so that figure could be way off.

Worse was to come for the English. On 29 August 1882, a team from the Australian colonies beat them at The Oval. At the ground, the reaction was one of both shock and excitement, with one man in the crowd dropping dead. A suitable response. The English press called it the day English cricket died, placing obituaries in the papers. Unfortunately for the English, English cricket seems to have an amazing ability to keep dying over and over again.

This event really awakened Australia's competitive streak on the international sporting stage, as well as the populace's addiction to sporting triumph to shore up low self-esteem. In every other field of endeavour – the arts, science, wealth, history, pasty white skin, comical dentistry – Australia was far behind, but cricket was something where Australia could eclipse the English.

The triumph helped to cement cricket's popularity back home, and that meant people became interested in controlling it. As Australia moved towards federation a battle for control of the game emerged, fought between the Melbourne Cricket Club (MCC) and the NSW Cricket Association (NSWCA). In the MCG and SCG, both had grounds that enabled them to do something incredibly important in establishing a sport: charge entry.

Revenue from tickets delivered a variety of advantages for sports administrations. It enabled the underwriting of overseas tours (often profitable exercises in themselves) and provided equipment, player payments and promotion. The Melbourne–Sydney divide resulted in ludicrous situations where both organisations put together their own 'Australian teams' to play England, further diluting the already small pool of top players.

In a trend that's marched on through the sporting landscape right until the modern day, this conflict eventually led to the centralisation of power, including the right to organise overseas tours, in the hands of a single body. Cricket's 'Board of Control' was formed in 1905, and is now known as Cricket Australia. This central body controlled cricket at a national level with a strong hand. That strong hand was over the players and state associations, helping the sport grow but coming back to bite them in the seventies when they were up against World Series Cricket.

The various football codes also consolidated their positions following the gold rushes. In Victoria, a new sport emerged from those played at various English elite schools. With no consensus in England, Victorians had no real idea which one to adopt. The earliest games of football in Melbourne resulted in all sorts of arguments over the rules. Again, timing was key to how things played out. The 'Victorian Rules', as they first came to be known, were written in 1859*; in England the Football Association (the FA) only formed in 1863 and the Rugby Football Union (RFU) in 1871.

There was no clear code to follow, or at least there was no agreement over which one to follow. So instead they sat down and thrashed out a set of rules everyone could agree on. Basically, inventing Australian Rules was like when you sit down to watch something with your partner and, not being able to agree, you compromise and settle on something neither of you really wants to watch. In this case, it turned out the compromise worked. 'Hey, that movie was actually okay.'

The Victorian game began to spread quickly across the country. South Australia initially had their own rules but, in 1877, twelve of their footy clubs met to establish a governing body. They formed the South Australian Football Association (SAFA) and voted for similar rules to Victoria.

Western Australia was a rugby hotbed until their gold rush, which saw a seismic shift to the Victorian game, following the Fremantle rugby club switching codes in 1885. One day they were playing rugby and the next a completely different sport. As supporters, following a rubbish performance we've all occasionally thought

---

* At first they were known as the 'Victorian Rules', especially outside Victoria. The term morphed into 'Australian Rules' as the Victorians' religious crusade to spread the code took hold. These days, Victorians still think they're the centre of the universe and many of them would like it to go back to being called Victorian Rules.

our team should try switching to another sport but they never actually do it. Fremantle were followed by two other WA clubs and the Victorian game had a foothold in the colony that, while precarious at first, grew to push rugby aside and become the dominant sport there.

New South Wales and Queensland were not immune to the charms of Australian Rules either. While rugby was the major sport in Queensland, Australian Rules ran very close to becoming its major winter code, and in New South Wales it battled Union for supremacy over thirty years. The arrival of Rugby League finally shut the door on Australian Rules becoming the major code in either state.

In both cases, the decisive issues were access to grounds and the ability to centrally control the game. In Melbourne, enclosed grounds had delivered gate revenue, making both the competition and individual clubs strong. In New South Wales, rugby worked hard to exclude Australian Rules from the Sydney Cricket Ground and other stadiums, significantly damaging the code's ability to generate revenue. It was the sort of ruthlessness that the VFL/AFL later applied to its own business dealings, often against its own clubs. Even at this early stage, 'revenue streams' were a key indicator of which sports would succeed.

In Queensland, Australian Rules' main problem was that it was unable to reach agreement on a central body of control, making it hard to keep the code functioning well. A vote by private schools to play rugby was another major hurdle. Rugby was ascendant in the northern states, while the Victorian game became established in the southern states.

This battle between rugby and Australian Rules had another consequence, especially in New South Wales. Australian Rules could pay players, and that was a big threat to Union, which couldn't. When Rugby League arrived in 1907, it too had an advantage over Union, significantly raising its appeal with the working class. This allowed League to overrun Union and negate the early appeal of Australian Rules.

League quickly became the preferred rugby code of the working classes, who came to see sport less as an honourable pursuit and more of a way to make some money and change their lives. League also got its house in order relatively quickly, with the Australian Rugby League Board of Control, the precursor to the Australian Rugby League (ARL), established in 1924. It may be the one time in its history that Rugby League did have its house in order off the field. If League hadn't arrived on the sporting scene, amateur Union would likely have struggled against the professional Aussie Rules.

That brings us to soccer.* One of the strangest things about Australia is that it didn't embrace the game with the same fervour as the English working classes. Not only did the country not embrace it, it seemed to positively hate it for a very long time. Only in recent years has a notable contingent of Australians begun to care about it with any seriousness, and there are still many that dream of its demise, mainly people working in the media it seems.

Games certainly occurred from the 1870s on, and a more organised side, the Wanderers, formed in Sydney in 1880. But between Victorian Rules and (a little later) League, the working class were sown up in both the northern and southern states. The code was not revitalised until the post–World War II influx of migrants, and of course it's been all smooth sailing from then on.

By World War I, a lot of the Australian sporting landscape was set for the winter and summer team sports. Cricket, Australian Rules, League and Union were all well-organised, established in their key states and in the main controlled by central administrations that drew good revenue.

---

* The correct name for this sport is an issue more complex than polynomial algebra and with more emotion than an online *Star Wars* forum. See page 232 for a full discussion.

THINGS NEVER HEARD AT A STADIUM

That's pretty reasonable for a pie and chips.'

'You've only got mid-strength beer? Great, that's just what I feel like.'

'There are just too many ATMs at this ground.'

'Mate, could you get me some sushi?'

'I feel really bad that I'm missing a wedding for this.'

Other sports were being imported from England as soon as they were invented, especially around the time of federation. Netball, tennis, hockey and cycling, to name a few, while swimming and athletics – which had been popular pastimes since the colonial days – began to be more organised. The NSW Amateur Swimming Association was established in 1892 and the Australasian Athletics Union in 1897.

By federation sporting clubs were seen as essential to the fabric of the community. Swimming and athletics became aligned with the Olympics; League, Union and Australian Rules dominated winter in their respective states; and cricket held sway over summer, although tennis was beginning to emerge as an alternative.

Perhaps most importantly, by 1900 everyone's favourite game to play while drunk, the sleeping giant of Australian sport, badminton, had arrived.

THE GREAT DEPRESSION

Australia in the thirties was hit hard by the Great Depression, which makes the Global Financial Crisis look like a holiday in Ibiza. Australia reached an unemployment rate of 30 per cent in 1932, which despite the best efforts of our politicians has never been bested.

It was a key period in Australian sport. With so many people out of work, sporting clubs became a place for them to gather and pass the time.

Governments also started to invest in sporting facilities to try to provide work and stimulate the economy. They built swimming pools, tennis courts and a host of other important venues that ensured Australia's international success later on. Investing in sporting infrastructure became a great tradition in Australian politics, especially in marginal seats. At the time it was a new experience; governments had mainly seen sport as an amateur pursuit and not part of their domain.

The Great Depression also had people looking for anything to distract themselves from the tough times. As if on cue, sport provided two of the greatest legends ever, Don Bradman in cricket and Phar Lap in horseracing.* Crowds flocked to see them, and their efforts and success took on mythical status. Phar Lap was so important he was stuffed and put on display in the Melbourne Museum, something I have argued should occur to all Australian sporting heroes. The timing of Bradman and Phar Lap's feats ensured sport became even more important to the Australian people, giving them a sense of pride, just as Nick Kyrgios and Bernard Tomic do for us now.

WORLD WAR II

After the Great Depression, World War II meant the government took an even bigger role in sport, having realised everyone in the country was deeply unfit.** This didn't usually matter, but in wartime it was a serious concern. The Menzies government passed the Commonwealth National Fitness Act in 1941, which set up the Commonwealth Council for National Fitness, as well as state councils. The main aim was to get men fit before they enlisted.

---

* How our national flag isn't Don Bradman holding his cricket bat aloft while riding Phar Lap is something I'll never understand and goes to the heart of the lack of visionary leadership in this country.

** They should see us now!

This was the first time the government put any really framework in place for distributing taxpayer dollars towards sport, and after the war, governments would take a very long time to do so again in any major way.

The war disrupted sports across the globe and in Australia, like in so many other countries, a whole generation of young men never got to play sport again. Yet, within weeks of the war finishing, sport had resumed. It was a way of returning to some level of normalcy after the horrors of the previous years.

It did not take long for sport to be back up and running and, in September 1949, the sleeping giant of Australian sport, canoeing, established the Australian Canoe Federation.

THERE GOES THE NEIGHBOURHOOD

Like most people, I prefer the company of my own kind, and by 'my own kind' I mean 'just me'. As far as I'm concerned, I'm happy to sit alone at home and watch TV and never have contact with anyone else. After the war, people in Australia liked their own kind too, but they had a broader definition of it. In the main they meant 'white people'. They liked white people so much they even passed laws saying so, especially when it came to immigration, which is a lot of effort in my opinion and a bit too broad a brushstroke. I mean *all* white people? I could give you a pretty comprehensive list of white people I wish had never come here. Take my neighbour Geoff, for example, who leaves his bins out in the street for days. Even me regularly reversing over them on purpose hasn't stopped him.

After the war, especially from the fifties onwards, Australia started to change and let in some people who weren't quite as white as the English or Irish, so long as they weren't black or Asian. A lot of these 'New Australians' hailed from European countries, in particular Italy and Greece. They also came with a love of sport, and in many cases this meant soccer, which made 'normal' Australians uncomfortable and suspicious. The new arrivals were made to form their own clubs, often built around a particular ethnicity so that at least there'd be one familiar, welcoming thing in their life. While these ethnic divisions caused tension and difficulty in Australian soccer for decades, these early clubs did foster a devoted if relatively small cohort of players and fans who propped up the game. Luckily we've learnt from our mistakes and are far more accepting of immigrants these days.

Many post-war immigrants did try to take up some of the more established sports, including Australian Rules and League. Mainstream Australia started to realise that many of these new arrivals were good at sport, so they warmed to them. I mean, racism is fine and all, but not when it's directed at one of your own star players. That's just not on. Plus, Australians were enjoying commentators coming a cropper on names like DiPierdomenico, Schifilliti and Capobianco.

GREAT NICKNAMES

Bruce 'The Flying Doormat' Doull: Commentator extraordinaire Lou Richards came up with this bizarre but fitting nickname for the Carlton legend. Doull was bald on top with long hair and a long beard, all capped off with a headband.

Robert 'Dipper' DiPierdomenico: Australians took one look at that surname and thought, *Nope, not even having a go at that.*

Mick 'The Galloping Gasometer' Nolan: Another Lou Richards special, North Melbourne's Nolan weighed 135 kilograms and was 194 centimetres tall, making him one of the largest ruckmen to ever play footy. His size reminded Richards of the massive gasometer on Arden Street, near the Kangaroos' home ground.

A NATIONAL EFFORT

By the 1950s, Australia was having enormous success internationally, peaking with the Melbourne Olympic Games in 1956. Australia dominated swimming, athletics, tennis and cricket, while also being strong in both rugby codes and having our own national game. Australians now demanded success; losing had the dramatic effect of pulling the federal government into sport in a way it had never been before.

After the war, the state and federal fitness councils had stayed in place, but the lack of an imminent invasion meant their funding was minimal at best. Sport was still mainly considered an amateur pursuit. The bigger sports like League, cricket and Australian Rules had some revenue from gate receipts, but it was nothing like the money that flows through these codes today.

Olympic sports required athletes to raise any funds they needed themselves, but with the incredible success Australia had been experiencing – coming third in the medal tally in 1956 and fifth in 1960 – this was not seen as a problem that needed fixing. We were punching well above our weight. There were, however, changes afoot overseas. Other countries were pouring government money into sport, and in some countries performance enhancing substances too.

Europe's Eastern Bloc countries were investing all sorts of government money in facilities, talent identification and development, and the shady voodoo world of 'sports science'. America was also using taxpayers' money to build up a modern sports system, built around their colleges. The Australian government couldn't have been less interested, so Australia's amateurs were increasingly going head to head with professionals and losing.

By the seventies, the Olympic community in Australia was screaming out for funding and assistance. The government didn't want to actually *do* anything, so they did what all governments do in that situation and commissioned a report. The Bloomfield Report of 1973 made numerous recommendations to improve the co-ordination of amateur and professional sporting efforts, as well as the use of community facilities. Perhaps its most prominent recommendation was the establishment of a national institute of sport.

What was done to move on this recommendation? Why, another report was commissioned, of course. The Coles Report in 1974 recommended the national institute be established in Canberra, probably to ensure athletes had no distractions in the form of restaurants, bars, cafes, nightclubs, bands, shops, family, friends, or really any reason at all to go outside.

WORST THINGS A PERSON CAN SAY

'Why are you watching this? Your team isn't even playing.'

'We'll get a great rate if we have our wedding on grand final day.'

'The government should be giving money to health and education, not sport.'

'Why would you watch a replay of a game you just went to?'

'Are you just going to sit around and watch cricket all day?'

Despite the findings of these two reports, the government had no real incentive to put money into an area of public life it never had to before. There just wasn't the political pressure to commit.

MONTREAL: THE GREATEST DISASTER EVER

Now, you may have read the heading of this section and used context to infer I mean 'the greatest disaster in Australian sporting history'. That would be a mistake. The performance of the Australian team at the 1976 games was the greatest disaster in Australian history.

While many focus on Gallipoli as our nation's greatest failure, the Montreal Olympic Games in 1976 are a clear contender.[*] Australia did not win a single gold medal at these games. Not one! Not even in one of those silly sports no one cares about the rest of the time, like athletics.

In total, out of 613 medals on offer at these games, Australia brought home just five. Let us be perfectly frank: silver and bronze might be fine for Estonia or one of those African countries I don't know anything about, but this is Australia. It was an unmitigated disaster. We ended up thirty-second on the medal table and a lot of truly rubbish countries were above us.

The public and the media exploded with white hot anger. Our old enemies the English had a field day. Obviously this situation could not be allowed to stand. My suggestion at the time – that the team shouldn't be allowed to ever return home – was ignored.

What did happen – and this is peak Australia – was a NATIONAL CRISIS. Other countries have famines, civil wars or terrorism for their national crises, but in Australia this was something so much worse. The government did not exactly handle it well. Prime Minister Malcom Fraser found the win-at-all-costs, only-gold-matters attitude perplexing. The minister

---

[*] Gallipoli is also cited as the most inspiring example of Aussie resolve; the same cannot be said of the Australian team's performance in Montreal.

responsible for sport, Kevin Newman, said the government had 'an important role in developing Australian sport' but balked at going all-in for a centralised, highly regimented approach or putting much money forward.

This approach misjudged the concerns of the great people of Australia. We had been embarrassed in front of the entire world, this was a matter of national pride. Australians were a genetically superior race of athletes, supreme amongst all nations on earth. It became increasingly clear that the Fraser government saw pouring lots of taxpayers' money into amateur sport as a waste of resources. I guess they just didn't value happiness.

The Australian reported that the government believed public anger would subside after the Montreal Olympics. Their assessment was a bit off, with a Gallup poll showing 70 per cent of Australians thought our athletes should get more money. The public pressure only increased. Lobby groups were formed, articles were written, the people stormed parliament and refused to leave (well, they thought about it), all bringing enormous pressure to bear on the Fraser government.

In a nutshell, the Australian government put every sports fan offside and then ignored them. That's like a French government cracking down on wine lovers.

AUSTRALIAN INSTITUTE OF SPORT

A new minister, Bob Ellicott, came along at just the right time. His Home Affairs and Environment portfolio included sport, and not only was he prepared to listen to the sporting community, he was a sports fan himself. That is, he was a true Australian.

Ellicott was keen to secure greater funding for sports, in part due to the Montreal Olympic debacle but also to help fight preventable diseases. It was becoming apparent that, without an enormous war to train for, Australians were getting unfit again (damn this peacetime) and this was costing the health system. Luckily we got healthy eating and fitness sorted out back then, hey?

Ellicott was keen to push forward with an institute of sport. He announced it would focus, in the beginning, on eight key sports: basketball, gymnastics, netball, swimming, tennis, track and field, soccer, and weightlifting.* On 26 January 1981, Prime Minister Fraser officially opened the Australian Institute of Sport (AIS), a facility he had no interest or belief in. Despite this, opening a national sports institute on Australia Day may have been the most Australian thing anyone's ever done.

Early on the AIS had a small sports science unit, whose job was not to just inject athletes with steroids all day, I'm told. For the first intake, 153 AIS scholarships were given out, from a pool of 800 applicants. That's an incredibly high amount of interest considering that if you were a successful, you had to live in Canberra.

THE DEPARTMENT OF JUNKETS

The election of the Hawke government in 1983 meant the arrival of a prime minister and cabinet who placed sport where it rightly belonged: above health, education, defence and basic infrastructure. There were, of course, exceptions; the treasurer, Paul Keating, preferred antique clocks to footballs for some bizarre reason.

Just one week after being elected, Hawke announced the new Department of Sport, Recreation and Tourism. It was a dream-come-true portfolio for any minister, just wandering the country handing out grants and going to sporting events. It should have been called the Department of Junkets.

Just two years later, Hawke established the Australian Sports Commission (ASC), a statutory body whose brief was to ensure funds were being distributed in a balanced way. Its job was to

---

* Surprisingly, the sleeping giant of Australian sport, squash, was not among the eight.

POLITICS AND SPORT

Politicians often give sporting codes enormous amounts of taxpayer money, and the favour is returned when retired athletes become political candidates – a very poor deal for politics. Some former athletes have succeeded in politics, like tennis player John Alexander and AFL ruckman Justin Madden. Others, like Dawn Fraser, make little impact before leaving.

Clive Palmer's political party proved a boon for ex-athletes, with former League star Glenn Lazarus elected to the Senate, while AFL star Doug Hawkins and boxer Barry Michael were unsuccessful candidates. Lazarus quit Palmer's party, accusing Palmer of bullying. Bullying Lazarus would be the sort of thing I imagine you only do once.

please everyone, which is always a sure-fire way to have everybody think you are doing a bad job. The ASC purview included funding arrangements for disabled sport (as it was then known) and women's sport, with funding newly going to both. It was one of the first acknowledgements by anyone with power or money that these groups played sport.

By this stage, the focus on elite sport and the AIS was seen to be delivering results. In 1989 Senator Graham Richardson (the Minister for the Arts, Sport, the Environment, Tourism and Territories) announced a $239 million package that the ASC would use to develop elite sport and grassroots participation programs. Sports had a clear pathway for professionals and the era of amateurism at the top level was mainly in the past. This was a sign that the government, once so hesitant to commit any money to sport, was all-in.

Sport in Australia was now political, in every sense of the word. Where there is money, there is corruption. With speed that would impress all those newly funded elite athletes, taxpayers' money started to be directed to the electoral seats that were most important to the government of the day.

In 1993, Ros Kelly, Minister for Sport, was asked on what grounds she had allocated $30 million worth of sport grants. She confessed that there were no actual criteria and that instead she'd gone off verbal advice from her staff. You'd be shocked to learn her staff overwhelmingly favoured projects in marginal seats that Labor had just about won in the previous election. Amazing! Famously, no records were kept, Kelly arguing they just worked on a whiteboard and then rubbed everything out. I've never trusted whiteboards myself, I think they're up there with other untested technologies like the internet and beepers.

A House of Representatives committee looking into the matter said nothing illegal had happened, the whole process was just 'deficient'. Hmmm.

Kelly resigned from the ministry before leaving parliament altogether, a salient lesson for future ministers to be more careful and to at least pretend to go through a rigorous process when pork-barrelling.

SUCCESS

All this investment was certainly having an impact on performance. As we approached the 2000 Sydney Olympics, Australia delivered one of the most successful years in its entire history, sporting and non-sporting.

The year 1999 was marked by two things: an unfounded fear of the Y2K bug and Australia's total domination of sport. In that year alone, Australia won twelve team world championships and twenty-one in individual sports. These included:

- Rugby World Cup
- Netball World Championship

- Rugby League Tri-nations
- Cricket World Cup
- Davis Cup
- Mark Occhilupo, Men's World Surfing Champion
- Layne Beachley, Women's World Surfing Champion
- Kostya Tszyu, WBC Super Lightweight Champion*

It was a great time to be alive. I remember watching almost all of these, especially the Cricket World Cup final. The bar I was at handed out shots every time an Australian hit a boundary. Whoever had done the maths on that particular promotion hadn't done it very well and within a few overs the bar was covered in drinks and the patrons were struggling to keep up. By the end of the night the bar had gone bankrupt and the Aussies were hoisting the cup. Not to glorify the consumption of alcohol but it was the greatest night of my life.

---

* Kostya Tszyu is a perfect example of how we learned to claim New Australians as our own. People welcomed Kostya with open arms, because he delivered sporting success and also because it's a bad idea to be racist towards someone who knocks people out for a living.

HERE COMES THE MONEY

Once upon a time, after a big win sports stars would thank their teammates, the fans and their family. These days, sponsors are the first to be thanked, given they are now more important than everyone else. After all, when was the last time your family gave you a million-dollar promotional deal? And children, well, they're really just domestic cost centres, which actually reduce the productivity of family profit centres.

Sponsorship is now a huge source of revenue for all sporting codes, as well as for individual athletes. Up until the seventies, the biggest source of revenue in sports was gate receipts. Controlling your own venues, or having access to the best ones, was crucial to making money. But the seventies not only saw the continuing moral decline of society, it also saw the rise of sports sponsorships.

There had been sponsorship deals before, of course, but television was giving sporting teams a reach they could have only dreamed of previously. On top of that, in 1976 tobacco was banned from being advertised on radio or television, for the flimsy reason that it killed people. Yet there was a rather large loophole in the legislation: sports sponsorships were basically exempt from this ban.

A tsunami of money flowed into sports. Philip Morris, Amatil and Rothmans all become the largest sponsors of sport in Australia. It was a wonderful synergy between our fittest athletes and lung cancer. In 1989, for example, the New South Wales Rugby League (NSWRL) got $20 million from tobacco advertising while cricket got $14 million. It was a difficult moral conundrum for the sporting bodies for all of about ten seconds.

Governments, however, were a bit less keen on the whole thing, especially as they were having to pay for much of the healthcare these dying smokers needed. They made moves to close the loophole. Well, the sporting codes reacted like a child being told that they can't have chocolate cake for breakfast. They screamed that this would mean the death of sports. Basically they were saying to the governments: do you want sports to die or smokers? You have to pick one!

By 1992 the loophole was shut, preventing any new tobacco sponsorship deals from being put in place, and by 1998 all existing ones had run their course.

Can I let you in on a little secret? Sports didn't die, despite the predictions of the administrations' CEOs. Amazing! The codes

THINGS YOU DON'T WANT TO HEAR FROM YOUR CLUB DURING PRE-SEASON

'We're actually alarmed at the condition the guys have come back in.'

'Some of our players haven't even shown up yet and it's week three.'

'We're just taking it easy. The season is still ages away.'

'I'm petrified by how we'd go in an intra-club match let alone against another team.'

'Sometimes the fans watching training have to look away. Many of them are fitter than our players.'

quickly moved on to alcohol, junk food and then gambling sponsorships. In recent times there have been noises about limiting these sponsorships too. In response, the CEOs of the various codes have once again claimed that this would end sport as we know it. When Andrew Demetriou was CEO of the AFL, he said that banning alcohol sponsorships 'would cripple football'. Now, where have I heard that before?

THE REVOLUTION WILL BE TELEVISED

In the nineties, TV rights delivered more money to the top sports than they could have ever dreamed of – and they could dream of a lot.

Early on, media rights were viewed as competition to gate receipts. When radios became a major consumer product in the twenties, sporting bodies were immediately wary of live media coverage, worried that people might not show up to games. Radio was one thing, but television was another. When TV first began broadcasting in Australia, just in time for the 1956 Melbourne Olympics, it scared the living daylights out of administrators. They worried TV would decimate crowds, who'd just stay at home to watch, without generating enough revenue to make up the shortfall. Back then they were right: in 1956, the ABC paid £25 for the rights to broadcast the cricket, while the first VFL deal, in 1957, was worth about $500 a week.

The fear of losing gate receipts led to all sorts of novel solutions. In the sixties, the NSWRL only allowed the second half of matches to be shown on TV. The VFL went even further, allowing only the last quarter to be shown, and even that was on delay. Despite these measures, the VFL still worried it was costing them money so in 1960 they stopped allowing any TV coverage at all. In 1962 they allowed footy back on television, but only replays.

It was also common at that time for TV deals to be non-exclusive, meaning any channel could show a match if they paid a tiny amount. As often as not, no one showed it. In the early seventies, neither the TV channels or the sports codes themselves saw any value in media rights. NSWRL chairman Kevin Humphreys said his attempts to sell the competition's TV rights in 1973 were met with no interest and he ended up having to beg the ABC to take them. They got about $1000 per game.

It was Kerry Packer who noticed that sport was both cheap to produce and filled up a lot of TV hours. He began to innovate with various sports, finding great success with golf. It wasn't long until he turned to cricket, and the battle sparked by his World Series Cricket made TV stations and sporting bodies sit up and take notice of the potential value of media rights.

In the eighties TV deals were given greater importance, as it was now understood they attracted sponsors and helped to grow a sport. In some cases TV supported other strategies; the VFL had decided to wipe out their competitor, the VFA, but they weren't allowed to play footy on Sundays in Victoria, while the VFA was. A TV deal with Channel Seven allowed the VFL to play games in Sydney on Sundays and broadcast them back into Melbourne. That's called honouring the letter of the law, not the spirit.

> **DID YOU KNOW?**
>
> ⤖
>
> At one stage, Eddie McGuire was hosting every AFL TV and radio show in existence.

Rugby League went even further, going to war over TV rights in the mid-nineties. Pay TV had entered the arena, and with media rights suddenly hot property Kerry Packer and Rupert Murdoch spent hundreds of millions of dollars fighting for control of Rugby League. Known as the Super League war, it didn't really have anything super about it at all.

The 2002–2006 AFL broadcast deal was a real coming of

age for the industry, with Channel Nine, Ten and Foxtel paying $500 million for the rights. Amazingly, later deals dwarfed this.

These days live sports is one of the few properties to still work for advertisers; audiences have become increasingly segmented, and people record things to watch later or stream them, often skipping or avoiding ads entirely. On top of that, sports attracts large groups of men who are ridiculously easy to market to, due to the fact that their brains cease to function if an attractive woman is used in the ad.

Today, the AFL has a six-year, $2.5 billion TV deal, the NRL has a five-year, $1.8 billion deal, cricket's deal is worth $590 million, the A-League's is $346 million over six years and Rugby Union has $285 million over five years. That's the sort of money usually reserved for published authors like myself.

ACROSS THIS WIDE BROWN LAND

In the seventies, sponsorship and media rights money, the reach of television, and the plummeting cost of air travel shook up the Australian sporting landscape for the first time since the start of the century. TV and sponsors both wanted 'content' and 'properties', and the various sporting codes were more than keen to provide them.

Since the emergence of League in 1907, sporting competitions had pretty much stuck to their own patches. Now they were expanding across the nation. First the National Soccer League (NSL) was founded in 1977, then the National Basketball League (NBL) in 1979. In the case of both League and Australian Rules, rich state-based competitions like the NSWRL and the VFL had continually sucked in the best players from around the country, so they were primed to expand.

In Australian Rules, the Western Australian and South Australian teams were interested in forming a national competition, but the VFL was only interested if they were the ones in control.

No wonder everyone hates Victorians. Through a mixture of ruthlessness and cash, the VFL emerged as the dominant league, with teams based in Sydney, Adelaide, Brisbane and Perth.

The NSWRL took a similar approach of ignoring local leagues where they existed. For example, they just ignored the competing Brisbane Rugby League, bought all their best players, and had private owners set up the Brisbane Broncos. Easy.

Union was slightly different. A century of amateurism meant their reach was limited to the richest private schools and a few key clubs. In 1995, however, the administrators decided that they would actually quite like some revenue and the sport became professional. It raced to set up teams in Queensland, New South Wales and then Canberra. Later on it added teams in Perth and Melbourne.

This all meant that, by the end of the nineties, the major sporting codes were all national, if you pretend Tasmania and the Northern Territory don't exist, which most Australians do. The parochial approach still remained, however, with many people thinking it was a cardinal sin to like more than one sport. Depending on where you lived, either League or Australian Rules was considered an alien invasion that must be resisted at all costs. But younger generations saw the appeal of following multiple codes, often on the back of watching elite overseas competitions like the NBA and the Premier League, as well as their local NRL or AFL club.

This explosion of national codes means Australia now has one of the most crowded sporting

IT'S ALL IN THE NAME

Brisbane Bears (VFL/AFL)

This expansion side was not based in Brisbane and its mascot, a koala, is not a bear. In some ways, this all made sense, because in reality they weren't a professional sports team, more an experimental comedy troupe. After ten seasons, they finished up in 1996 (72 wins, 2 draws, 148 losses), merging with Fitzroy to become the Brisbane Lions.

markets in the world. In some ways, it's a zero-sum game. Cricket's success hurts the A-League and basketball, while in winter the NRL and AFL duke it out, especially in the northern states, while Union quietly dies.

And yet it may not be as Darwinian as that. Australians seem to have an appetite for sport that only grows the more there is on offer, and the ever-growing TV deals seem to confirm that. It's rare to meet a sports fan these days who doesn't at least have an opinion on every sport, and they're only too happy to share it with you.

LET'S DO A REPORT

While the big professional team sports had nationalised and grown richer, the Olympic sports in the country shifted from their amateur roots to being substantially funded by government and, in some cases, sponsors.

The lessons from the Montreal dumpster fire had been learnt; the voters wanted success, and their taxpayer dollars were going to fund it. The Hawke/Keating government was followed by the Howard government, which continued to fund sport. The argument was no longer about whether the government should spend money on sport, it had become more about where it should go: grassroots sport or elite programs? Should funding be allocated on the basis of participation numbers or the likelihood of gold medals? Oh sure, occasionally someone complained about taxpayer funds going to sport, but these people were not taken seriously.

Where there are governments there are reports, and sport has been no different. Sports administrators, government bureaucrats and politicians love a report. Interim reports, never-completed reports, reports no one actually reads, reports that conclude the same thing the previous reports concluded. It doesn't matter, they love them all. The only thing they like almost as much as a report is a strategy or, if they're feeling fancy, a framework.

We've had:

- *The Bloomfield Report* (1973)
- *The Coles Report* (1974)
- *The Bloomfield Report (WA)* (1978)
- *The Master Plan for Sport* (1980)
- *Sport and Recreation: Australia on the Move* (1983)
- *Going for Gold* (1989)
- *The Next Step Program* (1989)
- *Maintain the Momentum* (1992)
- *The Olympic Athlete Program* (1994–2000)
- *Backing Australia's Sporting Ability* (2001)
- *Game Plan* (2006)
- *The Crawford Report* (2009)
- *Australian Sport: The Pathway to Success* (2010)
- *Australia's Winning Edge* (2012)

There have also been a lot of task forces, like the Sport 2000 Task Force, which generated a report called *Shaping Up*. Perhaps my favourite report was *A Case for Additional Funding to Further Develop Sport in Australia*. Imagine the hours they put into the title: 'Do you think they'll understand what we want?'

Apart from wiping out several forests, these reports have mostly shifted Australia towards having more and more elite-sports funding. Politicians want to appear to support grassroots sports, but they know it's much better to stand next to a gold medallist than some six-year-old hockey player who's never won anything.

Yet by the late 2000s, even politicians were wondering if all this reflected glory was becoming too expensive. So they got David Crawford to do a report. Crawford is a businessman who has been the chairman of KPMG and director of companies like BHP Billiton, Foster's Group, Lendlease, National Foods and Westpac Banking

Corporation. He is the go-to person to do a report on sport. In his time, he has done four major reports, which have each had a significant impact on Australian sport.

In 1992, he did a report into the Australian Football League, which led to the creation of an independent commission to oversee the sport, a decision widely regarded as catapulting the AFL to the forefront of sport in Australia. In 2003 he was called in by the federal government to sort out soccer, which was a mess, to put it kindly. His recommendations led to a complete overhaul of the sport's administration, reconstituted as Football Federation Australia (FFA), and the creation of the A-League, ushering in the brightest era in Australian soccer's history. He also did a report on Cricket Australia, in 2011, recommending a similar independent commission to the one the AFL had implemented.

The 2009 Crawford Report looked at the overall funding of sport in Australia and was described as a 'new strategic direction'. That's a dangerous phrase. Essentially, it recommended more funding should go towards sports Australians *actually play* rather than towards sports that had the potential to haul in gold medals. The report cited examples like this: more government funds were provided for archery* than cricket, despite cricket having more than 100 times the number of participants; water polo received as much high-performance and AIS funding as golf, tennis and lawn bowls combined.

Perhaps most controversially, the report said Australia needed to get away from its obsession with measuring success as winning gold medals. Well, this was sacrilegious and treasonous thinking. The President of the Australian Olympic Committee (AOC), John Coates, called the report an insult to all our past Olympic

---

* The sleeping giant of Australian sports.

champions.* I'd say that, more accurately, the report was an insult to every Australian who has ever lived. As he read the report, Coates, never the shy and retiring type, could be heard yelling right across the country, and when he finished reading it he just kept yelling. In fact I can still hear him now, as I type this.

The AFL, NRL, FFA and Cricket Australia all praised the report. Coincidentally, the report recommended they should all get more money. They pretended it wasn't about the money, of course, talking about how we needed to get more kids playing sport and away from the TV but, really, they were mentally shopping for new beach houses. Coates made the point that these sporting competitions already had huge revenue streams from sources the smaller sports couldn't access.

While the report was welcomed by many, governments don't really like 'new strategic directions'. They threw $1.2 billion at the problem in 2010–11 to keep everyone happy. The memory of Montreal was possibly also still lingering in their minds.

Even with that money, Australia's Olympic team has declined in recent years. The disastrous outing by the Australian swimming team at the 2012 London Olympics triggered two reviews, just for good measure.** It shows that the nation still sees failure as unacceptable.

The public's response to the London Olympics caused much hand-wringing at the top levels of Australian sport. The chair of the Australian Sports Commission, John Wylie, did what any good bureaucrat would do and came out with a new strategy with a fancy name. *The Winning Edge* strategy recommitted Australia to

---

* Coates would know all about insults, once saying that a staff member who had cancer and was receiving chemotherapy needed to 'get out in the real world', because the AOC was not a 'sheltered workshop'.
** Swimming Australia's *Bluestone Review* as well as the Australian Sports Commission's *Independent Swimming Review*. One review is bad, but two and it starts to look like carelessness.

GREAT MOMENTS IN AUSTRALIAN DARTS

In 2015, Etihad Stadium in Melbourne hosted the Darts Invitational Challenge, a high point for darts in Australia. During the finals, drunk fans suddenly realised they were at a darts tournament and started upending tables and throwing the plastic chairs into a massive pile in the middle of the arena. After the first pile, a second and third pile were started. The ensuing chaos proved that going to watch darts can be a fun group activity.

measuring success by gold medals. Funding would only go to sporting associations if they could contribute to Australia ranking in the top five nations at the summer Olympics and Paralympics, in the top fifteen at the winter Olympics and Paralympics, number one at the Commonwealth Games and producing more than twenty world champions each year.

This all sounded very nice, and $376.7 million was given to the sports most likely to win Australia medals ahead of the 2016 Rio Olympics. But another failure to perform well in Rio saw the pressure rise and now the AOC's John Coates and the ASC's John Wylie are flinging insults at each other in the media, both of them claiming they know what's best for elite sport in this country. It's great and very productive.

I'd argue they're both wrong. Fighting over how we divide up government funding between the sports is wrong. What we need is more funding for sport. We have too many hospitals, kids don't need to be at school past twelve years old and police forces are a luxury.

A MAJORITY MINORITY

I was going to begin this section by pointing out that some of my best friends are women, but that would be a lie. I do not have any friends, be they male or female, real or imaginary. Now don't feel sorry for me. This is a life choice. They say friends are the family you choose, but I say: choose neither friends nor family. Do you have any idea how much sport you can watch on TV, unencumbered by human entanglements? It's a lot. And in Australia, it works out that about 8.7 per cent of that is women's sport.

Have you also noticed that, in talking about women's sport, I've managed to make it all about myself, a man? It's a skill us men are born with.

Women's sport has for a very long time been an afterthought in Australia, considered inferior and, damn it, unladylike. Women have been shut out of so many areas of sports for so long it's no wonder that the recent launch of the AFL Women's league (AFLW) and a major TV deal for Super Netball* have been met with such joy.

Now, I initially had trouble understanding all this, as so many men do. The world of sport has always been open to me, even though I'm not very good at it. Then I remembered what it feels like to be denied entry to a nightclub while a group of women are let in. I then extrapolated that feeling across centuries and to every facet of society, every industry and every bastion of power. Then I thought, *Oh, I get why they're angry.*

Women are denied the top sponsorship dollars and media coverage even if they are ridiculously good at a sport. Historically they were shut out of actually playing sports, at first completely, then later just when they reached a certain age, at which point they weren't allowed to play with boys anymore. Barring over half the population from your sport does seem an odd approach for administrators to take, but sports in the early days saw the absence of women as a key selling point.

Early in the history of organised sports, part of the reason for shutting women out was that medical authorities said playing sport

* See page 317.

could kill a woman. These medical professionals were all men, of course, and they constantly worried that a woman would die if she did something unseemly like sweat or move faster than a brisk jog. I guess back then there were already plenty of opportunities for women to die in childbirth, so why add to the risk?

This wasn't that long ago, either. In 1922 a government committee was set up to investigate the benefits of physical education for girls. They determined that girls should never play some sports for 'medical reasons'.* Sports like tennis, netball, lacrosse, golf, hockey, cricket and football were all identified as potentially lethal. Sports identified as safe for women to participate in without instantly keeling over were swimming, rowing, cycling and horseback riding. The committee did say that these would only be safe so long as they were not played in an 'overly competitive manner'.

Apart from believing that women were perpetually on the verge of death, men were also be terrified of involving women in sport because people might catch a glimpse of a woman's ankle or a shin.** The fear women's bodies instilled in sporting administrators is really something to behold. Even today, various tennis tournaments get in a flurry over what a woman wears on the court, despite every ad played during the coverage featuring women in far more risqué outfits.

Swimming, of course, caused a lot of problems in this same area. In 1907, Annette Kellerman, a great Australian swimmer, was arrested on a beach in Boston for wearing a one-piece costume.

---

* These 'medical reasons' were only ever outlined very vaguely. It's almost like the men just didn't want women involved and used this all as an excuse!

** I glimpsed a woman's shin once and was surprised to find it neither repulsed me nor sent me into a crazed sexual state. In many ways, shins are fairly similar regardless of gender. What I do know is that shins are important in sport; not only did the kicking of shins split rugby and soccer, the threat of seeing a woman's shin held back women's sport for years. Come to think of it, shins might be the most important body part in the history of sport.

The concern was that it was possible to actually see a bit of her leg. I don't think they were particularly interesting legs, but they scared people nonetheless.

Clothes were a huge issue in women's sport. At first they were incredibly limiting; the rules of netball were an adaption of basketball, designed to make it easier to play in long skirts.

As well as being impractical, women's athletic attire was often a barrier in itself. Take swimming, for example. Not only were swimming costumes originally designed to cover the whole body, it was often mandated they be made out of wool. Now, I'm no scientist, but being dressed head-to-toe in wet wool seems to be more likely to drag you to the bottom than help you set world records. I can understand a lot of women not wanting to take up a sport that was actively trying to drown them.

This too wasn't as long ago as you might think. In 1956, the year of the Melbourne Olympics, the Australian Swimming Union rules said women's swimsuits must be semi-woollen and have a skirt.* That's so ridiculous on so many levels it's hard to know where to start.

Swimming had another dubious honour. The Australian Swimming Association Olympic Committee demanded women going to tournaments have chaperones. This effectively doubled the cost for women. Better still, it was then used as an argument to not send them, or make them pay for the trip themselves.

Over the years, women finally got to wear more sensible clothing when playing sport, at which point people of course turned around and accused them of trying to use sex to sell their sport. Aren't women lucky?

As well as 'medical' concerns and clothing issues, a common argument was that women just shouldn't be playing sport. People

---

* Seriously, a skirt.

felt they were not very good at sport, were kind of a downer to have around, and the games they played were boring. The Frenchman behind the modern Olympic movement, Pierre de Coubertin, said he felt that including women would be 'impractical, uninteresting, anaesthetic and incorrect'.

Australia did not send any women to the Olympics until 1912, and that was in small numbers. Olympic sports were one area where women could at least get a little public recognition. Tennis also received some media coverage, but in other sports there was barely any.

A telling example is Betty Wilson, often referred to as 'the female Don Bradman'. Wilson played for Australia from 1947 until 1958. At ten years of age, Wilson was so good she was playing against adults. By sixteen she was playing for Victoria. Wilson could both bat and bowl, and she was the first cricketer to ever to make 100 runs and take 10 wickets in the same test. While Wilson had a career as storied as the best men, she received none of their coverage or adulation.

The lack of coverage means that there are few role models for young girls to follow. A lot of women's sport has gone unrecorded, in effect making it invisible. In researching this book, I've uncovered volumes and volumes on the history of men's sport, yet in sports played by women, there are whole eras that are barely mentioned and significant moments that are covered only sparingly.

Off the field women haven't had a look in either. Representation of women on the boards of clubs and administrative bodies was unheard of for a long time and remains dire. It took until 1984 for the MCC to allow women into their Long Room, and this only happened after the Victorian government threatened to withhold funding for the construction of a new stand if they didn't.

But there are signs the world is changing, slowly. In 1967 women were allowed to be jockeys and, in 2015, Michelle Payne* won the Melbourne Cup. That only took forty-eight years!

The AFL poured a lot of resources into their new women's league and then seemed genuinely surprised (but pleased) when it proved popular. It's not the first women's league – the W-League (soccer) was ahead of it and netball is even more established – but it was important because, in many southern states, Australian Rules runs through all levels of society. In Melbourne it's the most important thing in the world, ardently discussed everywhere from boardrooms to worksites. Ending women's exclusion as players sent a huge message, and the success of AFLW is one of the biggest indicators things may just be changing for real.

Signs can be seen everywhere. The Collingwood Football Club, to their credit, now boasts a women's AFL team and a netball team, which is great as I enjoy watching the Magpies lose regardless of gender or code. The success of AFLW has also caused sponsors and TV networks to realise that women exist in a sporting context. It's been quite fun watching them rush out media releases sounding like they've just made an amazing new discovery. 'Women like sport too!'

Regardless of motive, it's becoming a virtuous circle; increased coverage boosts sponsors, which increases revenue, which is reinvested in the sport. Women players now have more role models and a path to the elite level. It's not there yet in terms of equal pay, but finally women can play a sport like Australian Rules at a young age

> ## DID YOU KNOW?
>
> One of the biggest issues facing the development of professional women's sport is cross-contamination of girl germs at sporting venues.

---

* Payne later tested positive for a banned substance, proving women really can do anything men can.

and then not get a tap on the shoulder at eleven and be told they have to stop.

For so long, women's sport has been judged as inferior to men's sport, but really, it's just different. Give any sport decent coverage and Australians will love it. We'll know we've achieved equality when a women's football team's Mad Monday makes the front page of a paper with IN CRISIS plastered across it.

Come on, we can do it, Australia.

PART
II

CENTRES OF
CRISIS EXCELLENCE

Sport is what they like to call 'an issues-rich environment'. It brings together money, an alarming oversupply of alpha males, high stakes, glory, and intense pressure to maintain the upper hand.

With sport being Australia's national religion, all the issues that run throughout society – around racism, sexism, drugs, sexuality, gambling – become magnified until they're almost cartoonish. Sport has both shaped these issues and been molded by them.

The steady influx of money and overwhelming media coverage means sport is often the canvas upon which these complex issues play out. Money means the stakes are ludicrously high, the temptation to cheat is commensurately great, and media scrutiny is intense, with journalists* competing to be the first to report the latest crisis.

Sport is the number one generator of public scandals in Australia. Sure, the politicians try to keep up, but we don't care about them that much. Even at their worst, they don't affect anything important, like whether our team wins on the weekend.

Remember that when sports administrators and athletes do ridiculously stupid things, like setting up complex schemes to cheat the salary cap or experimenting with questionable sports science practices, it's because the stakes are so high they've decided it's worth the risk. Also, it makes for very fascinating reading.

---

* Or worse than journalists: bloggers. Trust me, bloggers are the worst.

GAMBLING

Drinking, sports and gambling make up the holy trinity of Australian social life. It's been that way since the first boatload of convicts showed up on these fair shores. Australia has always tried to balance our love of gambling with a desire to curb its excesses. The story of gambling in Australia is governments first curbing it, then trying to figure out how to tax it, then saying, 'Ah to hell with it, go for your lives.'

Right now we live in an unprecedented era of 24/7 gambling where you can bet on almost anything. It shows, too, with Australians losing $23 billion in the 2014–15 financial year. That's serious money.

In the early days, betting was closely linked to horseracing and, as that sport grew, so did the infrastructure that supported it. To say horseracing and betting are essential to each other is probably understating it. They're as vital to each other's existence as your beating heart is to yours. Sure, there are people who just love the sport of kings without betting on it, but only five of them remain alive today.*

---

* And hello to Henry, Walter, Doris, Vernon and Mabel if you're reading.

By the 1820s, betting on a wide range of sports was incredibly popular, simply because there was nothing else to do in the colonies. People bet on boxing, cockfighting, sailing, athletics and later on the various football codes and cricket. Cycling became incredibly popular with punters and, by the 1890s, fixed bike races had become so obvious that governments around Australia banned betting on any sport other than horseracing. Horseracing somehow avoided the ban; the governments acknowledged that without gambling the sport probably wouldn't exist. It was a point that had some precedent; in 1883, South Australia banned betting from South Australian racetracks and crowds deserted the sport. The ruling was reversed.

Underlying the ban on sports betting was the ascendency of anti-gambling forces, often led by church groups. In their minds gambling was closely linked to all sorts of immoral behaviour, and their views were in the majority. It took almost a century for the gambling lobby to claw back a freewheeling regulatory environment, with no legal sports betting on anything but horseracing until 1996, when the NT opened the door.

Racing had started to introduce the 'totalisator' to some racecourses, just before sports betting was banned. What was popular about the 'tote' was that all the bets were placed in a pool and the odds were worked out by dividing the pool amongst the winners. It was seen as a lot less corrupt compared to previous forms of gambling and, more importantly, it was easier to tax. The various state governments saw this new form of betting as a wonderful way to gain revenue and minimise the amount of money that flowed to SP bookies – the unlicensed starting-price bookmakers who operated off-track.

THE ORIGINAL COLOURFUL RACING IDENTITIES

SP bookies were a massive problem for governments. They operated from anywhere, making it very hard to track their revenue and tax it.

They were early converts to the great Australian tradition of tax avoidance, which corporations based here have now have embraced with such relish. The various governments took a two-pronged approach to stopping them. They allowed tote betting at racetracks, to give punters a legal option, while banning all off-track betting.

Illegal off-track betting proved pretty hard to stop, especially as Australians loved it. Trying to stop it was like fighting a war in a country where the local populace was actively sabotaging you. It's hard to convey just how much Australians love betting. Perhaps the best example is a friend of mine who barely passed Year 10 and then became a mathematical genius overnight in order to calculate odds, thereby proving all you need in life is the appropriate motivation.*

The racetrack totes of the day required a huge amount of manual calculation to determine payouts,** meaning betting often had to stop an hour before the race started and then the results might not be known until the next day. In sharp contrast the SP bookies, using fixed odds, could simply pay out the agreed amount as soon as the race was over and could take bets right up to the start of the race.

Enter an engineer by the name of George Julius, who was working on a machine to tally votes for elections. On completing it, he found governments didn't want it, leaving him in a bit of a quandary. It didn't take long, though, for him to work out that the machine could function as an automatic totaliser, able to calculate odds and payouts faster than punters could hand over their hard-earned. Julius was not the first or the last person to discover that you could make a lot more money out of vice than community good.

Julius sold the first of his machines in New Zealand, where it was installed at the Ellerslie Racecourse. Before long, electric versions

---

* Hello to Simon, too. I can't wait to see you when you get out in five to six years, pending good behaviour.
** The best solution was to get lots of people doing the calculations at once, and we all know that people are both slow and expensive, which is why machines will be taking all our jobs in the next few years.

were installed across Australia. So successful was the automatic tote that Julius's company made it through the Great Depression and soon found success in the UK and America. Julius later became the head of an early version of the CSIRO and was even knighted. Perhaps people would have more respect for science these days if it devoted more of its research to speeding up how quickly we could lose money betting and spent a bit less time pointing out we've ruined the planet for future generations.

With off-course betting now illegal, a whole dark subculture built up around it, linked to race- and match-fixing, police and political bribery, and other crimes. It would be the subject of several royal commissions. Things only got worse when radio began broadcasting racing in the thirties, enabling off-course betting operations to offer instant odds and payouts, leading to the broadcasting of horseraces being banned several times.

SP bookies usually set up shop in a pub and were the original 'colourful racing identities'. As phones became common, people didn't even need to visit the bookies in person, which lead to an explosion of larger illegal operations that took phone bets. Unlike most call centres, gambling ones always answer your calls promptly. We should get gambling companies to run Centrelink. People would always get through to someone to discuss their dole, and then they could use it to place a bet at the same time.

To beat the SP bookies, governments decided they had to join them and, in 1961, the Victorian Government introduced the Totalisator Agency Board, or TAB, to run legal off-course betting shops that they could tax. The idea spread, with each state eventually operating its own TAB system. While it was seen as a way to tax a practice that was going on either way, it turned out to be the thin edge of the wedge. Dependence on gambling-tax revenue is something Australian governments have found hard to shake.

FOLLOW THE MONEY

In the eighties, betting was a booming industry for governments, and when there's money to be had, people tend to 'innovate'. This meant the introduction of dedicated satellite broadcasting of races through Sky Channel (now Sky Racing), which was shown in TABs and sports clubs from 1985 on, before being made available to individuals in 1998. Now people could bet on all sorts of races, all the time. But Sky and the TABs needed lots of betting to be viable, so the push was on for racing to take place on more days of the week. Soon there was Friday racing, night racing and mid-week racing. A national betting market was created so smaller states could get a cut of interstate betting. It was a wonderful time: you could lose your life savings across multiple states and on any day of the week.

With governments now owning a fair chunk of the betting market – surprise, surprise – betting on other sports was made legal again. Can you believe it? Yes, of course you can. It was a development as unsurprising as one of Geoffrey Edelsten's 'relationships' ending badly*. To be honest, the world isn't that complicated; just follow the money, not what people say, and suddenly everything makes a lot more sense.

With the TABs turned into profitable legal businesses, governments started to think about selling them off. Like toddlers, the states wanted instant gratification: a big pile of money right away rather than an ongoing revenue stream. It was the end of a long era. Attempts to ban, then minimise illegal gambling had ended in the states essentially legalising off-track gambling on horseraces and some other sports. Now gambling was back in the hands of private operations with a pure profit motive.

---

* A betting market for those would never work because the outcome is too predictable.

PLEASE PRETEND TO GAMBLE RESPONSIBLY

And still there was more to come. Soon Australia returned to the regulatory framework of the 1890s, best described as the 'bet on anything you want' framework. The main driver was the internet. Online gambling reshaped the betting landscape in ways governments are still getting their head around.

The Northern Territory was the first to legalise internet sports betting in 1996 and the other jurisdictions quickly followed suit so that everywhere in Australia had it by 1999. Imagine if our governments moved that quickly on positive stuff?*

It was a big move but most bookmakers were only allowed to operate in the state or territory they were based in. Still, it was a start, and the various operators started to chip away at the remaining pesky regulations. In 2008, the watershed moment came: the High Court found in favour of the James Packer–backed Betfair, ruling that it was unconstitutional to prohibit bookmakers from advertising in one state and operating in another.

That decision transformed the industry. It meant betting companies could set up anywhere they wanted and flood the entire market with ads. Almost overnight watching a game on TV became more like watching gambling ads occasionally interrupted by sport. It got to the point where bookmaker Tom Waterhouse was on Channel Nine's official coverage of the NRL

> ### DID YOU KNOW?
> ⟳
> Your mate who said they won a lot of money at the races didn't.

as well as almost every ad break. People were angry about the saturation of gambling ads – but mostly about Tom Waterhouse – and the federal government made noises about potentially, maybe, doing something about it, one day.

---

* That's how you fix climate change: let people bet on it.

The online betting industry quickly made up a new self-regulatory code for advertising, which was as effective as all self-regulatory codes: the number of ads increased. Self-regulation of companies is like expecting your children to decide and enforce their own bed time. Not going to happen.

At least Tom Waterhouse was gone,* replaced by massive international gambling corporations such as Sportsbet, William Hill and Betfair. In the 2014/15 financial year, sports betting grew by 30.1 per cent and Australians lost $814 million to it, indicating we're really bad at it. Hardly surprising if you've ever actually listened to your mates' theories on sport.

A FOOL AND HIS MONEY

Now governments are in a position where they want to be seen to be doing something about the situation while also keeping the tax dollars they've become reliant on. With the betting happening online, the states and territories – once the regulators of gambling – are no longer relevant. Only a federal approach will work. That seems unlikely.

All the major sports are in it up to their necks. The AFL, NRL, Cricket Australia, FFA, Golf Australia, Basketball Australia, Formula One, MotoGP and many sporting clubs all have 'official' betting partners. Each of them contorts themselves into justifying taking the betting companies' money by positioning themselves as part of the community and caring about the impact gambling can have on families and children. They argue that only their involvement limits excessive gambling, but that's nonsense. Sure, people were betting when it was illegal, but that was nothing compared to the current barrage of advertising and infrastructure designed to

---

* Only after selling his business for $34 million. What a feel-good story, hey?

separate a punter from their money with minimal friction. What the codes really mean is, 'Please don't take away all this nice money.'

Today's regulatory framework means that only one barrier really remains when it comes to betting on sports, with in-play betting still illegal in Australia. It'll be interesting to see how long it takes for that to change.

This rise in sports betting has seen match-fixing scandals and other betting-related corruption in cricket, tennis, horseracing, greyhound racing,* soccer and League, to name just a few. The various sporting administrations have responded by putting in place the wonderfully named 'Integrity Units', pretending the root cause of the trouble is something other than the massive amounts of gambling money flooding into sport – money in which they have a vested interest.

Surprising only those who haven't engaged their brain past first gear, the more gambling there is in sport, the more corruption follows. It's really like most of human life: set the incentives right and people will respond in a depressingly predictable way. So, the more the major sport administrations try to convince us they've got everything under control, the more you know they don't.

---

* You know something's not right when you can't even trust greyhound racing to not be corrupt.

CORRUPTION

As money and media coverage have turned sports into a life and death matter, people have tried to find ways to cheat. I know, I know – I'm as shocked as you are.

There are more ways of cheating than there are sports. In fact, while some consider art as the pinnacle of human creativity, cheating would have to be right up there too. I mean, there's a reason we call them con artists. The problem is, the artistry and creativity that goes into developing a good scam is almost always matched by the stupidity of the people executing it. This can be expressed mathematically by the 'Fine Cotton correlation coefficient'.*

THE BEST TEAM MONEY CAN BUY

Some ways of cheating have become incredibly complicated, but just using buckets and buckets of cash to buy a better team than everyone else is a long and proud tradition. Clubs have always found ways to pay players extra, whether directly or indirectly, starting with handing over paper bags full of cash. John Wren, for example, ran an illegal tote in Melbourne in the early twentieth century, and

---

* You can read about the Fine Cotton scam on page 298.

was rumoured to have helped out his team, Collingwood, by finding jobs and money for players.

In the VFL attempts were made to stop a few rich clubs from dominating as early as 1897. Both the NSWRL and the VFL placed restrictions on where clubs could recruit from and implemented rules against poaching, as well as setting maximum amounts individual players could be paid. But for a long time so little money was coming in, it wasn't really an issue.

Following nationalisation of the codes and the increased revenue from TV and sponsorship, leagues started to think about more drastic measures to stop inequality. This led them to the introduction of the salary cap, a limit on how much each club could spend on players all-up. The VFL introduced one in 1987 and the NSWRL in 1990. The NSWRL's initial salary cap was between $800 000 and $1.5 million per club; by 2017 it had risen to $7 million. The AFL's has grown from $1.25 million to $12.45 million.

As soon as the salary cap was introduced, clubs tried to cheat it. In the very first year it was implemented in the VFL, Sydney were caught cheating. The NSWRL's Canberra Raiders at least managed to keep things under wraps for twelve months before getting caught.

The AFL was rocked at the end of the 2002 season when Carlton was fined just under $1 million for cheating the cap in 2000 and 2001*. They also lost draft picks for the next two years, a brutal punishment that set Carlton back decades. You'd think that'd stop salary cap cheating in the AFL but there's always someone who thinks they're a bit clever and the Crows gave it a go too, sneaking Kurt Tippett an undeclared payment of $170 000. They got caught and were fined $300 000 and barred from the first two rounds of the 2013 draft. Tippett and chief executive Steven Trigg were also fined.

---

* Despite all that cheating, Carlton finished dead last in 2002, which takes some doing.

While AFL clubs have put in a decent effort breaching the salary cap, the NRL made them look like amateurs. In 2001 the Canterbury Bulldogs had a massive clean out of its players and by 2002 the restructure was bearing fruit; they were on the cusp of securing the minor premiership and had won seventeen games in a row. But they had one big problem: they had put their wonderful team together by ignoring the competition's salary cap. Even worse, they were caught.

It wasn't cheating by a little bit either. Then NRL CEO David Gallop described the cheating as 'exceptional in both its size and its deliberate and ongoing nature'. That's not what you want to hear. In fact, they were in breach of the salary cap by about $2 million over the space of three years. That seems excessive to me. Surely $1 million gets you sufficiently ahead of everyone else.

The punishment was just as exceptional in its size: the Bulldogs were handed a $500 000 fine and stripped of 37 premiership points, ending their season. The CEO, president and entire board resigned. It was a sobering lesson and all Rugby League teams heeded the message for at least five minutes before salary cap cheating resumed.

In 2005, the New Zealand Warriors were caught out, their new management revealing that the previous management had been over the salary cap to the tune of $1.1 million over two years. The club received a $430 000 fine and started the next season with a four-premiership-point penalty. It all came as a bit of a shock, just a few years after the Bulldogs had come undone.

Would these teams ever learn? The simple answer was no they would not.

The next major salary cap scandal would make the Bulldogs look like novices. Since its formation in 1998, the Melbourne Sto. had quickly established itself as a powerhouse in the NRL. The late 2000s were especially impressive, the club winning minor premierships in 2006, 2007 and 2008 and premierships in 2007 and 2009.

I remember watching the team at Olympic Park during that period and thinking, *This is the best team money can buy.*

Unfortunately, this was more true than I knew. In 2009 the NRL discovered that the club was keeping two sets of books, one for the NRL and one with the actual accounts. Further to that, this system had been in place for five years. Under the scheme, invoices from certain suppliers would be for a lot more than the services provided. The club would pay the inflated invoice and the extra money went to players. It was breathtaking in both its scale and organisation. The whole saga was also a good lesson to not write things down if you're committing fraud, as the NRL got their hands on some of the Storm's meticulous paperwork that outlined the illegal payments.

Records showed one player, who was officially getting $400 000 a year, was actually getting $950 000, including a $20 000 gift voucher and a boat. I don't know about you but I could get interested in receiving gift vouchers for Christmas if they were worth $20 000 not $20. Awkwardly, the Storm were owned by News Limited, a part owner of the NRL, who were quick to throw as many club officials under the bus as they could get their hands on.

The punishment was brutal. The two premierships and three minor premierships the Storm had won in that period were stripped from them and the club was unable to earn premiership points in 2010, confining them to last place for the season. They had to offload stars to get back below the salary cap.

Yet, again, a good scandal didn't affect the game for long and, in 2012, the Storm faced off against the Bulldogs in the Grand Final. The Storm won the battle of the salary cap cheats.

You'd think all these cautionary tales would have put a stop to salary cap cheating but to show you that no one has a monopoly on stupidity, in 2016 the Parramatta Eels were found to have been systematically cheating the salary cap since 2013, using inflated invoices and third-party payments. It seems rather than learning from the past, club administrators use it as a template for future endeavours. Again the punishments rained down: a $1 million fine and the stripping of 12 premiership points in 2016.

It seems the NRL's revenue model might be based around fines for salary cap breeches, but that's probably okay as they seem to be a sustainable resource.

In happy news, the A-League has also gotten in on the action, with Perth Glory fined $269 000 in 2015 for breaching the $2.55 million salary cap by $400 000.

History suggests that the next big salary cap scandal is already occurring right now and we're just a few years away from finding out about it. Exciting!

DRUGS

I'd like to preface this section by saying no Australian athletes have ever taken drugs and that they are all fine people of high moral character. So anyway, here's a long history of all the drugs Australian athletes have taken.

In 1988 Australia started to get serious about testing sports people for performance-enhancing drugs. Before that we'd been doing a lot of losing to Eastern Bloc countries, so we were probably more worried that we weren't giving our athletes *enough* drugs.

THE WINNING EDGE

Once the government started giving sports a lot of money at the start of the eighties, they felt they needed to ensure that money wasn't going towards illegal drugs, which is probably a sensible position to take. They were also motivated by a *Four Corners* episode called 'The Winning Edge',* which alleged steroids were being used at the AIS. Nothing better than a media exposé to focus the minds of government officials.

---

* Not to be confused with *The Winning Edge* government strategy that followed Australia's meek performance at London 2012.

In 1990 the Hawke government established an independent statutory authority, the Australian Sports Drug Agency (ASDA). The establishment of ASDA reflected the wider realisation that athletes were juiced almost all the time. The Olympics in particular were being rocked by positive tests, most famously Canadian Ben Johnson being stripped of the 100-metre gold medal he'd 'won' at the 1988 Seoul Olympics. As a result, sports fans and the media needed to talk about urine samples a lot more than they had ever wanted to. The new focus on catching drug cheats led the ASC and ASDA to release a 'tough on drugs in sport' policy, replacing their 'we don't really have a drug policy' policy.

TOP FIVE WAYS I COPE WITH SUPPORTING A BAD TEAM

1. Excessive drinking
2. Stress eating
3. Venting on social media
4. Ranting to friends and family until they stop returning my calls
5. Lying in the fetal position, sobbing, until a neighbour calls the police

Generally, Australians were convinced that drug cheating was something other countries' athletes did, not our Aussie heroes. While athletes in international sports, especially those in the Olympics, were forced to comply with drug testing rules if they wanted to compete overseas, our domestic sports officials dragged their feet. For instance, when Richmond player Justin Charles tested positive for an anabolic steroid in 1997, the AFL didn't even have an anti-drug policy. So they just made up the penalty – a 16-match suspension.[*]

This seemed shambolic at the time but future events proved that making up penalties is actually the AFL's official policy.

---

[*] Charles returned to the game but didn't last long, in part due to injuries and in part due to not being on drugs anymore.

By 2004, the ASC had become compliant with the World Anti-Doping Code, which included recreational drugs like marijuana and cocaine. You know, the fun ones. This caused enormous problems for the AFL; they preferred a more lenient approach to recreational drugs because they didn't want to lose all their players.

Events overseas continued to push performance-enhancing drugs to the front of administrators' minds. The news that absolutely every single rider in every Tour de France ever was doped up to their eyeballs caused ASADA* to investigate Australian cycling in 2012, with cyclists Matt White and Stephen Hodge admitting to doping.

THE BLACKEST DAY

While the cycling finding was significant, it was nothing compared to the release of the Australian Crime Commission (ACC) report *Organised Crime and Drugs in Sport* in February 2013. This involved a media conference with about 200 people on stage, all tut-tutting and trying to outdo each other in explaining how serious it was. It was described as the blackest day in Australian sport.**

The report said prohibited substances such as peptides, hormones and recreational drugs were rife in professional sport. The AFL's Essendon Football Club and six NRL teams – Canberra Raiders, Cronulla Sharks, Newcastle Knights, Manly–Warringah Sea Eagles, North Queensland Cowboys and the Penrith Panthers – were implicated. ASADA struggled with the task of investigating a lot of this. What followed were investigations that centred mainly on Cronulla and Essendon.

---

* The Australian Sports Drug Agency changed its name because they kept going to meetings and being mistaken for pro-drugs campaigners, so in 2006 they became the Australian Sports Anti-Doping Authority. Everyone was like, 'Oh, you're *anti*-drugs, that makes a lot more sense.'

** This wasn't the blackest day in sport by a long shot. What about when they stopped letting you bring a slab of beer into the cricket? That was a pretty black day.

The Cronulla case was settled relatively quickly, and when I say relatively, it's because anything is quick relative to the Essendon saga, including the heat death of the universe. It was alleged that in the 2011 season, Sharks players had taken the banned peptide CJC-1295. ASADA offered the players involved a six-month ban if they pleaded guilty; if they maintained their innocence but were then found guilty, they'd receive a two-year ban. Many of the Sharks players pleaded guilty. In total fourteen players received suspensions, the coach Shane Flanagan received a one-year ban, and a $1 million fine was handed down to the club.

The Sharks went on to win the NRL Premiership in 2016, further proof that there's no such thing as karma.

The Essendon Supplements Saga, as it came to be known, accurately, would drag on for years and years. Bizarrely it ended up in the Federal Supreme Court of Switzerland.* It ended careers and funded more beach houses for lawyers than a royal commission. To recount the whole tale would take several books but, quite simply, the Essendon saga was a vortex and anyone who came near it came out of it worse for wear.

Basically, in 2010, former superstar Essendon player James Hird was appointed coach, with another Essendon legend Mark Thompson joining him as a sort of wise counsellor.** These were exciting times for the Bombers faithful, but it later came out that a supplements program was in place for their players. In media coverage of sport, 'supplements' is a nice way of saying 'a host of stuff, some legal some potentially not'. At worst the program was sanctioned by the two men; at best they, and other club officials, didn't do enough to stop it.

---

* It was like the morning after a bad night out. 'And then we woke up in the Federal Supreme Court of Switzerland with no idea how we got there.'
** Never would that term be less accurate.

Running this program was Stephen Dank, a sports scientist. This is a class of scientist that has recently inundated clubs. Some are about as scientific as those that supposedly work in the Pond's Institute. Working with Dank was a fitness specialist Dean Robinson,* a former rodeo clown (I kid you not) who had recommended Dank to Essendon. Dank had been at Cronulla in 2011, too – he was really versatile and could ruin clubs regardless of what code they played.

One thing that is indisputable about the whole affair, and even Essendon have acknowledged this, is that they ran the program with an alarming lack of paperwork and oversight. Basically, no one really knows what they injected the players with, only that they injected the players hundreds of times.

This all came to a head with the Bombers self-reporting just before the release of the ACC report. James Hird claimed that this move was the result of a tip-off by then AFL CEO Andrew Demetriou, who has strenuously denied this from day one.

The following years saw claim and counterclaim, numerous court cases and never-ending media stories on the recklessness of the program. The one big problem at the centre of it all was that there was no smoking gun, only a trail of very convincing evidence that some of the injections had been banned substances. Essendon had no records to prove this wasn't true, instead they offered up the faith-based defence that they didn't believe any of the substances used were banned.

The AFL fined the club $2 million for its poor governance, suspended them from the 2013 finals, took away draft picks, suspended Hird for a year and fined Thompson $30 000. Essendon, in response, extended Hird's contract, the worst decision they'd made since hiring Stephen Dank.

---

* Robinson had given himself a nickname 'The Weapon'. Anyone who gives themselves a nickname should be treated with the utmost suspicion.

Dank would continually claim he was about to produce the evidence that would clear the players, but he never did so. He was banned from the AFL for life. He appealed the decision but then failed to turn up to the appeal hearing. He was also the victim of a drive-by shooting at his home, with a bullet grazing his head. Everyone in Victoria was a suspect.

Hird returned to coach Essendon after his suspension but performances on the field were terrible and eventually he was sacked. Clubs can put up with illegal supplement programs but losing is just unacceptable.

By 2015, the AFL tribunal finally heard the case and – I'm sure you're incredulous – they found all thirty-four players involved not guilty. Many observers believed this was the AFL covering for its players and protecting its own brand; ASADA simply saw it as the wrong decision. They went running to their international big brother, the World Anti-Doping Authority (WADA), who decided to appeal the case in the Court of Arbitration for Sport. That court reversed the AFL tribunal's decision, satisfied that the evidence showed the players had been injected with a banned supplement. The players decided to launch an appeal of their own, to the Federal Supreme Court of Switzerland – as if this wasn't all ridiculous enough already – but that was dismissed very quickly and the players were suspended for two years.

To say the AFL community has not taken this outcome well would be an understatement. Many believe that the players did nothing wrong, others argue they couldn't have been 'innocent pawns'. The fact that all athletes are individually responsible for what goes into their bodies was largely ignored by the AFL and many fans. Some in the game have

DID YOU KNOW?

NRL and AFL players represent 73 per cent of revenue for the tattoo industry in Australia.

claimed the WADA rules don't work for team sports, on the logic that players in a team are forced to go along with the group. This is the sort of peer-pressure nonsense we wouldn't accept from a child but there it was, being spouted in the media by grown adults.

The whole affair has shown how, for all its money and power, the AFL is still an organisation that prefers to run on feelings and deals more than processes and procedures. The fact that thirty-four players were found guilty by the highest sports court in the world has been met with pure denial by many within the AFL community. They claim it's all a stitch-up and really unfair. Australians still like to believe *our* athletes are clean. The fact remains that in a major Australian sporting club a supplements program was run that was reckless at best, drug-cheating at worst. People in positions of authority and responsibility either had no knowledge that it was going on, which is hardly acceptable, or were complicit in it. We'll probably never know the full truth but the idea this was all some massive misunderstanding is an insult to the public's intelligence.

Since then, the AFL has had a few other athletes test positive. Fremantle's Ryan Crowley was given a twelve-month suspension for taking a banned painkiller. Collingwood players Josh Thomas and Lachlan Keeffe received two-year bans for taking clenbuterol, which they first claimed was from a New Zealand steak but turned out to be from illegal party drugs.

While Australia is hardly up there with Russia, it's clear our athletes are at best naive when it comes to doping, and many administrators are not properly equipped to deal with it. But when it comes to not being properly equipped to deal with challenges, just wait till we get to more complex social issues.

RACISM

We've already discussed that Indigenous people had been on this continent for tens of thousands of years when the First Fleet arrived, and there is anecdotal evidence of many sporting pursuits throughout the myriad of Indigenous groups that existed. We know they played sports that ranged from spear throwing, hockey-type games, wrestling and many ball games – the ones we don't know about would be in the majority.

One thing we know for sure is that from European settlement on, the history of Indigenous sport is one of exclusion, overt, covert and institutionalised racism, punctuated by very occasional moments of glory.

Australians like to think that sport is at least one thing that has brought people together across the divide that often separates Indigenous people from the rest of the population. Reality suggests that this has rarely been the case. Even today there are so many examples of racism in sports that demonstrate progress has been slow, and sometimes it feels like there's been little at all.

For a long time the problem of Indigenous participation lay in geographical remoteness or economic circumstances. But of course there were more direct means of denying them access, like in 1869, when the Central Board of Aborigines ruled that it was illegal to take any Aboriginal person out of the colony of Victoria without the approval of the government minister. That kind of made it hard for Aboriginal players to go anywhere, especially overseas, like the team of Aboriginal cricketers who had toured England in 1868.*

Some sports like Rugby Union were completely inaccessible because they were a sport of the upper class, which the Indigenous population were certainly excluded from. Later the Wallabies played some games in South Africa during apartheid, which hardly made the sport more appealing to Indigenous players.

Cricket was a stranger case, because, as the 1868 tour showed, some Indigenous players were highly skilled and in the early days of colonisation did play cricket. In fact, they were often some of the best cricketers of their era. There is a lot of evidence that, as time passed, the white cricket community just didn't want Indigenous players to be part of their sport.

Eddie Gilbert, the fastest bowler of his time, once bowled Bradman for a duck – but he still had to get permission from the 'Protector of Aborigines' every time he wanted to play. Even when allowed to play he could not travel with his teammates or stay with them. He was also regularly harassed by umpires and cricket officials for being a 'chucker' and, in 1936, the Queensland Cricket Association pushed him out of the game. They wrote to the Protector of Aborigines: 'The matter of Eddie Gilbert has been fully discussed by the committee and it is decided, with your concurrence, to arrange for his return to the settlement.' It's hardly any wonder that Indigenous players didn't flock to the game in those circumstances and, to be clear, Eddie wasn't the only one to experience this sort of treatment. Jack Marsh, arguably the greatest bowler of his time, had the English team refuse to play against him in 1902, denying him

---

* The full story of this Aboriginal tour of England is on page 102.

the ability to play for Australia. He, too, was forced out of the game with bogus no-ball decisions.

Some sports are seen as welcoming to Indigenous players, but they often don't have as good a track record as you'd think. Australian Rules has done a lot of good in this area but the switch to supporting Indigenous players is actually very recent, and has often fallen more into the marketing arena than anything structural or transformative.

There are records of Albert Austin playing for Geelong in 1872, and Joe Johnson played for Fitzroy in 1904, but Indigenous participation in Australian Rules was sporadic at best. Those who did play had to overcome relentless racism. In the twenties Doug Nicholls wasn't given a jumper because players and coaches said he smelled. After six weeks of being shunned he left and, fully five years later, he ended up playing for Fitzroy.* Personally, I'm amazed that he hung around at Carlton for six weeks. It showed what a determined man he was, and gives us another reason to hate Carlton.

BLACK AND PROUD

Events like those are not just confined to the dim dark past. Indigenous players have regularly experienced abuse from the crowd, opposition players and sometimes even teammates. On 17 April 1993, St Kilda's Nicky Winmar received constant racist abuse from the crowd throughout a game against Collingwood. Even some of his opponents admitted they were embarrassed by it. After the final siren, which marked a St Kilda win, Winmar famously lifted up his jumper and pointed to his skin. He later said of the moment, 'As an Indigenous person, I wanted to show that I am a

---

*   Nicholls lived an incredibly interesting life. He was part of Jimmy Sharman's travelling boxing show, was an activist for Indigenous rights, an ordained pastor, appointed an MBE then an OBE, and became Governor of South Australia. He was knighted in 1972, making Pastor Sir Douglas Nicholls the first Aboriginal person to receive a knighthood.

human being as well, no matter what colour I am. I said I was black and I was proud.'*

At the time, many saw it as a sign that things needed to change, but nothing really happened. In fact, in 1999, when Nicky Winmar was late to appear on Channel Nine's *Footy Show* due to car trouble, Sam Newman went on TV in blackface and pretended to be him.

In 1995, during the inaugural Anzac Day game at the MCG, Collingwood ruckman Damian Monkhorst called Essendon's Michael Long a 'black bastard'. Long, an amazing player and well respected, couldn't stomach the racism any longer, and he decided something need to change.

The AFL, in full damage control, organised a media conference with then CEO Ross Oakley, Long and Monkhorst all awkwardly sitting on stage together. It was a show of contrition for the cameras and was meant to signify how seriously the sport was taking things but again, in reality, no one committed to anything concrete. Long, however, showed the same determination as he did on the field and didn't let the AFL off that easily. He pushed for an actual process for dealing with such incidents. The result was a code of conduct called Rule 30: Discrimination and Racial and Religious Vilification.

Of course this rule fixed everything and there's been no trouble since. Except in 1999, when Melbourne's Scott Chisholm was called a 'black c—' by St Kilda's Peter Everitt, who was fined $20 000 under the code. And actually, it's still going pretty much today; most notably Adam Goodes, one of the greatest players ever, was booed out of the game by crowds across the country.

The racial taunts began during a Collingwood–Swans game in May 2013, which was part of the AFL's Indigenous Round. Goodes

---

* Collingwood president Allan McAlister made matters worse a week later: 'As long as they [Indigenous people] conduct themselves like white people, well, off the field, everyone will admire and respect them.' He wasn't the last Collingwood president to find this racism stuff tricky.

called out a girl in the crowd who had called him an 'ape'. Helpfully, a few days later Collingwood president Eddie McGuire suggested Goodes should be used to promote the musical *King Kong*. McGuire apologised several times, each apology more confusing than the previous one, to the point where two years later he said it was all down to the fact he was on painkillers at the time.

The vitriol towards Goodes escalated after he was named 2014 Australian of the Year and used the platform to push for racial equality and recognition of the plight of Indigenous people. Goodes was booed at almost every game he played. The torrent of racism set the game back years on this issue. The AFL Commission themselves were torn on how to handle it, with some believing Goodes had brought it on himself by being so outspoken. It was a perfect example of how Indigenous people who speak out on the very real problems they face are torn down for doing so. The reaction to Goodes calling out racism only proved his original point that racism is still an issue that this country needs to confront.

Rugby League is the other code that has done a lot to reach out to the Indigenous community but, up until 1960, it was a barren wasteland when it came to Indigenous players. That started to change in the sixties, in line with changes in broader society. There had been Indigenous players before then, but they had been few and far between. To get a game, Indigenous players had to form their own teams at lower levels, a prominent example being the Redfern All Blacks Rugby League Football Club, formed in 1944.

In 1973, Arthur Beetson captained the national team, the Kangaroos, but racism on and off the field was still common. In 2010, a high-profile case involved Andrew Johns, arguably the greatest player the game has ever seen. Johns racially vilified Greg Inglis, his upcoming State of Origin opponent, telling his NSW teammate Beau Scott he'd need to stop 'that black c—'. Johns' teammate Timana Tahu walked out of the NSW training camp as a result. That's often the problem – players have to make a scene to get anyone to pay attention, never mind instigating change, and then they're described as soft or overly dramatic.

This is not to say progress hasn't been made, but it's off a low base. Where once Indigenous players were just straight out excluded from certain sports, now they are actively recruited. Where once racism was overt, now it's more covert or dressed up as being about something else.

There can be no doubt that seeing the likes of Lionel Rose, Cathy Freeman, Buddy Franklin, Greg Inglis and Jade North perform on the big stage is a great thing, but it also reinforces the fact that sport is one of the very few ways for Indigenous people to gain broad acceptance and respect.

One thing that has certainly changed is that professional sports in Australia, already competing in the most tightly contested sports market in the world, can't afford to exclude entire groups of people anymore. The money involved means that any competitive edge must be exploited, and that means securing the best talent, wherever it is.

It would be nice if as well as sport opening up those pathways, other areas of society did so too.

SEXUALITY

As a heterosexual, white, middle-aged man, I apologise in advance for any mistakes I make in this section. To say I understand these complex issues or the way they make people feel would be an over-reach, to say the least. Let's be honest, I'm not even sure if the title of this section is correct. But to leave this out would have been repeating the mistakes of the past, where the topic of sexuality was either ignored or met with outright hostility. Despite the mistakes I'll possibly make in this section, the way a large section of society has been marginalised triggers in me a sense of empathy and anger.

The confluence of sexuality and sport is not something most Australians like to think about too much. Many are still coming to terms with women playing elite sports and the fact that not everyone is heterosexual. For most of my lifetime the most nuanced analy-sis of sexuality in sport was that any women who wanted to play sport at a decent level must be a lesbian and that no male athletes were gay. It has become increasingly apparent that this may not be a sophisticated enough model to reflect reality. Why, it might even be possible that people of all genders and sexualities enjoy watch-ing and playing sport, right up to the elite level! In fact, this has probably been going on for a very long time – and the world hasn't ended or anything.

The issue of sexuality is still a difficult one for sports administrators, fans and players because it requires a high level of empathy and emotional intelligence, qualities that are in short supply in the industry. This is all changing, of course, as younger people know that the nonsense and hatred of the past is not only wrong but also really weird.

In Australia we hold up sport as the greatest expression of our egalitarian society, yet when it comes to LGBTI people, inclusion has not been forthcoming. This is not an issue of the past, it's here and now. The first international study of homophobia in sport, *Out on the Fields,* in 2015, found that 87 per cent of young gay athletes in Australia feel forced to keep their sexuality from teammates. Australia was the worst in this area in the entire English-speaking world. Consider how bad some of the countries in the English-speaking world are! I mean there's England, for starters.

More than half of all gay athletes surveyed in Australia said they feared being openly gay would result in bullying. Now where would they get that idea? Well, in 2010, retired AFL footballer turned commentator Jason Akermanis wrote:

> If a player wants to out himself, then I say good luck.
> But I believe the world of AFL footy is not ready for
> it. To come out is unnecessary for a lot of reasons.
> Imagine the publicity associated with a current player
> admitting he's gay. It would be international news and
> could break the fabric of a club.

Break the fabric of the club? What precious flowers Akermanis must think AFL players are. All these tough men would go to water because one of their teammates is gay?

A lot of Akermanis's concerns revolved around the fact that there's a lot of nudity in dressing rooms. This seems to be a common theme; some straight men just assume gay men will lust after them, unable to control themselves. I've never seen any evidence for this claim. Most men I know can't get straight women to lust after them, let alone a gay man. I think a lot of these guys are overrating their own appeal.

More recently, in 2014, on a prime-time Channel Seven broadcast, AFL commentator Brian Taylor said of Geelong's Harry Taylor, 'And I've just seen that crap from Harry. He's a big poofter. I mean, give'em this one, Harry. [Makes an up-yours gesture.] You can't be doing the old royal wave, Harry.'

Such was the immediate reaction on social media that Taylor was forced to apologise during the same match: 'I sincerely apologise . . . to Harry Taylor and anyone – particularly Harry and any of his friends – that [sic] were offended by my remark.'

The fun thing about Brian Taylor's 'apology' was that it took the form of many modern apologies, where you apologise for possibly offending people rather than for what you've actually done wrong, in this case saying something homophobic. The implication seemed to be that what he said was not necessarily offensive. He seemed to think the problem was that he'd suggested Harry Taylor was gay, when it was actually that he'd used a homophobic slur.

> **DID YOU KNOW?**
>
> In South Australia, a marriage between a Crows and a Power supporter is known as a 'mixed marriage' and is illegal.

These aren't complicated concepts to understand, but the sentiment was repeated in the footballing world several times in the following days, with other commentators pointing out Brian was very sorry and had apologised to Harry. The impact on Brian Taylor's career was huge, of course: he had a few weeks off, received some counselling and has now been promoted to the *Friday Night Football* team. That'll show him!

These are just a couple of examples from mainstream football people, employed by the mainstream media. It's no wonder that *Out on the Fields* reported that most lesbian, gay and bisexual athletes don't disclose their sexuality.

In fairness to the major codes, there have been some efforts to change these attitudes. Six of Australia's major sporting codes signed up to the Pride in Sport Index (PSI), in response to the *Out on the Fields* survey. The ARU, NRL, AFL, FFA, Cricket Australia and Water Polo Australia will now regularly measure how they support their LGBTI players, staff, spectators and supporters. We might be world-beaters when it comes to sports performance, but this is another area where we have a lot of catching up to do.

ROLE MODELS

NBA player Charles Barkley once famously said, 'I am not a role model . . . Just because I dunk a basketball doesn't mean I should raise your kids.' The fact that he said this in a Nike ad that was using his profile to sell shoes to kids probably lessened the credibility of the message. I doubt anyone was expecting him to raise their kids, they just recognised he had a big influence on them.

Regardless of what Barkley thinks, athletes are role models to many people. The problem is that giving someone lots of money at a young age, treating them like they're special and placing them under a lot of pressure often results in them doing not very role model-y things.

Behaving badly in sports seems to always play out in some fairly predictable patterns. There are the alcohol-fuelled incidents, often featuring a lot of public urination. Like NRL's Todd Carney, who rather interestingly had a photo taken in a nightclub bathroom where he was urinating into his own mouth, or former Richmond captain Kane Johnson, who decided the St Kilda Road police headquarters was a good place to take a leak (it wasn't).

Urinating in public is not the worst thing that can happen when sports stars and alcohol mix. In 2008 swimmer Nick D'Arcy, in an incident at The Loft bar in Sydney's CBD, king-hit fellow swimmer Simon Cowley, telling police that 'it seemed like a good idea at the time'. D'Arcy was convicted of recklessly causing grievous bodily harm.

Swimmers have contributed more than their fair share of bad behaviour, with Grant Hackett tweaking a man's nipples on a flight in 2016 and once being found wandering semi-naked through Melbourne's Crown casino while looking for one of his children, whom he had lost.

Drug-related incidents are also common. Perhaps the most famous, really just one long continuous incident, is AFL Brownlow medallist Ben Cousins. Cousins' battle with drug addiction has moved right through the spectrum, from occasional amusing and silly episodes to downright scary ones.

Cousins' first major incident was in 2006, when he ran away from a booze bus, leaving his girlfriend in his Mercedes-Benz, sitting in the middle lane of Perth's Canning Highway. Not exactly a well thought-through plan.

Events like these continued for Cousins with alarming regularity. Numerous arrests for drug possessions followed, as his run-ins

HOW TO ENCOURAGE YOUR KIDS TO BE BETTER AT SPORT

- Explain to them that given their IQ, sport is probably the best chance they have of becoming rich
- Withhold your love unless they win something
- If they're playing sport and look like losing, don't stick around to give them a lift home
- Point out that even Bernard Tomic has made millions of dollars without really trying

with the law became ever more bizarre: he led police on a slow chase through the Perth suburbs, was found in the Special Air Service's Campbell Barracks, was involved in a strange incident involving a priest's wife at a Sikh temple and was found directing traffic on the Canning Highway (not in an official capacity). In late March 2017, Cousins was sentenced to twelve months in prison for drug possession and stalking offences relating to his ex-partner.

A FALLEN SPORTING IDOL

Geelong's Gary Ablett Snr was such a freakish figure on the field fans called him 'God'. Off the field, Ablett had frequent issues with drugs and, in 2000, a nineteen-year-old woman died in his hotel room following a drug overdose. Ablett admitted to supplying the woman with heroin and other drugs. He pleaded guilty to four drug charges and was convicted and fined $1500.

After providing drugs to a nineteen-year-old that resulted in an overdose, most people would feel unqualified to lecture people on morality, but not Ablett Snr. In a long rambling column in the *Herald Sun* in 2010, Ablett decried the decline of Australian society and its values, due to science and Australians turning away from religion. He then broadened his scope to argue that evolution isn't real:

> Now it is bad enough misleading us by telling us we descended from convicts but to tell us we descended from 'apes' – come on!
>
> Man might look like an ape, act like a goat, eat like a pig, think like a jackass, be as stubborn as a mule and as cunning as a fox, but a man is still a man and has been that way right down through recorded history. I openly confess to being no scientist, nor will I try to pretend to be one.

Ablett Snr didn't really need to point out he's not a scientist, and I think most Australians felt he was not the moral leader we needed.

REAL CHARMERS

Unfortunately, treating women horribly is an alarmingly common trait among some of our top sports stars.

Wayne Carey, perhaps the greatest player in VFL/AFL history, had more than a few misdemeanours off the field. As well as having an affair with a teammate's wife, he pleaded guilty to indecent assault after grabbing a women's breast in the street, provided a character reference for gangster Jason Moran (later murdered in Melbourne's gangland war), assaulted police in the US, had to be subdued with capsicum spray by Victorian police, struck his girlfriend in the face with a wine glass and was found to have traces of cocaine on his clothes when entering Barwon Prison to mentor Indigenous inmates. All this has not gone unpunished, as Carey is now forced to have a high-paying gig as part of the Channel Seven commentary team.

Not to be outdone, NRL legend Andrew Johns had a variety of issues too, including one incident in 2015 where he was photographed lying on the floor of the Toowoomba airport, heavily under the influence of alcohol. This was after he propositioned a married woman, who reported afterwards, 'He was severely intoxicated. I am a 42-year-old woman that he asked to kiss him. When I refused to kiss him and replied I was happily married and had three sons, his question to me was "Did you have a caesarean birth?"' What a charmer.

Nick Kyrgios is the perfect example of a sportsperson who is just a goose. During a match against Stan Wawrinka, Kyrgios told him, 'Kokkinakis [Australian tennis player Thanasi Kokkinakis] banged your girlfriend. Sorry to tell you that mate.'

There's no doubt that the immense pressure of sport causes people to do odd things, but that's not the only reason for this

DID YOU KNOW?

Due to numerous NRL players being involved in unsavoury incidents with dogs, the NRL has appointed a member of the RSPCA to their Integrity Unit.

sort of behaviour. When you're young, you usually have no money, and in the main young men experience more rejection than adulation. That's a necessary step to smooth out their rough edges. There's nothing like life pointing out you're not all that great to make you a nicer person. A lot of sports stars miss this step completely and therefore never really grow up, instead going right through adulthood with the life skills of a thirteen-year-old, thinking they're invincible and can do no wrong.

What's the effect of all this bad behaviour, dodgy practices and crisis mismanagement? Looking at the trail of destruction, it's tempting to think, as the media often claims, that this all damages a sport's 'brand'. Nothing could be further from the truth. With every crisis, sports dominates the public consciousness, saturating the media even when no games are being played. A history of all Australia's major codes is a history of scandal, with some athletic feats thrown in.

PART III

THE DOMINANT FIVE

CRICKET

THE GENTLEMEN'S GAME

Every summer, a common scene in households across Australia goes like this:

'Are you going to sit there and watch cricket all day?'

'Actually, for five days.'

Some of my favourite memories are of wasting a day on the couch watching cricket. What appears to be a boringly glacial pace is actually what makes this great game appeal to cricket fans. So little seems to be going on but so much is happening. It's meditation for people who think veganism is right up there with extremist Islam.

Then there are the individual moments that stay with you forever: Shane Warne's ball of the century, Dean Jones's 210 against India in Chennai and Andrew Symonds shoulder-charging a naked man who ran onto the field at the Gabba.

The impact cricket has had on making Australia the sporting nation it is cannot be overstated, and even more important has been its glorious contribution to the art form that is facial hair.

THE CONVICTS TAKE TO CRICKET

There are tales of cricket being played in Australia going back to around 1800, which is no great surprise. The game was a strong reminder of home and allowed the convicts, guards and free settlers to forget they were on a continent that mainly seemed to be trying to kill them through drought, poisonous animals and bushfires.

As the community developed, cricket increasingly became the sport of choice, with hotels often organising competitions. From the very beginning, gambling was a big part of cricket, along with drinking. It is a heady combination that continues to this day, although now fried chicken has been added to the tradition. That people wear the buckets the chicken comes in on their heads at cricket matches is a clear sign that civilisation is on the verge of collapse. Not that we need to look particularly hard for signs of civilisation's collapse these days.

Club cricket emerged from these initial pub games and the foundations of the modern sport began to take shape. By 1826, the Currency Cricket Club, the Military Cricket Club and the Australian Cricket Club had been formed in New South Wales, with the Melbourne Cricket Club set up in 1838 and the Launceston Cricket Club in 1841. By 1859, the New South Wales Cricket Association was up and running, meaning the two powers of cricket pre-federation – the MCC and the NSWCA – were in place. Being from Victoria and NSW, they got along like a house on fire.

THE ENGLISH ARE COMING

While cricket was well established by the 1860s, what sent its popularity skyrocketing was professional English cricketers touring the colonies. These early tours were met with great excitement by the people of the colonies, like having their existence acknowledged by someone popular. It didn't take long, though, for the colonists to go from appreciative to antagonistic; intimidating English people became a much loved Australian pastime, with cricket just a convenient vehicle for it.

This only increased as more and more people were born in the colonies. These new Australians went from wanting to impress the English to wanting to beat them. This was originally thought to be a challenge but has since proven to be not very difficult.

The first tour, in 1862, was organised by two caterers from Melbourne, Felix W. Spiers and Christopher Pond, who underwrote the tour and made a tidy profit from it too. Making money off sports fans is something caterers have been doing ever since, usually by charging the price of a medium-sized apartment for a single cold pie.

The arrival of the 1862 English team in Melbourne was met with huge crowds. Melburnians turning out for absolutely any event soon became one of their defining features, along with wearing black, drinking coffee and pronouncing Es like As.

For the first match of the tour, against the Victorian XVIII on 1 January 1862, 25 000-odd people turned up, with many taking the day off work to watch the match. This created another Australian tradition: chucking a sickie to go to the cricket.

In Sydney, parliament was adjourned so MPs could go to the match, beginning another rich Australian tradition: politicians going on junkets to sporting events. Back then they just said they were knocking off work to go watch the cricket; now they get us to pay for it by pretending they're 'engaging with key stakeholders'.

As the tour wound its way around Australia, it became clear that cricket had a future. Especially when we were playing England. There was a wide gap between the cricketing abilities of the English and the Australians at this time, with the English team winning ten of their twelve games.

But the great response made tours like this financially viable, despite the fact it took months to get to Australia by ship. A second English touring team quickly followed in 1864, with similar levels of popularity and profitability. That side went undefeated. Australian cricket still had a way to go.

Further tours took place in 1873/74 with the great W. G. Grace leading the English and then again in 1876/77. It was during the 1876/77 tour that the first official test match was held at the MCG between the English and a team comprised of both New South Wales and Victorian cricketers. This first combined side was notable for the fact that the New South Wales contingent complained heavily that the Victorian selector didn't pick enough of their players. Peace was only restored after the final remaining spot was awarded to a New South Welshman. This problem eventually sorted itself out: in the future selectors would just pretty much always pick New South Wales players for the Australian team.

To everyone's surprise, Australia won the test by 45 runs, following an unbeaten 165 by Charles Bannerman. The result demonstrated that these cricketers from the colonies were improving significantly but, a fortnight later, the English won the second test, and they could resume their sense of superiority for a while. Later, the English explained that the loss was the result of playing so far away and being on such a long tour. The English making excuses for losing would become a tradition too.

A REAL RIOT

A tour in 1879 saw a match between New South Wales and England that threatened to derail the rivalry the two countries had built up. At the centre of events was Lord Harris, the English captain and a powerful man in the English cricketing hierarchy: he was also the captain and secretary of Kent County Cricket Club. Harris had picked the umpire for the game, a Victorian no less, which endeared him to the New South Welshmen no end. On the first day, Harris was given not out by the umpire despite what was perceived as a snick on the ball as it carried to the keeper. The crowd was incensed.

Later in the match, the same umpire judged a New South Wales player run out, despite the opinion of the crowd and the NSW team that he was well in his crease. The crowd began yelling and the

New South Wales captain, Dave Gregory, was so outraged at the decision that he stopped the next batsman from coming in. Harris and Gregory began to argue on the field, with Gregory demanding the umpire be stood down. Harris was not receptive to this unsolicited suggestion.

As the argument went on, spectators jumped the fence and someone from the crowd hit Harris with a stick (which was frowned upon even back then); the English players grabbed the stumps to protect themselves and the umpire. It wasn't a great look and pretty quickly made the quality of umpiring a secondary concern, which you'd have to say was counterproductive to the crowd's strategic goals. That's the problem with angry mobs: they do tend to lose sight of the overall picture pretty quickly.

Harris blamed a lot of the problems on the bookmakers in the crowd, who he felt were egging people on. Bookmakers and betting became a lifelong hatred for Harris, believing them to have ruined many great cricketers by seducing them with money and leading them to tarnish the game.*

Things settled down enough for the match to resume the next day, but Harris went home furious. He saw the behaviour as typical of a nation of convicts and, when the Australian team toured England in 1880, Harris used his considerable power to prevent local teams from playing them. It meant the Australians spent months at sea only to find on arrival that no county sides would play them, and tests against England were a pipedream.

That could have been the end of the rivalry right there, before the Ashes had even gotten started. Luckily, the secretary of Surrey County Cricket Club, Charles Alcock**, was a bit more measured

---

* As we all know, he needn't have worried, as bookmaking never leads to any corruption in cricket these days.
** Alcock was also the secretary of the Football Association and was the creator of the FA Cup.

when it came to judging the men from the colonies. He could sense something building that would be good for cricket. He met with Harris and told him that the game needed to continue to grow, even if it did mean playing against a group of rioting criminals. Alcock wanted Harris's approval for Australia to play England at The Oval as a way for the Australians to recoup at least some of the losses they'd made on the tour. He went even further, telling Harris that he must lead England against the Aussies, to show that cricket was bigger than the incident in NSW the year before.

Harris took a moment to think before saying, 'You find the timber and we will find the workmen to build a bridge that will last forever.'

We don't know what Alcock's response was but I like to think he said, 'You could have just said "okay".'

The match at The Oval was a huge success, with packed crowds, and ended in a narrow victory for England. It captured the imagination of both the English and Australian publics. It should be recognised that Alcock saved the day for Australian cricket, as did Harris by putting the good of the game ahead of his personal grudge. But that's enough nice things said about English people for this book.

ABORIGINAL TOUR

Before these official tours of England, there had been another: the Aboriginal tour of 1868. It was the first time a team from the colonies had ever toured England. Perhaps the strangest thing about this quite amazing fact is that cricket went on to become a game that involved very few Indigenous people. For most of Australia's cricketing history, 'cricket whites' described more than just the clothing worn.

A decade before this tour of England, a group of pastoralists from the Western District of Victoria put together a match between a team of Aboriginal cricketers from their area and the MCC. The pastoralists were impressed by the sporting prowess of their team, which was mainly made up of Jardwadjali men working on their properties. They were also aware that the novelty of the match would attract a fair crowd; the promise of a financial windfall trumped the racism of the time.

To ensure the best possible showing they hired Tom Wills to coach the team of Aboriginal players. Wills was arguably Australia's best sportsman at the time, seen as a wonderful cricketer both in England and Australia. He would go on to be part of the group that drafted the original rules for Australian Rules.

On Boxing Day, 10 000 people turned up to the MCG to see the Aboriginal team take on a full-strength MCC team, with the MCC winning.

The popularity of the match meant the pastoralists were keen to take the team to England and they spent the next few years raising the necessary capital. The tour was a gruelling marathon, with forty-seven games being played over five months, and in a completely alien culture. Luckily the English welcomed them with open arms, *The Times* calling them 'a travestie upon cricketing at Lords' and 'the conquered natives of a convict colony'. Subtle racism and dog-whistling newspaper articles were obviously yet to be invented.

While the British press may have criticised the team, the public turned out in droves, and the tour was a financial success. It would be false to paint the tour as some enlightened moment where the English public recognised the Aboriginal players as equals, but the team did win a lot of respect for their abilities, with a record of fourteen wins, fourteen losses and nineteen draws.

One of the stars of the team, Johnny Mullagh, hit 2489 runs and took 245 wickets on the tour. English fast bowler George Tarrant said, 'I have never bowled to a better batsman.'

The tour marked a high point for Indigenous Australians'

participation in cricket. The skill of these players and the few that followed should have seen them welcomed into the sport, but unfortunately humans don't follow the sensible path very often. Instead, a series of racist measures saw the Indigenous community pushed out of cricket. There were fabricated charges of throwing the ball instead of bowling with a straight arm and in 1869 legislation was introduced that made it illegal to 'remove' any Aboriginal person from Victoria without written approval from the government.

Jason Gillespie is the only player with Indigenous heritage to have officially played for Australia, and he didn't debut until 1996. It's surely one of the saddest outcomes in Australian sport that their early prominence didn't lead to more Indigenous cricket players. The exclusion of Indigenous people from a central part of Australian life undoubtedly denied cricket fans around the world the opportunity to see great players; players that were never even given the opportunity to start playing.

When people rail against inclusion, just think of this case: exclusion benefited nobody and cost everybody something. I mean this isn't like education, health, the economy or something else frivolous. This is sport. You don't mess around with sport.

OTHER AUSTRALIANS ARE THE WORST

While tours by the English did a lot to boost the popularity of the sport after 1860, intercolonial rivalries were another big reason for the game's early success. It sounds strange to us now but back then some colonies, especially Victoria and New South Wales, had a deep-seated need to prove they were the 'best' colony. This has now subsided and instead everyone recognises that every part of Australia is unique and amazing in its own special way, except for Canberra, which is the worst.

The first intercolonial match took place on 11 February 1851, between Victoria and Tasmania, at the Launceston Racecourse.

Victoria had only just become a colony – previously they were part of New South Wales – and this was one of the first things they did to celebrate, showing that they had their priorities straight right from the start. The only thing more Victorian they could have done is to open a cafe in a graffiti-filled alley. Perhaps they did but it's lost to the historical record because no one could find it.

The Tasmanian team won that day, possibly due to it being an overseas tour for the Victorians. Anyone who has been on the *Spirit of Tasmania* knows a sea voyage across the Bass Strait is enough to put you off food, physical activity and going to Tasmania.

The return game was won by the Victorians. Intercolonial cricket was away.

New South Wales first played Victoria in 1856, at the MCG, giving that sporting edge to the existing animosity over whose colony reigned supreme.

The rivalry between New South Wales and Victoria can best be described as a disagreement about how to go about being arrogant. People from New South Wales prefer a loud, showy form of arrogance, while Victorians go for a more reserved form based around a lot of pretence about not being arrogant. New South Wales arrogance is about showing how good you are through public displays. In Victoria it's about hinting that you know what's happening around town and then withholding that information from others. Like a theological argument, while this disagreement seems incredibly important to the participants, people from other states have always just lumped them both into the 'arrogant' category to save time.

Soon South Australia was also playing against the other colonies, and the intercolonial games seemed to be heading for great success. However these rivalries did not always lead to positive outcomes off the field. In the late nineteenth century the colonies, especially New South Wales and Victoria, started to see cricket as a zero-sum game.

They believed only one of them could be the promotor of both tours to England and of the English teams visiting Australia. This attitude saw them organise competing tours, resulting in farcical events like two different English sides touring Australia at the same time. In the 1890s Australia's tours of England were so shambolic (competing and therefore weakened sides were sent) that they threatened to put an end to touring all together.

Once again an Englishman had to step in and save Australian cricket from itself, as seemed to be happening with alarming regularity. Henry Holroyd, the Earl of Sheffield, was so worried about the rivalry, he paid a huge sum to have the leading cricketer of the age, W. G. Grace, lead an English tour of Australia. He gave a total of £150 to New South Wales, Victoria and South Australia to do with as they pleased. The colonies met and voted to set up an intercolonial tournament, named after the Earl: the Sheffield Shield. Divisions between the colonies didn't exactly dissipate; the vote was only six in favour to five against. But at least it had the colonies trying to work together, and the W. G. Grace tour revitalised the international rivalry.

Commencing in the summer of 1892–93, The Sheffield Shield competition would go on to power Australia to great heights on the international stage and help centralise control of Australian cricket.

In recent years, despite its success, administrators have played down the competition's importance in favour of more lucrative forms of the game – and then acted shocked when national team performances declined. Short-sighted sporting administrators with no sense of history are the viruses of the sporting world; they've been around forever, cause great damage and we don't really have a cure for them.

For example, in 1999, the Australian Cricket Board announced a sponsorship deal that renamed the Sheffield Shield 'the Pura Milk Cup'. This was allowed to happen with no repercussions for those

CRICKET FIELDING POSITIONS

Cricket fielding positions have some of the best names in sport, fine leg and gully are just two examples. By far the best, though, are silly mid-off, silly mid-on and silly point. You don't need to know exactly what they mean, just that they are all fielding positions where you stand dangerously close to the batsman. It means you regularly get a rock-hard ball hit at you at a terrifying speed with little time to react. See? Silly.

who approved it. I thought at the time that a proportional response was to fire the responsible administrators into the sun. Since then my views on the matter have only hardened and it's not too late for the Australian government to revisit this punishment.

THE DEATH OF ENGLISH CRICKET

Despite the intercolonial rivalries, Australian cricket took some huge steps in the late nineteenth century. Perhaps the biggest was pulling even with the English on the international level. On 29 August 1882 a combined team from the Australian colonies beat the English at The Oval.

The match was a close one; England needed to make 85 runs in their final innings to win, believed to be an easy target. At the time, it must be remembered, the Australian colonies were still seen as a dumping ground for England's worst. The last convict ship had been sent in 1868, just fourteen years before. No one in England thought they could be beaten at home by a bunch of criminals and their offspring.

Yet the English had not counted on Fred Spofforth, a New South Welshman known as 'The Demon Bowler'. Spofforth was a proponent of overarm bowling, something that was still not the universal style at the time. In fact, underarm bowling was still practised by some, so I assume the New Zealanders complained a lot back then.

Spofforth was fast. He used pace to intimidate the batsmen and he proceeded to knock the English over in what proved to be a dark afternoon for English cricket.* He took 7/44 and the match was Australia's. The English couldn't believe it. A team from the colonies had defeated a full-strength English side on its own soil.

This was the match that lead to the birth of the Ashes.

THE ASHES BEGIN

After the defeat, Reginald Brooks produced a famous satirical obituary for English cricket in the *Sporting Times*. 'An Affectionate Remembrance,' he wrote, 'of English Cricket which died at the Oval on 29th of August 1882'. He ended with the line, 'The body will be cremated and the ashes taken to Australia.' The line took on a life of its own when the English captain, the wonderfully named Ivo Bligh, vowed to 'regain those ashes' on their tour of Australia in 1882/83. The press took up on it and regaining those ashes suddenly became a point of national pride.

There were no actual ashes at this time. It was just a bunch of sports fans massively overreacting to something, as is our way. Overreaction is our resting state. On the tour, the English team visited Rupertswood mansion, the stately Sunbury home of Sir William and Lady Janet Clarke. Sir William was a member of the Victorian Legislative Assembly but also held a job of actual importance: president of the Melbourne Cricket Club.

After a picnic, a social game of cricket was played and, as a bit of a joke, Lady Clarke burnt the bails (the two bits of wood resting on top of the wicket, if you're not a cricket fan but have read this far, in which case thank you for sticking around) and presented the remains to Bligh in a velvet bag embroidered with '1883'. Basically,

---

* Actually, all afternoons in England are dark.

the actual physical ashes were the beginning of a proud tradition of Australians sledging Englishmen.

The gift was taken in good humour at the time, but sport is serious, not funny, and instead of being seen as a joke the Ashes have taken on spiritual overtones, with many cricket tragics making the pilgrimage to visit them at Lord's, where they are now held.

Typical of sport fans, really. Something intended as a light-hearted joke has become deadly serious. Like a stray comment I once made at a family Christmas about Uncle Geoffrey's chronic alcoholism.

The English don't let the physical Ashes leave the country very often; they've only come to Australia twice. They claim it's because of the brittle urn, which could easily fracture. If there's one thing watching English top orders has taught me it's that they are a nation that would recognise brittleness when they see it.

The Ashes series is now one of the truly great rivalries in sport, right up there with Yankees vs Red Sox, Real Madrid vs Barcelona, Lakers vs Celtics and Stone Cold Steve Austin vs Vince McMahon.

THE GOLDEN AGE

Thanks to the Earl of Sheffield stepping in and getting the Australian colonies to play nicely with each other, Australia went on a run of success that would become known as the 'Golden Age of Australian Cricket'.

In this period, from the end of the nineteenth century up until the Great War, Australia won eight out of ten tours, setting new standards for the quality of their play and their depth of talent. Cricket centralised its power in the newly federated country, and Australia's first truly great batsman, Victor Trumper, was ushered onto the world stage. Australia had gone from being a backwater to the dominant team in the world.

Trumper was a beautiful player of the ball and would torture the English attack, even on their home grounds. It was said that he would hit the ball out of the ground so often at Redfern Oval that on the surrounding lawn bowl rinks play would be abandoned until he went out. Being clocked by a Trumper six was considered a great honour at the time.

Despite this golden age, events off the field were marred by conflict. Cricket was now successful enough to attract people who wanted to run it. Given the importance of sport to Australian life, being a sports administrator instantly catapults you into the ruling class. Equally, it helps to start off in the ruling class if you ever want to run a sport in Australia.

THE BATTLE FOR THE BOARD

In 1905 the Australian Board of Control for International Cricket was formed to oversee the organisation of international tours, previously the domain of state-level cricketing bodies such as the MCC or the NSWCA. In the past competing tours had created chaos and the Board of Control was an attempt to move past that.

In fact the early days of the Board saw arguably more strife than ever before, which was not an easy thing to accomplish. The Board of Control was quick to brutally underline that it alone had the power to organise tours, at one point suspending the entire New South Wales XI for being part of the MCC's attempts to organise a tour of England.

The tension between the states, the players and the Board steadily built up. The players were used to controlling their own destinies, picking who played for the national team and negotiating a lot of the financial components of the tours. The Board set out to change all that. It probably hasn't escaped your notice but people are not exactly thrilled when they go from being able to do whatever they want to being told what to do. I still get angry at those 'no glass in the pool area' rules.

Clem Hill and Victor Trumper, the highest profile players of the time, were regularly in conflict with the Board, and in Clem Hill's case it was often in spectacular fashion. In 1909, the Board appointed ex-player Peter McAlister as chairman of selectors, a new position that replaced the captain picking the touring party. It was not a popular move, and then McAlister – forty years old and well past it – proceeded to select himself for the upcoming tour of England. If that was salt in the wound, McAlister added some acid, making himself vice-captain and treasurer for good measure.

Clem Hill exploded. He saw McAlister as nothing more than a plant by the Board, someone to watch the players on the tour. Hill boycotted the tour and the remaining players voted Frank Laver as manager for the tour, a role still decided by their vote. Laver and the other players then went out of their way to make the tour miserable for McAlister, refusing to help him in any way.

Hill returned to captain the team the next year, but the tension was far from over. McAlister remembered what Laver had done to him and, in 1912, he moved to take away the players' right to vote for the manager position. This went over about as well as you'd imagine and the simmering animosity between Hill and McAlister was quickly brought back to the boil.

As a result the 'Big Six' players (Warwick Armstrong, Vernon Ransford, Victor Trumper, Tibby Cotter, Hanson Carter and Clem Hill) boycotted the 1912 Triangular Tournament in England, forcing the Board to send a second-rate side. Underlying the personal issues between the Board and the players was a power struggle over the control of revenue by the South Australian Cricket Association and, to a lesser extent, the Melbourne Cricket Club.

But the personal animosity was what turned this row into a flashpoint, with long-term ramifications for Australian cricket. An argument between Hill and McAlister over a test in Melbourne, conducted via telegram, escalated things considerably, with McAlister recommending Hill stand down from the team. It was the equivalent of a workplace dispute over email – something we'd advise against these days, instead recommending that the combatants meet in person to thrash out their workplace issues.

Luckily, Hill and McAlister got the chance to thrash out their workplace issues on 3 February 1912, at a selectors' meeting. The insults flew thick and fast. McAlister criticised Hill's captaincy and Hill responded, 'In England, Armstrong wouldn't play under you. Did you ever win any except second-rate games?'

McAlister retorted, 'I am a better captain than Trumper, Armstrong and yourself put together. You are the worst captain I have ever seen.'

Hill at this point responded by punching McAlister and the two fought for ten minutes. That's a long time to fight. Even boxers need a break every few minutes and those guys are fit. By all accounts it was a vicious fight that ended with a bloody McAlister on the floor and Hill standing over him.[*]

DID YOU KNOW?

While being great cricketers, the majority of players who have represented Australia have been awful people.

Hill may have won the battle but he lost the war. He resigned from the Board and he would never play for Australia again. The Board would move on, player power having been crushed so forcefully it wouldn't reassert itself until the seventies, at great cost to the game. It's like when you repress something for a long time, only for it to come up when you're on a date with someone you really like and then they never call you back. But I digress.

What this meant for cricket in Australia was strong, centralised

---

[*] An afterthought: perhaps stick to email to settle workplace disputes.

control of the sport, which in many ways (players aside) helped the game to grow. The Board of Control would go on to be renamed the Australian Cricket Board in 1973 and then Cricket Australia in 2003. These days things aren't settled by punch-ups in the board-room, instead long PowerPoint presentations are used to beat opponents into submission.

The McAlister–Hill incident was the beginning of the end of Australia's golden era, and it was soon followed by the violence that was unleashed across Europe and decimated a generation of young men. No more first-class cricket was played until the 1920/21 season, eight years after the previous season.

World War I marked the end of the golden age and would directly lead to the death of Tibby Cotter, one of the Big Six who had boycotted the 1912 Triangular Tournament. He was shot by a Turkish sniper in Palestine, having never played test cricket again. He was thirty-three.

BODYLINE; OR, THOSE CHEATING ENGLISH

Following the war, the resumption of cricket in 1920 was welcomed, but Australia had mixed results throughout the twenties. The thir-ties saw the emergence of Australia's greatest ever cricketer, Don Bradman, who arrived just when Australia needed him: during the Great Depression.

'The Don' towered over Australian and world cricket, and he still holds a revered position to this day. He was a player of almost superhuman abilities. For example, English captain Walter Hammond said, 'On one or two occasions, when he was well set, and when he saw me move a fieldsman, he would raise his gloved hand to me in mock salute and then hit the ball exactly over the place from which the man had been moved!'

The period between the wars brought us other great cricketers like Bill Ponsford, Stan McCabe and Bill Woodfull. Ponsford and

Bradman were so good together they twice put on partnerships of over 380 runs.

England and Australia, so recently great allies in an awful war, managed to almost fall out of diplomatic relations in this period because of cricket. The cause was Bodyline, the most important event in the history of Australia. Not just Australian *sport*, but all Australian history.* It took the Ashes rivalry to new heights and proved once and for all that Australians are morally superior to the English.

The English side that toured Australia in the summer of 1932/33 were the worst tourists to ever visit our shores.** They lived in constant fear of one man: Donald Bradman. To these Englishmen, Bradman was scarier than the temperature going over 25 degrees or a visit to the dentist.

Their captain, the purely evil Douglas Jardine, ordered his fast bowlers, Bill Voce and Harold Larwood, to bowl short-pitched balls aimed at the bodies of the batsmen, Bradman in particular, while setting a packed leg-side field. The tactic was highly effective but not within the spirit of cricket. In fact, it was the most egregious attack on the fabric of cricket ever. My theory is this series led directly to the fall of the British Empire and has left a permanent stain on the soul of England.

The series was full of spite, as our Aussie heroes were hit twenty-five times by the bowlers. Bradman was hit twice. On the second day of the third test, in Adelaide, a day that shall live in infamy, the simmering anger erupted. Larwood hit Woodfull in the heart, causing him to double over in pain for several minutes. The crowd almost rioted and police had to come onto the boundary to stop a pitch invasion. With Woodfull bent over and in serious pain,

---

* It's probably the most important event in world history now that I think about it.
** This is a fair effort considering all the rubbish backpackers the British have sent here over the years.

Jardine simply said, 'Well bowled, Harold,' and ordered his fielders to take up positions on the leg side to further inflame tensions.

The Australians considered Woodfull a symbol of all that was good about cricket. He never complained in public about the bodyline tactics and refused to respond by taking the same approach with his bowlers, despite the media and public demanding he do so. Things got so heated that one of the Australians called Jardine a bastard on the field. Back then, that was one of the worst things you could call someone, far from the term of endearment it is today.

Things were so tense that after the day's play England's team manager, Pelham Warner, visited Woodfull to see if he was okay.

'I don't want to see you, Mr Warner. There are two teams out there; one is playing cricket, the other is making no attempt to do so,' Woodfull famously said, adding, 'This game is too good to be spoilt. It's time some people got out of it.'

The next day was equally fraught. Bert Oldfield mis-hit a hook shot, off Larwood's bowling, and fractured his own skull. Probably the only thing that prevented a riot is that the field was not set as a bodyline field; it was more an accident on Oldfield's part, something he admitted later on.

Still, the incident raised tensions even further and the Australian Board of Control for Cricket sent a cable to the MCC in London:

> Bodyline bowling has assumed such proportions as to menace the best interests of the game, making protection of the body by the batsman the main consideration. This is causing intensely bitter feeling between the players, as well as injury. In our opinion it is unsportsmanlike. Unless stopped at once it is likely to upset the friendly relations existing between Australia and England.

The English reacted with outrage at the tactic being called unsportsmanlike. All I can say is the English were lucky emoticons had not yet been invented.

Things then escalated to a level that underscored just how serious the Ashes were to both countries. The South Australian governor took up the issue with the British Secretary of State for Dominion Affairs, suggesting the ill feeling could affect trade between the two countries. That didn't go down well either and the English threatened to boycott the final two tests. How rich is that? They were the ones trying to knock our players' heads off and they threatened to boycott the series because we wouldn't let them.

At this point Prime Minister Joseph Lyons stepped in and told the Board to withdraw the 'unsportsmanlike' remark, as the damage to the Australian economy would be severe if trade with Britain was affected.

To me, Lyons' actions were pure treason. Defending the Australian cricket team is the most solemn and paramount duty of the office of Prime Minister of Australia. Selling out on the team turned this bleak chapter in Australian history into one of the darkest. I think I speak for all Australians when I say the government should have let them withhold trade: us Aussies would have lived in bush shacks to defend the honour of the Australian cricket team.

Needless to say, the Board of Control withdrew the remark and the series continued.

The final two tests were played and the English continued to use bodyline. The English departed Australian shores with a 4–1 series win and the Ashes. They also left hated, with Jardine reviled to this day. It was a pivotal time – Australians were no longer the criminals, it was the English.

The use of bodyline tactics declined after this series and was eventually outlawed. Australia returned to England in 1934 and, as England's ability to cheat had been taken away from them, the Australians regained the Ashes, with Ponsford and Bradman dominating the English bowlers.

WAR AGAIN AND ITS AFTERMATH

In 1939, another annoying war interrupted test cricket. When will humankind learn?

Unlike what happened during World War I, the government initially wanted to proceed with a business-as-usual approach, and Robert Menzies asked the Board of Control to continue with domestic cricket. I mean if you can't play cricket, the Nazis have already won, right?

But by the summer of 1941, with a rather large amount of Japanese soldiers – never big fans of cricket – heading towards Australia, devoting a lot of manpower to playing cricket seemed a tad excessive and first-class cricket ceased for the rest of the war.

After the horrors of the war, the return of cricket was a pleasant reminder of civilised society. The public in both England and Australia were keen for the return of the Ashes. In fact, a series of 'Victory Tests' were held within a fortnight of the end of the war in Europe, which is pretty bloody keen indeed.

They were contested by an English side and an Australian Services XI made up of servicemen who had played Sheffield Shield before the war, who were technically still a military unit. The team included an up-and-coming batsman by the name of Keith Miller. To give you an idea of how tough people were back then, Australian bowler Graham Williams had only been released from a German prisoner-of-war camp a few weeks earlier. He was 31 kilograms below his pre-war weight. That's just ridiculous. He occasionally had to stop and drink water with glucose to keep his energy up. The next time your mate is saying they're too tired to go out, remind them of Graham Williams.

ORDER VERSUS CHAOS

One of the most interesting storylines of the post-war period was the clash of two very different personalities, Don Bradman and Keith Miller. Bradman was consumed by cricket and winning. You don't get as good as he was without a singular focus that excludes almost everything else. It meant Bradman often had trouble relating to his teammates, who described him as aloof.

Miller, on the other hand, was a man who enjoyed all aspects of life. For Miller, playing cricket was the fun bit and winning was just a by-product. To Bradman, this was a concept so foreign it might as well have come from an alien civilisation. Bradman squeezed every last drop out of his talent, with superhuman efforts of concentration. Miller had all the talent in the world but preferred to spend his efforts off the field, partying, visiting the racecourse and generally having fun. Miller's talent was arguably up there with Bradman's, and his record is all the more amazing when you consider how recklessly he played, and often while hungover. He once deliberately lost his wicket quickly because he wanted to go to the racetrack in between innings.

The two cricketers represented two very different approaches to life: The Don, in both his captaincy and his long career as a cricket administrator, would come to represent authority and order. Miller, on the other hand, was the rebel, an agent of chaos.

Miller's view that cricket is just a bit of a laugh is often attributed to his time as a pilot in the war, where he racked up 550 flying hours, many of them flying missions over Germany and other parts of Europe. Perhaps most famously, when asked about the pressure of the game, he replied, 'Pressure is a Messerschmitt up your arse, playing cricket is not.'

However, Miller's rebelliousness wasn't purely a result of his wartime experiences. In fact, Miller seemed to take the same approach to fighting the war as he did to life generally. During his service, he threatened to punch his commanding officer, went AWOL to watch a concert and once broke formation on the way back from a mission over Germany so he could fly over Beethoven's birthplace (he was a fan).

That's not to say Miller didn't experience real danger in the war – he narrowly avoided death several times. But it seems these moments simply confirmed his existing view that life was not to be taken too seriously.

After the war, Bradman and Miller would clash repeatedly. In one testimonial match they played against each other, Miller bounced Bradman three times in a row, and a week later Miller was not selected for the upcoming tour of South Africa. Miller clearly believed Bradman used his power as a selector to block him, in retaliation for the bouncers.

Miller didn't agree with Bradman's ruthless approach and humiliation of opponents. In one case, Miller deliberately went out for a golden duck in response to Australia scoring 721 runs in a day, against Essex.

The idea of two diametrically opposed styles of sportsmanship is not uncommon in Australian sport: ruthless efficiency and a win-at-all-costs mentality versus a larrikin approach to what is meant to be a fun pastime. But rarely have we seen two exponents at such extreme ends of the spectrum, especially together in the same team. What Miller saw as harmless fun – turning up hungover to a game

THE DUCKWORTH–LEWIS METHOD

No, not a method of contraception; a mathematical formula to work out the target score of the second batting team if rain affects the first team's innings. The Duckworth–Lewis method is so complicated that only four people in the world understand it and they aren't allowed to fly on the same plane.

in a hearse, having twelfth man Sid Barnes bring out cigars, mirrors and combs during the drinks break while dressed as a flight attendant – Bradman saw as affronts to the game.

Australian sports fans want it all – the ruthless efficiency of Bradman and the fun of Miller – but it's an almost impossible line to walk. Most players tend to walk a bit on either side, rather than taking things to the extremes these two did. You could argue the only person who has managed to do both on the field is Shane Warne, who seemed to have all the waywardness of Miller as well as the ruthless winner's mentality of Bradman.

THE INVINCIBLES

After the war, Australia was able to rely on a new breed of cricketers as well as its pre-war players, the most notable being The Don himself, to keep themselves at the top of the cricketing world. This period produced 'The Invincibles', arguably the greatest team in any sport that would ever play for Australia.

The Invincibles toured England in 1948. It was Bradman's last tour of England. The team batted deep and had a terrific attack. Despite the fact that the Aussies belted the living suitcases out of the English, the crowds still showed up in droves. By this stage, Bradman was a cricketer without peer. Like Michael Jordan, Babe Ruth or Pelé, Bradman was so far above his peers that his popularity extended beyond the normal boundaries. Considering the pain he'd inflicted on the English, he and the team still received a warm welcome. They proceeded to win twenty-three of their thirty-one matches, drawing eight; they did not lose a single match.

Famously, Bradman's batting average going into his final innings was 101.39, about 50 runs higher than most top batsmen's. On the second ball he faced he was bowled for a duck, meaning he finished his career with an average of 99.94. He needed just 4 runs for it to be above 100, so really: a bit of a loser.

A story that has long persisted is that he couldn't see the ball because of the tears in his eyes from the emotion of the occasion – a vicious rumour that Bradman denied to his dying day. As he should. Australian men do not cry; we push our emotions deep, deep down within ourselves and only let them come out when we are alone, drinking beer in the shower while listening to Cold Chisel.

THE POST-BRADMAN ERA

The long shadow Bradman cast over Aussie cricket didn't go away when he retired from playing. As a member of the Board of Control, he had a far-reaching and long-lasting administrative influence. Bradman was the key figure in resisting the professionalisation that was encroaching on the game. Cricket was changing and The Don was keen for it to be glacial change.

The fifties saw the Australians take on South Africa and the West Indies a lot more; the team struggled against England, losing the Ashes series of 1953, 1954/55 and 1956. As captain, Richie Benaud managed to reclaim the Ashes in 1958/59, but it would be fair to say the fifties were marred by boringly defensive play, so interest in test cricket was on the wane.

The sixties threatened to be exciting for test cricket but, for Australia, it was a false dawn. Doug Walters exploded onto the scene, but his exciting style stood out mainly because it was unlike how most other players were approaching the game. The sixties seemed to be a time when players and captains too often played timid cricket, preferring to settle for a draw rather than risking a loss by pushing for the win. Bill Lawry's ascension to the captaincy in the late sixties was the epitome of this style. Nicknamed by an English journalist as 'the corpse with pads on',* Lawry once batted

---

* The journalist was Ian Wooldridge, who had a fabled career as a sportswriter, including covering ten Olympic Games, the last of which was Sydney in 2000. He once went three rounds with Ugandan dictator Idi Amin for a story – he wisely chose to lose the bout.

for a draw when victory required just 3 runs an over. Instead, he stayed at the crease for four hours, making just 49 runs. Funnily enough, that sort of play didn't bring fans flocking to the grounds. Even in the sixties, when attention spans were slightly longer than today, the public and media crucified him.

But if excitement and drama was what cricket fans were after, the seventies would deliver more gripping drama than an HBO series.

UNCIVIL WAR

The seventies brought the introduction of exciting players like the Chappell brothers, Dennis Lillee, Jeff Thomson and Rod Marsh. One of the greatest ever tests, the Centenary Test, was played in March 1977, which, in an incredible coincidence, was exactly 100 years after the very first test. Australia won by 45 runs, an identical result to the first ever test match, proving once and for all that cricket is more fixed than WWE.

As well as the return of some excitement to test cricket, this was Australia's golden age for facial hair. Some of the great moustaches of all time were in this team. Dennis Lillee's mo was named Australian of the Year in 1973 and sweat from it was known to cure blindness. Bob Massie sported the best sideburns since the gold rush; they were so big he had to turn sideways to get through doorways.

Unfortunately, even an exquisite handlebar moustache can't hide the world's problems. It turned out that all this facial hair was actually masking a lot of tension between the players and what had, by 1973, been renamed the Australian Cricket Board (ACB).

Even before Clem Hill's eventful selectors' meeting in 1912, cricket had been run by old white men. It had been the sport's longest tradition: good solid upper-class white men of English stock or ancestry were in charge. They ran the game autocratically and they ran it as a monopoly. Sure, the occasional Australian with Irish heritage got a seat at the table, but that was as close to diversity as things got. Since Hill's fisticuffs, in many ways the players had been relegated to indentured servitude, paid almost nothing and often treated very poorly.

By the seventies things were changing. Slightly younger white men sought to wrest control of the game, wanting to drag it kicking and screaming out of the eighteenth century. This cricket civil war emerged in Australia, dividing families and more importantly, teammates. It changed cricket forever.

Cricket was in a bubble, untouched by the modernising world around it. A bit like when they find a prehistoric tree in a deep rift valley, only alive because it's been isolated from the environmental changes all around it. Now the evolutionary pressure was well and truly upon it. Cricket, that is. Not the tree. The tree was just a metaphor. Look – forget about the tree.

Cricket administrators in Australia savoured their monopoly over the game more than anything else. They were part-time amateurs themselves, as were the players, who shoehorned in games while working as architects, accountants and car salesmen.

The Australian Cricket Board acted like most monopolies do: they were slow, bureaucratic and wanted things to remain that way. They paid the players little. They signed the TV rights over to the ABC without talking with any other broadcaster. Those rights were not even exclusive; technically any other channel could have paid to broadcast matches too, but it was hardly a recipe for ratings success when the ABC was showing the same thing but without ads.

Innovation might have occurred outside the halls of cricketing power, but it wasn't something encouraged within them. For example, limited-overs cricket had been experimented with by the ACB but, despite it proving popular, they just didn't bother to do it again. You have to admire how much the administrators were not interested in making money, something the modern version of the body, Cricket Australia, has more than corrected. At the time, a sponsorship deal with Benson & Hedges was about as commercial as it got, and that was mainly to keep cricketers in cigarettes, which were essential to controlling their weight. Exercise and cricket had not met each other yet.

Overall, the game was still an amateur one. There were few revenue streams and no interest in really developing them. The national team players were growing dissatisfied with the increased demands on them while their match fees stagnated. The tension was heightened in 1971 when captain Bill Lawry was sacked in the middle of a tour, replaced by Ian Chappell. Chappell, rather than being appreciative of the Board appointing him, saw it as a lesson in how brutally the end could come. Not only was there no money, there was no loyalty. In Ian Chappell, the Board had a headstrong, smart person who could see where the game was going and he began to clash with the governing body over player payments almost immediately.

The ACB had no interest in increasing the professionalism of the game. In 1975, after a request to increase match payments, ACB Secretary Alan Barnes told the media: 'These are not professionals [. . .] they were all invited to play, and if they don't like the conditions, there are five hundred thousand other cricketers in Australia who would love to take their places.'

Compounding one stupid thing with another, Barnes then went into the Australian cricket team's dressing room, where bowler Ian Redpath promptly threw him up against the wall, held him there, and said, 'You bloody idiot. Of course five hundred thousand would play for Australia for nothing but how bloody good would they be?'

THE PACKER REVOLUTION

This was the world of disharmony Kerry Packer stepped into. He was destined to be Australia's richest man but, at the time, was not well known. With the subtlety of an Adam Sandler movie, Packer would turn the game of cricket on its head and haul it into the professional era.

Packer needed content for his TV station, Channel Nine, and cricket's glorious five-day format was the ultimate schedule filler. When the TV rights were up for renegotiation in 1976, Packer expressed his interest to the ACB. The response was the traditional one. In a meeting between Packer and the ACB, they told him a handshake deal had already occurred where it was agreed that the rights would go to the ABC for the next few years. The cosy relationship between the ACB and the ABC went back to 1956, when the ABC purchased the broadcast rights for a whopping £25.

Being told the rights had effectively been sold without any negotiation made Packer about as unhappy as is humanly possible. He was offering a lot more money than the ABC. Huge money in fact. The ACB wouldn't even commit to Packer's offer to buy, there and then, rights for the three years following the one year they had promised to the ABC. They said they'd consider it.

The ACB didn't want things to change. They saw the ABC as part of the fabric that ran Australia. Plus, they were getting that sweet cigarette advertising money and that would surely never end.

What the ACB (and many other sports bodies) didn't realise was that TV revenue would make them richer than their wildest dreams. It would overtake every other revenue stream and then some. Unlike smoking cigarettes, everybody watched TV, and it didn't lower your life expectancy. Well, except for all that obesity.

Through their complete rejection of Packer, war had been declared – the ACB just didn't know it. This is always a bad position to be in during a war. It's like arguing with your partner: if you don't know you're having an argument, it counts against you.

On 16 August 1976, Packer registered World Series Cricket Pty Ltd. Packer's plan was simple; if he couldn't have the ACB's cricket tours, he would create his own and poach their best players. And not just the best Australian players, Packer's World Series Cricket (WSC) would go after every country's best players.

He was ridiculously successful in doing this. Ian and Greg Chappell, Tony Greig, Dennis Lillee, Rod Marsh, Doug Walters, Imran Khan, Michael Holding, David Hookes, Rick McCosker and Clive Lloyd were just some who signed on for the generous salaries Packer was offering. Turns out not paying people properly and treating them like serfs makes them susceptible to receiving lots of money from someone else. It was something the Rugby Union administrators had not understood in 1908, and the cricket authorities had allowed history to repeat.*

When word finally leaked – and that took a surprisingly long time – the move was met with outright hostility from cricketing administrators, fans and the media. Ian Chappell and Tony Greig, who were incredibly important in getting other players to sign on, received a reception previously only reserved for Judas. Tony Greig became the most hated man in England for some time and this was before people had even heard him commentate.

Richie Benaud was advising Packer on messaging. He recommended Packer strike a conciliatory tone with the ruling bodies, even suggesting this new tournament could co-exist alongside their existing schedule. Packer took Benaud's advice but added a gentle persuader to it: 'We'll do all we can to co-operate with the cricket board, and if they co-operate with us, there is no reason why test cricket as it is now will be affected. But, if they don't co-operate, they'll walk straight into a meat mangler.'

---

* An interesting aside: future Australian prime minister Malcolm Turnbull was one of the people to sign players for Packer. He was more successful in this than governing the country.

Unsurprisingly, this didn't engender warm feelings. Suddenly, cricket was divided. The phoney war was over and the real one had started.

World Series Cricket had a range of early issues. For a start, the ACB had control over a lot of the stadiums, so finding somewhere to hold the games was a problem. But there were options. VFL Park (later Waverley Park), in the outer Melbourne suburb of Mulgrave, had cost the VFL $42 million to build and cricket was the answer to paying off some of that debt. Not a great answer, but an answer nonetheless.

There were options in other cities, like the Sydney Showgrounds, Gloucester Park in Perth and Football Park in Adelaide, but they all lacked cricket pitches. The solution was to use drop-in pitches, developed by the WACA curator, John Wiley, for WSC. Cricket pitches that are prepared away from the ground and then placed in the centre of the field for the match are common today, but they were unheard of back then. Moving the pitches into place without damaging the outfield was an engineering nightmare and they seriously considered putting them in place using hovercrafts. That didn't actually work, so they used rollers instead.

Packer wasn't allowed to call them 'test matches' so they played five-day 'supertests', as well as limited-overs internationals. Despite the stars and an iconic advertising campaign – 'C'mon Aussie C'mon' – early crowds were small. On top of that, the drop-in pitches seemed to be a lot more dangerous, especially with the newly ascendant West Indies' bowling. A bouncer broke David Hookes' jaw and cheekbones. Packer rushed Hookes to the hospital in his Jaguar, which was nice of him; I wouldn't let anyone into my Jag if they were bleeding. Almost overnight, helmets were introduced to the game.

The innovations WSC introduced to the game came thick and fast. On top of helmets and drop-in pitches, there were cameras filming from angles other than straight down the pitch. This was exciting stuff. Most people back then would need a good lie down if the camera angle changed more than twice an hour. Replays and coloured uniforms were introduced, and Dennis Lillee even experimented with an aluminium bat.*

After a slow start, these innovations began to have an impact. Crowds started to grow. Packer was also using political power to prise open doors that had been shut to him. He convinced the New South Wales premier, Neville Wran, to sack the SCG Trust so WSC could play at the ground. This was the same SCG Trust that Packer described as 'a group of crusty old men sitting behind closed doors', which was probably accurate, if a tad harsh.

While WSC's crowds were improving, especially for one-day cricket, the ACB wasn't going so well. Although the ACB initially had the public's support, with most of the top players in WSC the on-field performances of the official Australian team were suffering, as were their crowds.

The ACB and the state associations, never run with any commercial savvy, were now bleeding financially. Some were on the cusp of going broke. They knew Packer was losing money too, but not how much or for how long he could sustain it. They just knew they couldn't keep going as they were. On top of that, a 4–1 loss in the Ashes showed the dilution of the playing pool was unsustainable.

Packer wanted the TV rights, and the ACB wanted its precious monopoly back. Basically sporting administrators are communists who like making money – so, like Chinese communists. On 30 May 1979, peace was declared. Packer would have his TV rights and the ACB would get back its players, with WSC leasing them back to

---

* Lillee used the bat against the West Indies without incident but in a later match, the English complained. A heated argument sprung up on the field. Lillee's own captain, Greg Chappell, strode out and told Lillee to give up the metal bat as he thought it less effective than wood anyway. Lillee tossed the bat away in disgust. Metal bats were soon outlawed, but not before sales soared and Lillee got a cut of the profits.

GREAT FACIAL HAIR IN AUSTRALIAN CRICKET HISTORY

Jack Blackham: The wicketkeeper had a beard and moustache so glorious, a substantial cult formed in worship of it. At its peak, it was estimated to have seven million followers.

Dennis Lillee: A moustache so intimidating, an army division once surrendered to it.

Merv Hughes: Hughes's moustache is the densest naturally occurring element, six times denser than the next, Osmium.

David Boon: Boon's moustache released pheromones so potent that they once made a man fall pregnant.

George Bonnor: Bonnor's beard was so large that when he toured England in 1880, the royal family went hunting within it. They were never seen again.

Allan Border: I met Allan Border's moustache once. One hair from it drifted to the ground and landed on my foot, breaking it in three places.

Ian Chappell: The only moustache to be declared a World Heritage area by UNESCO.

the ACB. Limited-overs cricket was now a mainstay of the summer and Packer's Channel Nine would be the national broadcaster of cricket; the ABC was out.

The whole affair was another case of the fault line of employer–employee relations rupturing. But the outcomes here were slightly different to what happened with rugby, where an entire new code was created. Packer didn't set out to create a new competition. He only wanted to broadcast it, not run it. His strategic aim never changed. World Series Cricket was a tactic to achieve that aim, and the moment he got what he wanted he handed back control of the sport. The ACB still existed, and while the players were now being paid significantly more, Packer was no huge advocate of players' rights. Once he was at the table, in terms of controlling the game, Packer actively worked to stop any other rebel tours being organised.

Packer's Channel Nine innovated for decades, until it eventually grew complacent and became a sad, tired facsimile of its early days. Cricket itself may have been fixed off the field but players and administrators had taken their eye off the game and, as anyone with children knows, when you turn your back, things get messy.

THE AWFUL EIGHTIES

The retirements of Chappell, Lillee and Marsh, combined with rebel tours of South Africa, severely weakened Australia's playing stocks as the eighties began. Poor results followed.

The decade started with controversy, but this time on the pitch. In 1981, the infamous 'underarm incident' added to the history of cricket creating diplomatic incidents. As captain, Greg Chappell instructed his brother, Trevor, to bowl an underarm delivery to New Zealand's Brian McKechnie, preventing a six being hit on the last ball and denying New Zealand any chance of a victory. Trevor rolled the ball down the pitch like a man playing lawn bowls with a gun to his head.

The New Zealand team and public reacted like business people on a plane being told they have to turn off their phones for take-off.

Richie Benaud, then the host of Channel Nine's cricket, slammed the act as 'unsportsmanlike' in a passionate to-camera piece. Politicians on both sides of the ditch got into arguments over it. Underarm bowling was subsequently banned but, to this day, the incident is still a sore point with New Zealanders, making it something I like to bring up regularly when I'm around them. Is it really Australia's fault that McKechnie couldn't hit what was then a perfectly legal delivery for a six? Also, why were they in a position where they need a six on the last ball anyway? It's like someone who left their homework until the night before it's due complaining their internet went down.

Not long after the first major controversy of the eighties,

another hit: the rebel tours of South Africa. The South Africans had been banned from international sporting competition because of their apartheid policy. Where South Africa went wrong was in making apartheid an official policy; other countries have gotten away with similar policies for a lot longer by not making them law.

Of course, many cricketers are about as socially aware as bricks, so a lot were happy to take the money and tour anyway. Former test captain Kim Hughes, Terry Alderman, Rodney Hogg, Carl Rackemann, Trevor Hohns, Tom Hogan, John Dyson and Steve Smith all toured. There was enormous outcry and Prime Minister Bob Hawke called the group who went 'traitors'. The players were suspended for three years by the Australian Cricket Board. I think being made to live in South Africa would have been a better punishment.

Apart from the political, moral and social ramifications, the discord hit Australia where it mattered most: sporting results. With key players out of the side, Australians in the eighties felt the full might of the West Indies cricket team. They unleashed on the world some of the finest players ever, including some of the fastest bowlers: Joel Garner, Michael Holding, Curtly Ambrose and Courtney Walsh terrified us all. Even now I wake in the middle of the night in a cold sweat. Not because of them; my doctor thinks it's my diet. She says I have the body of someone who should have died years ago.

UP OFF THE MAT

It took the appointment of Allan Border as captain – and a great scowling effort from him – to turn Australia's fortunes around. He was the sort of man you don't mess around with. His nickname was Captain Grumpy (the worst children's character of all time). He hated losing, like any true Australian does, which unfortunately meant he hated a fair bit of his playing career.

New coach Bob Simpson and Border both formed a strong view that they needed players with more grit, players who didn't ignore whole components of the game, like fielding, or breaking out of a jog. The players they brought into the national team would form the beginning of one of the most successful dynasties in world sport: Steve Waugh, Ian Healy, Mark Taylor, Geoff Marsh, Mark Waugh, David Boon and Merv Hughes, to name a few.

Boon and Hughes would also return Australia to the top of the tree in the facial hair stakes. David Boon is perhaps the finest physical specimen the Australian continent has ever produced; even today, more than twenty years after his retirement, he remains at his playing weight.

Here were players who wanted to win more than anything else in life, to the point where they were probably unbearable in person but wonderful at winning tests. Border was keen to become less friendly with opponents off the field, the English especially. It was a doctrine that was later taken up to devastating effect by Steve Waugh, who called it 'mental disintegration'. It's the same strategy I use at social events. Or rather, I did when I used to get invited to them. To me, being unfriendly is not a tactic, it's my personality, and a key reason I'm lonely. So lonely.

The 1987 World Cup victory was the start of this uncompromising style of cricket, and it became a hallmark of the Australian game. It was followed by an Ashes victory in 1989. The Border and Simpson rebuild was complete. The Australian cricket team was now a ruthless winning machine, bristling with body hair and heavy drinkers.

PLATINUM AGE

Following Border's retirement, the captaincy moved to Mark Taylor and later on to Steve Waugh. This already formidable team was about to receive an obscene amount of talent, including two once-in-a-generation players who, through some cosmic mix-up, arrived in the same generation.

The first was a leg-spin bowler named Shane Warne and the second was fast bowler Glenn McGrath. The two would form a bowling attack so lethal that Australia could now win any game from any position. Any total could be defended; teams could be bowled out in an hour. Warne could make the ball do things it shouldn't really do. It would spin so far, it raised questions about our understanding of physics. McGrath, on the other hand, was so methodical that you just couldn't make the slightest mistake against him. He hunted batsmen like he would later hunt Africa's endangered animals.

Warne dominated cricket both on and off the pitch for fifteen years, finishing with 708 wickets for an average of 25.41. In that time, he delivered the greatest delivery ever, against English captain Mike Gatting, who to this day remains at his crease trying to work out what happened.

Warne lost the vice-captaincy for sending erotic text messages to a British nurse. He was fined for accepting money from a bookmaker for information about pitch and weather conditions.

GREAT NICKNAMES

Mark 'Afghanistan' Waugh: When his brother Steve was well entrenched in the Aussie test side, Mark was toiling away in state cricket, leading to him being called 'Afghanistan', as in, the forgotten war.

Allan 'Captain Grumpy' Border: Border's love of winning or, more accurately, his hatred of losing, often made him a difficult person to be around. Not only did he limit socialising with opponents like England, he made quite a few of his teammates miserable.

He received a fine and a suspended two-match ban for saying of Sri Lankan captain Arjuna Ranatunga, 'There is plenty of animosity between Arjuna and myself. I don't like him and I'm not in a club of one'. He got a one-year ban from cricket for taking a banned diuretic, which he blamed on his mum. So, yeah, he was busy.

But Australia kept winning. We didn't lose the Ashes from 1989 to 2005, and at one stage put together a sixteen-test winning streak. In that time, some true greats of Australian cricket emerged, including Adam Gilchrist, Matthew Hayden and Ricky Ponting.

It's hard to convey how good the nineties and early 2000s were for Australian cricket. The relentless winning led some Australians to say winning all the time was boring – some even barracked against Australia. These people should have been deported. But our politicians only seemed to be interested in stopping people from coming into the country, not culling the idiots among us, a policy position that continues to this day.

MORE BUT SHORTER

The 2005 Ashes were the end of Australia's greatest ever era. England won the series 2–1, claiming the Ashes for the first time since 1986/87. I wore only black for the following two years, including to a wedding, which the bride and groom described as 'tasteless'.

Losing the series saw fingers pointed in every direction, and management was completely reorganised, but shuffling deckchairs couldn't cover the retirements of Steve Waugh, Glenn McGrath and Shane Warne. Australia was still a decent side and still produced quality players: Ricky Ponting was a fantastic batsman, as was Michael Clarke, whose batting prowess was only matched by his ability to put his teammates offside. Currently, Australians get to watch Steve Smith, arguably the greatest batsman since Bradman.

But cricket is changing. India, with its massive population and fanaticism for the game, has become the new centre of cricket.

Today, money from TV rights makes India to cricket what the United States is to baseball. The money in India is so immense, they basically took over the ICC in 2014, along with England and Australia, who had no real choice. They weren't about to forsake the riches India offered. India offered such a large audience they could afford to tell the rest of the world to take it or leave it.

Alongside these changes at the international level, Cricket Australia finally approved plans to move towards being an independent body, free of state control. It's a model that has served the AFL well, except if you're from Tasmania of course.

The biggest recent change to the game is the focus on the shortest format of the sport, Twenty20. The 50-over one-dayers made popular by Packer – once so exciting – are now considered boring time wasters, while tests are the preserve of the cricket true believers.

Now Twenty20 cricket is the most popular format of the game. Throughout the ebbs and flows of cricket's history, the Australian people have never lost their love for the game, but they do now want to see it in shorter bursts. That's the pattern of any long-term relationship really.

Schedules now work around the Indian Premier League (a Twenty20 format) where players can make huge amounts of money. How much money? Well, in 2016 Glenn Maxwell made $1.24 million playing for the Kings XI Punjab. Glenn Maxwell! Not bad for two months' work.

In Australia, the success of Twenty20 has hardly gone unnoticed, with the formation of the Big Bash League (BBL) in 2011. Cricket Australia saw what happened when the ACB failed to take up one-dayers in the seventies and they were not going to let history repeat itself. They also seemed keen to help sell even more fried chicken to the nation's already obese children.

The BBL has been ridiculously popular, reinvigorating cricket for younger generations and in the TV ratings. There's no doubt

IT'S ALL IN THE NAME

Hobart Hurricanes (Big Bash League)

This is what happens when the marketing department comes up with a team name. The coke session that developed this must have been amazing. Never have so many people with ponytails worked so hard to deliver such an inaccurate name.

Hurricanes only occur in the northern hemisphere and Tasmania is a fair way outside the northern hemisphere. Cyclones would be more accurate and, as we all know, Tasmania is constantly ravaged by cyclones due to its tropical climate.

that Twenty20 is the format of the future, which raises a few questions. What is the future of the one-day internationals, which now sit there awkwardly like an unloved middle child? At the moment, players on the Australian ODI team are removed from the BBL to play in series no one is particularly interested in. While many people want to scrap the one-dayer, it's still the format of the World Cup, so that's not going to happen anytime soon.

Tests, on the other hand, have a quality problem. With Twenty20 teaching players to hit out, the craftsmanship of test cricket threatens to go the way of sock darning. Gone are the days of test cricketers grinding away in English county cricket just to get ready for an Ashes tour. No self-respecting cricketer is going to do that when he can make a small fortune in the Indian Premier League.

Is the future of cricket shorter games? The ICC is certainly not conceding that, but the money might dictate otherwise. Either way, Australia's love affair with cricket continues like a long, hot, lazy summer.

RUGBY UNION

THAT SPORT YOUR DOCTOR PLAYS

Ah Union. The oldest of the footballing codes and, like all old things, a bit set in its ways. Union is the code that has changed the least since its birth and it now faces challenges from younger, better-looking sports.

Union's biggest problem is it's seen as elitist and not interested in appealing to poor people. That hardly seems fair, so let's get NSW Waratahs CEO Andrew Hore to explain what's so great about the sport:

> A kid could grow up and be a pretty ordinary rugby player, but that young man might also get in with a good peer group, goes to school, gets an education, puts his headshield, mouthguard and boots in a bag, flies over to London, jumps in a lower grade footy club there, meets a guy who works in a bank, and before you know it, earning millions.

See? Not elitist at all.

MUSCULAR CHRISTIANITY WITH NONE OF THAT EXCESSIVE INTELLECTUALISM

Despite conventional wisdom, Rugby Union was not invented to make New Zealanders feel relevant, it actually began at the Rugby School in England as part of a push to install 'muscular Christianity' into their young men. Muscular Christianity was a philosophy for 'the expulsion of all that is effeminate, unEnglish and excessively intellectual'. That sounds fun, doesn't it?

In the earliest days of Australia, Rugby was the dominant sport. In colonial New South Wales, muscular Christianity seemed like a good idea, a view not shared by the godless hedonists that live there now. Back then, there weren't many schools, so guarding against excessive intellectualism was relatively easy, and colonisation was itself an attempt to expel anything that was 'unEnglish'. As for expelling anything effeminate, well, this was a frontier outpost; there weren't that many actual women, let alone men who didn't confirm to the strictest reading of masculinity.

Australian Rules, rugby and soccer all evolved from the early scratch matches that occurred in English schools, but Union is the code that has changed the least in terms of style, with its rucks and mauls (those bits when they all hug each other for minutes with nothing happening). Those early school games involved a lot of competition for the ball with few rules about what should happen when someone was tackled. Union to this day sees every moment after a tackle (the breakdown) as an ongoing competition for the ball, with both sides trying to get the ball, often in a mess of players.

In League and Australian Rules a tackle triggers a different outcome; a play of the ball in League, a free kick or a ball up in Australian Rules. Other sports that emerged from rugby made similar decisions to move away from a tackle being a contest. American football changed the most, deciding a tackle results in a break in play, several hours of TV ads, and finally another play. These evolutions came about because the other codes wanted their sports to be popular – the money from spectators, and later TV revenue, is what paid the players and kept the sport running. These games had to be appealing to the public. Union had no such need to impress the public because the sport remained the province of the English public schools, the upper class.

Rugby's unique position stemmed from the fact that the men who ran the game and those who played it were wealthy enough to play the sport and fund the pursuit themselves. This amateur approach was not a deliberate choice – it just wasn't even an issue. Only rich people played the sport and there was no need to change that. Despite its early dominance, it was this disdain for the working class that ultimately saw Union fall behind Australian Rules and League in popularity in Australia.

By 1864, Sydney University, the first recognised rugby club in Australia, was formed. By 1874 the Southern Rugby Union was in place to administer the code. As an organisation, it was heavily under English control, part of the Empire's push to install Britishness in the colonial population. Those in England and the powers that be in Sydney were keen to keep the game to the original set of rules; a tough physical challenge, designed to prepare upper-class boys for the rigours of administering the Empire.

TOP PROFESSIONS THAT PLAY UNION

1. Doctors
2. Lawyers
3. Idle rich
4. Captains of industry
5. Sons of captains of industry
6. Liberal MPs
7. Bankers

This lack of interest in making the game more appealing to spectators and less brutal on players did result in some early warning signs for the code. In 1877 the Waratah Rugby Club played the Carlton Football Club first at rugby and then Victorian Rules, as it was then known. The appeal of Victorian Rules was immediately apparent, in no small part because you could be compensated for playing it and not get injured all the time. The Waratah club decided almost right away to switch to Victorian Rules and the New South Wales Football Association (NSWFA) was formed the next week. The rugby administration resorted to banning the new competition from its grounds to contain its early spread.

Despite this hiccup, rugby was growing in popularity and expanding. In 1883, the Northern Rugby Union was formed in Queensland, again at a pub, the Exchange Hotel. By the late nineteenth century, rugby was the most popular sport in New South Wales, Queensland and Western Australia, with a league established there in 1882.*

CLASS DIVIDE

The split that would form Union and League was due to the oldest tradition in sports administration: spectacular incompetence.**

As had happened in England, rugby's increased popularity was attracting the less desirable elements of society: anyone who participated in physical labour. In NSW and Queensland, rugby was battling it out with Victorian Rules, which was seen as a challenger for attracting the best players. This made the rugby authorities in those states a bit more understanding in terms of making 'broken time' payments to players who missed paid work because of playing commitments or injuries. This was not a push for full-time wages, just money to cover missing work. Those overseeing rugby's

---

* Rugby's dominance in Western Australia was short-lived, with many clubs and schools converting to Victorian Rules in 1885.

** Spectacular incompetence to this day drives most decisions in sports administration. The next time you find yourself searching for a reason a sporting administration has decided to do something, stop yourself and remember: it's not rational, it's spectacular incompetence.

exploding popularity struggled to deal with the increase in working-class players and their demands to be compensated for playing.

In the administrators' eyes, rugby was about muscular Christianity and a sense of duty to the British empire. It was pure, and any move toward professionalism would taint this ideal. Of course some administrators just didn't like poor people, but the accounts from the time give a strong sense that the English Rugby Football Union (RFU) just painted themselves into a corner by making amateurism an unbreakable tenet of the game.

In England there was also a feeling that this was part of a push by trade unions and the working class to usurp the natural order of things. Challenging the administration of rugby and its sacred amateurism was not just an attack on the sport but on the Empire itself. Why, if this continued, where would it end? People in positions of power with little to no inbreeding? The barbarians were at the gates and they wanted to play rugby.

Even at the time, this was viewed as hysterical in Australia and New Zealand. The small populations meant it was impossible to build full teams from only men who could afford to play.

The defection to League of Dally Messenger,* the best rugby player of the day, was a perfect example of the difference between Australia and England. Messenger had previously received payments from the NSW Rugby Union to cover expenses, but he could read the play off the field as well as he could on it and, with the schism in England, he realised the Australian Union authorities would soon no longer be able to unofficially pay him. In 1907 he switched to the code that would.

The majority of the Wallabies national team joined him in defecting to the new code in 1908. Now the Australian Rugby

---

* He was the Israel Folau or Karmichael Hunt of his day, but without the cocaine possession charges of Hunt.

Union authorities were fighting an uphill battle with one hand tied behind their back.

With a large number of defections to League, Union found itself attracting smaller and smaller crowds, subsequently losing access to those same enclosed grounds it had prevented Victorian Rules from playing on. The loss of revenue meant that Union was forced double down on amateurism, like the person who makes a big deal of wearing only second-hand clothes but really is just broke. Those who remained had high enough salaries that they could afford to fund tours overseas and organise time off to play. It led to the old joke that the safest sport to get injured in was Union, as there were more doctors on the field than off it. This was further reinforced because the only places still churning out Union players were private schools, mainly in Sydney and Brisbane.

This commitment to amateurism, so zealously pursued by the RFU in England, meant that in Australia Union continued to slip behind League and Australian Rules in popularity and participation, where it still languishes today.

DOING ONE'S DUTY

The values of muscular Christianity, which permeated every part of Union, perhaps had no bigger effect on the Australian sporting landscape than during World War I. The sense of Britishness it instilled in young men meant Union players answered the call of the Empire in huge numbers. Union had to be shelved during the war as there simply weren't enough players to run a competition. The New South Wales Rugby Union reported that out of 220 regular first-grade players 197 were on active service, an amazing figure of duty-bound young men. I find that level of commitment amazing. Most people today won't commit to a social event that's a week away.

Rugby League certainly felt an impact from the war, but nowhere near the levels Union did. It was able to continue its competition during the war years, maintaining the momentum it had built up before the outbreak of the war.

Heartbreakingly, many of the men from Rugby Union's ranks would not return from the war. Those who did carried the wounds, both physical and mental, of the battlefields of Europe. The impact on the code can't be overstated. In Victoria it effectively stopped the game until 1926. In Queensland, a stronghold of the code, the Queensland Rugby Union was completely dissolved in 1919 because of a shortage of available players. Many clubs in Queensland simply switched to League and, in an even bigger blow, the Greater Public Schools all switched to League.

It took until the late twenties for Union to pick itself back up in the Sunshine State, a huge amount of time lost, to League's advantage. The push to revive Union came from the Greater Public Schools. I guess elites never truly lose their love of elitism. Nudgee College, the Church of England Grammar School and Brisbane Grammar School all eventually began to play Union again and by 1928 the Queensland Rugby Union was back up and running.

It was a big step forward for a game that had mainly become limited to Sydney and needed a slightly larger gene pool to flourish. While Queensland was in recess, leadership for the code in Australia fell to NSW. The decimation of its ranks meant the NSWRU appealed to the RFU in England, looking to increase the popularity of the code and attract more players. They suggested a raft of rule changes and asked if they could compensate some players, so they could compete with both League and Australian Rules.

To say this wasn't met with enthusiasm would be understating it a tad. The English Rugby powers saw this as a direct attack on the Empire and all who had just fought for it. To give you a flavour of it, here's a letter to the Sydney Referee in 1921:

The rugger game [is] a beautiful edifice, built up by years of patient labour, and over which is shed the lustre of a tradition that will live as long as red blood flows in Australian veins – this tradition (I quote from the 1919–20 Rugby Football Annual): 'On the last Saturday of the 1913–14 season the London Scottish [rugby club] placed four teams in the field, of these sixty players, forty-five have been killed. Altogether the club had seventy of three hundred members killed and fifty-two wounded. Some of the smaller clubs have lost almost all of the playing members.' [. . .] You know the record of the New South Wales and New Zealand rugby unions in the terrible but wonderful years of Armageddon. Before you and your friends, in this sudden, new found zeal of yours for 'improving the rules' destroy that edifice – think! And think again! In England it is imperishable and indestructible.

Now he seems like a chap you'd want to party with. I'm not sure World War I is best described as the 'terrible but wonderful years of Armageddon' but maybe you had to be there.

Given Australia back then was still very much a British country, this kind of thinking meant asking for rule changes equated to treason. In fact, in the eyes of the British and some in Union's ranks, League itself was in essence anti-Empire. The manager of the 1930 British Isles side on a tour of New Zealand, James Baxter, said of League, 'Every town must have its sewer.'

The course was set. Union would go forward as an amateur sport in Australia and with a rigid set of rules.

AUSTRALIANS MAKE UNION ENTERTAINING

Of course, it was Australians who found a way to make Rugby Union fun to watch. The 1927/28 Waratahs dazzled all who saw them on a tour of Ceylon, Britain, France and Canada. In another of those marathon tours they all did back then, they played five tests and twenty-six tour matches. Teams today complain if they get less than a seven-day break between matches, yet these Waratahs displayed exciting, winning running rugby despite playing every other day. Instead of the focus on strong pack play by the forwards, the Waratahs relied on their backs to use creative passing to open up gaps to exploit. It was the birth of a style that would come to define Southern Hemisphere rugby – 'running rugby' – and it has led to many of the greatest moments in Australian rugby history, even if today we've overdone it and everyone has figured us out.

At the time of the tour Queensland Rugby was still in hibernation, meaning the squad was exclusively made up of New South Welshman except for one Queenslander, sort of like the current ratio for the Australian cricket team. The Queenslander was Tom Lawton Snr, a brilliant fly half who was inducted into the Australian and IRB Rugby Hall of Fame. As well as being a legend of the game, he was a Rhodes Scholar. The captain of the team, Arthur Cooper 'Johnnie' Wallace, was also a Rhodes Scholar and he steered the team to a record of twenty-four wins, five losses and two draws, during which they averaged almost four tries a match. It's further proof that you can never have too many Rhodes Scholars in your team.

To give you an idea of the place they occupied in society, while on tour the team was given a personal tour of the Houses of Parliament by Lord Donoughmore, the Secretary of the House of Lords, and Sir John Whitley, the Speaker of the House of Commons. They also met the Prince of Wales and King George V, who invited them along on a shooting expedition before introducing them to Queen Mary.

If that wasn't enough, they also took tea with the Duke and Duchess of York, where they met the infant Princess Elizabeth, who you may know from being Queen Elizabeth II.

While Union struggled in Australia, internationally, the Australian players were recognised at the highest levels of society. This international connection kept Union strong and was a significant advantage over the more domestic codes.

THE BLEDISLOE CUP; OR, REGULARLY LOSING TO NEW ZEALAND

The Bledisloe Cup is considered one of the world's great rivalries, if you consider one team regularly annihilating another a rivalry. If you do, then I have a healthy rivalry with ice cream (my doctor says it's not healthy). The All Blacks hand out beatings to the Wallabies with such regularity that it has significantly affected the popularity of the sport in Australia. Despite the rather lopsided nature of the competition, it still evokes a lot of feeling, so much so that the two countries can't even agree on when it started.

The Australians believe it all started in 1931 at Eden Park in New Zealand, while the New Zealanders believe it started in 1932 in Australia. The Kiwis actually have some written evidence to support their claim but I'll be damned if I'm going to let that force me to side with them. I'm a patriot and even if my country is wrong, I'm going to maintain it's right.

What we do know is the cup was donated by the fourth governor-general of New Zealand, Charles Bathurst, 1st Viscount Bledisloe. He was known for creating awards and trophies – many regard the Bledisloe Cup the most important but I've always had a soft spot for the Bledisloe Gold Medal for Landowners of the Royal Agricultural Society of England, which is awarded each year to whoever has the best the application of science or technology in English farming. Unfortunately, the biased left-wing media don't give that award the same level of coverage.

The viscount himself was actually a very interesting man. He presided over New Zealand from 1930 to 1935, in what I can only assume was a punishment. He was a decent person who reduced his own salary during the Depression and worked hard to improve relationships with the indigenous population of New Zealand. He even happily referred to their leaders by their preferred title of 'king', which others at the time saw as controversial as it could be seen as recognising their sovereignty. Bledisloe, I imagine, figured he'd already been sent to New Zealand so the British king couldn't really punish him any further.

Up until the eighties, the Bledisloe Cup wasn't played with any regularity. Long periods of time would sometimes elapse without it being contested, a blessing for the Australians. Between 1931 and 1981 the New Zealanders won the cup nineteen times and Australia just four.

In the eighties, the pace of the Bledisloe Cup picked up significantly, and it became an annual event, often played as a best-of-three series. It was becoming apparent to the administrations on both sides of the Ditch that the Bledisloe was a popular drawcard. With the switch to professionalism, it became a regular part of the Tri-Nations tournament. The Tri-Nations saw South Africa, Australia and New Zealand play a tournament each year, providing another excellent platform for the Wallabies to let us all down. The Tri-Nations tournament is the only time I feel inferior to New Zealanders and South Africans. I don't care for it.

Following the switch to professionalism and the profit motive in full effect at the Australian Rugby Union (ARU), the Bledisloe was hyped to unheard of levels, culminating in 2008 when a fourth game in the series was played in Hong Kong. A quick check on Google Maps shows Hong Kong is in neither New Zealand or Australia but is in fact part of a country called 'China'. It was an overreach and, despite initial enthusiasm, the rivalry was now overexposed. It was very similar to the mistakes Cricket Australia has made with their sport, scheduling countless matches to the point of boring people. The specialness of the Beldisloe had been eroded.

It also doesn't help that the Australians haven't won the trophy since 2002, which makes it less a competition and more of an annual sacrifice. The Bledisloe Cup has served Australian sport very poorly, repeatedly making Australia look bad and, worse than that, making New Zealanders feel good about themselves. How this hasn't been the focus of a royal commission is beyond me.

THE IRFB, NSWRU, ARFU AND OTHER FUN ACRONYMS

Following World War II, the International Rugby Football Board (IRFB) began to pressure Australia to end the NSWRU's dominance of the code. Because the southern states didn't care about Union and the Queensland Rugby Union had disbanded after World War I, the NSWRU was in effect the national body. This wasn't a great position for a sport that wanted to grow beyond Sydney. It's also possible the IRFB just got sick of the Queenslanders constantly complaining to them.

The IRFB was mainly interested in doing this so Australia would finally become a full member, which we did in 1948. After so many men had lost their lives in both world wars, fighting for the Empire, it had become unsustainable for the IRFB to continue to treat South Africa, New Zealand and Australia as colonial outposts. This new world meant the southern unions would have a lot more power in the global game. A condition of Australia being recognised as a full IRFB member was the establishment of a national body, so the Australian Rugby Football Union (ARFU) was created.

As a full member, Australia managed to have several rules changed, including kicking out into touch on the full, using time-keepers and increasing the value of a try to 4 points. The northern unions still acted like elitist snobs, but it was progress.

The Wallabies continued to struggle in the sixties and seventies and domestically there was no major improvement in the code's participation numbers. Union remained an amateur code and the failings of the national side were of deep concern to the ARFU, who set up a committee to find ways to improve the Wallabies' fortunes. The committee recommended the establishment of a coaching unit, with the aim of improving the standard of play across the sport. It was a small but significant step. In the past the sport had been run with an emphasis on supporting the amateur game, the grassroots of the sport. Now, slowly at first, the ARFU was focusing more on the elite level, with success at the top a clear objective.

IS IT OKAY TO NOT UNDERSTAND THE RULES OF UNION?

Absolutely. Not understanding the rules of Union is one of the great traditions of the sport and places you in great company with both the players and the referees.

Like business jargon, the rules of Union were designed to confuse poor people and keep them away. Like business jargon, eventually those using it ended up not understanding what it all meant either but they continue to pretend they do.

THE PESKY PROBLEM OF APARTHEID

While in the main rugby had lived happily in its amateur bubble since the end of World War II, money from TV rights and sponsorship was starting to flow into other sports. These trends would one day overtake Union, but it was political events that thrust Union front and centre in the public's mind. All rugby nations had had a rather awkward relationship with South Africa since apartheid was officially introduced in 1948, which took centuries of racial segregation and somehow found a way to make it worse. The rugby nations were torn, as they wanted to play South Africa but didn't like looking bad by doing so.

At first the Australian public was slow to pick up on the issue. The White Australia policy was still in effect, so getting on the moral high horse was a bit tricky. In fact, those at the highest levels of government in Australia struggled to come to terms with South African apartheid. It was instead a surprising mix of activists, sports stars and the public who would drag the issue into the light and radically shift Australia's position.

Yet it took time. The first major ripple in the relationship between the Wallabies and Springboks was on a tour of South Africa in 1963. Lloyd McDermott, the first Indigenous person to play for the Wallabies, was forced to decide between sitting out the tour or signing a piece of paper declaring himself to be an 'honorary white' while in South Africa. McDermott made what in hindsight seems the obvious decision, but one that must have been very hard for him: he boycotted the tour, switching to League. It was a dark moment for Australian rugby, but the tour went ahead anyway.

On the tour many Wallabies experienced events in South Africa firsthand. Wallabies winger Jim Boyce was appalled by what he saw. At one stage during a game, spectators in the non-white section, who were cheering for the Wallabies in an act of protest, were outraged by a referee's call. The police moved in to quell the uproar in brutal fashion. Boyce was witnessing the oppressive South African regime firsthand – he went on to protest against future tours. During the tour, Boyce was told by John Vorster, then South Africa's justice minister: 'No black man will ever wear a Springbok jersey.'

In another tour of South Africa, in 1969,* Wallabies forward Tony Abrahams witnessed similar events firsthand. But in this case, Abrahams was using the tour as a fact-finding mission as much as

---

* Just two years after Australia's 1967 referendum that decided Indigenous Australians should be counted as people.

a sporting tour. Abrahams was only twenty-four but he was well across the moral issues involved. Before he went, he sought counsel from people like Aboriginal activist Charles Perkins, who encouraged him to go on the tour to see for himself what was happening. In a move that was perhaps braver than he realised, Abrahams met with opposition groups while in South Africa. It was only years later he discovered he'd been watched by South African secret police the entire time. Being followed by secret police is never a good thing. No one ever says, 'But then I found out these were the friendly kind of secret police.'

Upon leaving the country, Abrahams wrote a letter to the *Sydney Morning Herald* outlining what he had seen and putting forward the moral case for not touring there. It was a different era; no 24-year-old writes a letter to the editor these days, they just change their Facebook cover photo. His stance led to seven players – Jim Boyce, Paul Darveniza, Terry Forman, Barry McDonald, Jim Roxburgh, Bruce Taafe and Abrahams – refusing to be selected for the South African's tour of Australia in 1971.

The '71 tour was a turning point in Australia's stance against apartheid, with the seven Wallabies sending a clear message that this was a matter that could no longer be ignored. Lloyd McDermott would years later describe the Wallabies seven as his 'heroes'.

As well as sitting out the tour, some of the Wallabies seven actively campaigned against it, handing out pamphlets at matches and lobbying rugby and business leaders about the issue. Boyce, remembering the words of South Africa's justice minister that no black man would ever wear the Springboks jersey, gave four Springbok jerseys he'd collected over his career to Indigenous activists to wear while they were demonstrating. A bit like giving your ex's jumper to your new boyfriend.

There were large-scale protests, as activists and the broader public stood firm against the regime, with 700 people being arrested over the course of the tour. Luckily, this being Rugby Union, there were a lot of lawyers about.

In addition to the public protests, airlines and hotels refused to deal with the Springboks. It got to the stage where a month-long state of emergency was declared in Queensland by the state's premier, Joh Bjelke-Petersen, hardly a supporter of progressive causes. However he was not alone in how out of step political leaders were with the public; the Victorian premier, Henry Bolte, described the protests as a 'rebellion against constituted authority'.

Yet others realised the issue was one that need a stronger response and Don Bradman, the chairman of the Australian Cricket Board at the time, was surprisingly one of the key figures to provide it. Bradman had a reputation as one of the most conservative sports administrators there was, so it was surprising when he responded to 23-year-old activist Meredith Burgmann when she wrote to him. The five letters he wrote to her show Bradman as a rather complex figure. On the one hand, he didn't approve of the violence and disruption the protest caused, but, on the other hand, he was genuinely interested in the reasons for the protest.

He expressed the view that politics and sport shouldn't mix, while giving a rather dark account of Australian history. He wrote to Brugmann comparing the privilege of whites in South Africa with those in Australia, arguing they were not much different:

> If you'll pardon me for saying so, how did you come to get the chance of a university education in Australia? It was made possible because your forebears and mine plundered this country, murdered aborigines etc etc and took over the land.

The letters show Bradman willing to consider broader views while consciously grappling with a situation that didn't sit easily with those views; Bradman had a cricket tour by the South Africans coming up and he had to decide what to do about it.

Finally, in September 1971, Bradman announced the tour would be cancelled. Partly due to legitimate security concerns, but Bradman added that Australia wouldn't play South Africa in cricket until they selected teams on a non-racial basis. He added that he hoped South Africa's government would 'so relax its [apartheid] laws so that cricketers of South Africa may once again take their place as full participants in the international field'.

The outcome of the 1971 tour resulted in Prime Minister Gough Whitlam breaking off all sporting ties with South Africa the following year, a decision that would remain in place until 1994. It was situation that demonstrated that the argument that sport and politics can be separated is ludicrous. On top of that, it highlights that athletes can be great role models. In 2001, Nelson Mandela held a dinner to honour the Wallabies who had campaigned against the Springbok tour.

Mandela himself would go on to use rugby as a vehicle to try to heal race relations in South Africa during the 1995 World Cup, events that would be made into the movie *Inviticus*, an amazing film that shows just how good an actor Matt Damon is, making a Springbok player almost likeable.

THE EIGHTIES

In the eighties the Wallabies took their first steps out of the international doldrums they had been in since the end of World War II and start actually winning. The signs were there in 1979, when the Australians won the Bledisloe Cup for the first time in thirty years. That's a long time not to win something in a two-horse race. The only comparable example in sports is the Harlem Globetrotters versus the Washington Generals.

Things only got better when, in 1984, the Wallabies completed the 'grand slam', defeating the Home Nations of England, Scotland, Wales and Northern Island. The result not only catapulted Australian rugby to the forefront of the international pack, it got so much press that even people in the southern states of Australia heard about it. Players like David Campese, Michael Lynagh, Nick Farr-Jones and Simon Poidevin became well known to Australians as they underpinned an era of success previously unknown to the Wallabies, which to be honest didn't require much. Even today, David Campese is better known in most states than any current Wallaby.

One of the highlights of the 1984 tour was the play of Mark Ella, who scored a try in every test. Mark was one of the famous Ella brothers, the first Indigenous players to represent their country since Lloyd McDermott had left the code. Mark, Glen (his twin) and Gary all played for the Wallabies, which is just showing off really. Mark played from 1980 to 1984, retiring at the age of twenty-five. It's quite possible he did this because by then he had mastered the sport. To watch Ella was to watch a genius. He created oppor-tunities all over the field with his running and passing. Just trying to anticipate what Ella would do had opposition defences in chaos before he even actually started a move. Despite retiring so young, he is remembered as one of the greatest Wallabies ever and some believe the best player ever. That's a pretty remarkable achievement in four years. The only thing I've done in the past four years is watch all of *The Wire*.

The Wallabies' new-found success came at a time when the world was dragging Union off its chesterfield and into the harsh light of commercial reality. League was starting to push into markets

> ### DID YOU KNOW?
>
> To become a cult figure in a sporting team, you must have a funny haircut and not be that good.

previously the exclusive domain of Union: inbred aristocrats and captains of industry. Even the Victorians were bringing their aerial ping-pong to Sydney and Brisbane. Amateurism had only been sustainable because the money the other codes paid was less than what a doctor, banker or lawyer could make, but now the other sports' coffers were awash with cash they could pay players real money.

In response to this challenge, the idea of a Rugby World Cup was floated. At first, the Home Nations had no interest in the World Cup as they were so insular they almost folded back in on themselves. The Australians, New Zealanders and French, however, were all very keen. After all, the international component was one of the great assets of Union and a showcase event could certainly help grow the code.

In 1985, at an IRFB meeting in Paris, the issue came to a head. South Africa voted in favour of a World Cup, an odd decision since they wouldn't be allowed play in it on account of their ban for being really, really racist. Actually, just the fact that they were still a voting member at the IRFB was pretty odd. Still, we have the South Africans to thank for the World Cup, which we should just keep amongst ourselves. Don't want them thinking we like them or anything.

The first World Cup was held in 1987, hosted by both Australia and New Zealand. The All Blacks won it so let's not dwell on that one and instead fast-forward to the 1991 World Cup, where Australia defeated England in the final at Twickenham. It was a famous victory because it featured both Australia winning and England losing, the greatest combination since fish and chips.

PARADISE LOST

With the Rugby World Cup significantly boosting the profile of rugby and Rupert Murdoch launching the Super League war in

League, the barbarians were no longer at the gate but about to buy the castle. The fortress of amateurism could no longer hold against the tide of money. The money pouring into League meant there was a serious risk of a raid on Union playing stocks, but Union itself was awash with sponsorship and TV rights money too – it just wasn't going to the players. Back in 1895, it was easy for Union players to ignore the small amounts League players got, but now it was different. Playing professionally in the modern age, you could set yourself up for life, without the hassle of going to medical school.

The Southern Hemisphere Unions, always less hidebound than their northern counterparts, saw professionalism as the only way forward and, after signing a broadcast deal with Rupert Murdoch, they declared the sport professional. The International Rugby Board had no real choice but to follow. Either the sport could split itself again, which would look careless in anyone's eyes, or they could join in. And so, on 27 August 1995, the IRFB voted that the game was now professional, just two days short of the hundred-year anniversary of the split. Amateurism was dead.

It was the end of one of the most boneheaded and stubborn crusades in the history of sport. Rugby should have never split in the first place. If the early administrators could have found ways to integrate working class players into the sport, it could have become unstoppable. In the end, the reality of the larger sporting landscape had swamped the code, and the importance of Empire and Britishness had diminished to the point where it could no longer hold it together.

THE GOLDEN AGE

With the pesky amateurism thing out of the way, the Southern Hemisphere Unions quickly got to work trying to make money. In 1996 they formed SANZAR (South Africa, New Zealand and Australia Rugby), which oversaw the new Super Rugby competition, featuring several club sides from each country, and an international Tri-Nations tournament.

It was an exciting time in Australian Rugby. Rod Macqueen was appointed head coach of the Wallabies in September 1997 and he built a team that would go on to sweep all before them. Featuring John Eales as captain, Tim Horan, Matt Burke and George Gregan, the side completed a clean sweep of the Bledisloe Cup series, won the 1999 World Cup and defeated the British and Irish Lions in a series for the first time ever. They were palpably exciting times and the game was certainly growing. Watching the Wallabies play was becoming a tradition around the country, not just in the normal strongholds.

Part of the excitement was that the All Blacks and the Wallabies were equally matched for once, providing some of the most thrilling sporting events ever. In 2000, the two countries contested 'the greatest game of rugby ever played'. Australia went down by 24 points in the first 11 minutes of the game (which is actually hard to do), but came back to tie the score by half-time. The second half proved just as dramatic, with New Zealand's late Jonah Lomu scoring the winning try. The final score was 39–35. Although, can it really be 'the greatest game of rugby ever played' if Australia lost? I tend to call it

SOME RUGBY UNION TERMS

Forwards: The players doing all the hard work

Backs: The players that get all the glory for the forwards' hard work

Ruck: When a group of players all lie on top of each other and hug for ages

Maul: When a group of players all hug for ages but while standing up

Scrum: When a group of players all hug each other, then ram into another group of players hugging each other and then a little guy throws a ball under them

the 'greatest but ultimately disappointing game of rugby therefore arguably not the greatest game of rugby ever played'. I grant you it's not as catchy.

Rugby Union seemed destined to challenge other codes, with the 2003 World Cup to be held in Australia. But, in 2001, the winning combination of Rod Macqueen and John Eales retired, handing over to Eddie Jones as coach and George Gregan as captain. It was like replacing Meryl Streep as your lead actress with Madonna.

THE DOLDRUMS

Appointing Gregan and Jones didn't immediately mean the end of the good times – they had to work at it for a few years. The 2003 World Cup in Australia was a successful event, as much as an event can be a success when the English win it. Australia met the old enemy in the final, losing 17 to 20. It was a brutal night and I can still remember sitting there with my head in my hands, English back-packers celebrating all around me. Yes, there is a hell, and I visited it that night.

What appeared to be a new dawn for Rugby Union in Australia became more like a sunset; since then the code has struggled for relevance and attention, like a reality TV star whose 15 minutes ended several years ago. The Wallabies' play declined in the period after the 2003 World Cup, and they haven't won the Bledisloe Cup since 2002. The NRL and the AFL secured huge free-to-air television deals; Super Rugby didn't. The competing leagues began to see Union as a threat and fought harder to compete at the grassroots.

The ARU did keep trying to grow the game, putting a new Super Rugby team, the Western Force, in Perth in 2006 and starting the Melbourne Rebels in 2011. But unfortunately the delay in putting a team in Melbourne meant the ARU failed to capitalise on the interest the game had back in 2003. The decline in the Wallabies' success has seen their profile fall significantly, to the point where many of

FULL SUPPORT OF THE BOARD

Nothing signifies the imminent end of a coach's tenure more than people offering them support. Once the board does it, you know that coach is on borrowed time. Here are some of the most famous sackings in sport.

Norm Smith: Smith was the reigning premiership coach in 1965 and his team had a record of 9–3 when he was sensationally sacked. Smith had coached Melbourne to ten successive finals appearances including six premierships; the committee was worried he was becoming bigger than the club. It turns out he was. Despite being briefly reinstated after the public backlash, the Demons have not won a premiership since, leading many to put the premiership drought down to the Norm Smith Curse.

Mickey Arthur: Arthur's sacking as coach of the Australian cricket team started with him dropping four players, including vice-captain Shane Watson, for not completing an assignment he'd given them. Dubbed 'homework-gate', it was seen as a ridiculous overreaction. After all, athletes don't do homework in school, let alone when they're members of the Australian cricket team.

David Nucifora: ACT Brumbies coach David Nucifora had arguably the strangest sacking in sports history. He was appointed in 2002, taking the Brumbies to the finals in 2002 and 2003. In 2004, he was sacked after the players told the board it was him or them. He was allowed to stay until the end of the season. The problem was that the Brumbies went on to win the title that year. Watching Nucifora celebrating with the people who had sacked him was brutal.

their games are non-events on the scale of a Nicole Kidman movie. All in all the ARU have really struggled to generate interest in the sport from anyone but hardcore rugby fans.

This hasn't been all the ARU's fault, although at times they seem to lack a clear vision. The SANZAAR arrangement is the real problem for them. Unlike the AFL and ARL, the ARU can't make all its decisions on its own, it has to please South Africa, New Zealand and now Argentina (the new 'A' in SANZAAR). This has led to a lot of strange decisions in recent times, including expanding

Super Rugby to eighteen teams by adding clubs from Japan, Argentina and another one from South Africa. This has made the competition so complicated as to be almost unintelligible – there are now four conferences across two groups (the Japanese Sunwolves are in one of the African conferences, obviously), teams play each other an uneven number of times depending on which conference they're in, and even that lopsided fixture schedule rotates from year to year. Amazingly, this move has resulted in falling attendances, as well as higher costs, not an ideal combination. The competition is now in a crisis, with clubs like the Brumbies in Canberra regularly making a loss each year.

At the time of writing, the ARU are trying to shut down the Western Force, hardly good for the game in Australia, but demanded by SANZAAR. Even shutting one of these clubs down has been handled with the skill of a drunk person trying to unlock the front door after a big night out.

The problem for the ARU is leaving SANZAAR would mean forsaking the international broadcast revenue they so desperately rely on. An Australia-only or Australian/New Zealand competition wouldn't arouse as much interest from television stations. They view club rugby as ratings poison and are becoming indifferent to Wallabies games too.

Rugby Union stands on the precipice of losing any hope of being a staple of the Australian winter sports market. It threatens to become more like an Olympic sport: interesting when the World Cup is on and ignored by the majority of Australians the rest of the time. Only time will tell if it can turn things around.

You may come away from reading this chapter with the impression that I'm not a fan of Union but that would be incorrect. It's a great sport and at times has produced some of the most entertaining play I've ever seen, yet it has repeatedly been mismanaged in a way that few codes can match.

AUSTRALIAN RULES

THE SCIENTOLOGY OF AUSTRALIAN SPORT

As Australia's own code, Australian Rules football holds a unique position in our sporting landscape. It's also the only code (that we know of) whose players have set a dwarf on fire and that has fined a club for being found not guilty of something.

I've loved Australian Rules ever since I found out if you played it you could get out of the last period at school for training. That's how it works in Melbourne: your education is secondary to footy. Actually, everything in Melbourne is secondary to footy.

Memories of footy are foundational moments in my life. I remember watching the VFA Grand Final in 1990, where Bill Swan booted a famous goal to cap a remarkable comeback by Williamstown against Springvale. I remember seeing Leigh Matthews run into the point post and break it. And I remember Ted 'Mr Football' Whitten going around the MCG on his farewell lap while Mariah Carey's 'Hero' played.[*]

The story of Australian Rules is one of administrative ruthlessness and insane levels of fanaticism. It is basically the Scientology of Australian sports.

---

[*] This was the one and only time in my life where I allowed myself to cry and enjoy a Mariah Carey song.

ORIGINS

Discussing the origins of Australian Rules will almost immediately lead to an argument. As the official religion of Victoria, the fact there are sectarian divisions over its origin myths is hardly surprising. The debate is fierce and it's a minefield to step through without offending the different camps. Like most religious debates, the different schools of thought think it's a matter of life and death, while outside observers wonder what all the fuss is about. I will handle the debate with my usual sensitivity, which means I'll probably offend everyone but hopefully equally.

Invented down south, in the land of black clothing and communist values, 'Victorian Rules' quickly spread across the country, almost conquering the entire continent before being confined, until recently, to the southern states.

The argument over its origins tends to be about how much, if at all, Indigenous sports influenced the game. One theory put forward is that champion sportsman of the day Tom Wills, often described as the father of Australian Rules (even though he wasn't really), would see Indigenous games, namely marngrook, played around where he grew up in Western Victoria. The story goes that these early memories influenced him when he was part of the group who drew up the first rules for the game.

Others argue there is no real evidence that Wills saw these games and that, in fact, he was keener to push for rules closer to the game played at the Rugby School in England, where he had been a student. Yet another group argues that Wills pushing for rugby rules had less of an impact on the first set of rules than some suggest. It's all very confusing.

Not all sides of this debate have 'facts' on their side, but facts mean nothing when compared to the power of emotions. For example, I'm a firm believer that the game originated partly from Indigenous roots and partly from the Vikings that colonised Victoria in the eighth century. I'm almost sure that's accurate, but Australian history was the subject I used to miss for footy training, so I concede it's possible the Vikings didn't arrive until the ninth century.

Really, no one knows the truth, but the idea of Indigenous roots is a nice one, and the romanticism of it means many fans hope one day we find some proof it's true.

Another popular theory is that the game emerged from Gaelic football, which ignores the fact the first rules for the Australian version were written down a quarter of a century before the Gaelic ones. But again, let's not allow facts to get in the way of a good story. Coming from Irish stock, I know that's what my extended family would want.

What is clear is that Australian Rules didn't emerge from another code but as a result of a complete lack of agreed-upon rules. The early games were a mess. People from different backgrounds were playing together and they all did whatever they wanted, with people on the same side often playing by different rules.* It was just a group of people running around doing whatever they wanted with no real thought given to the greater whole. Federal parliament, basically.

All that chaos led to some rough rules being worked out on the fly. Melbourne wasn't the only place this was occurring. Geelong had created its own version of the rules, which possibly predate Victorian Rules. South Australia had their own version too, which involved quince paste and stopping the game every five minutes to tell everyone they weren't founded by convicts.

A set of rules that could be written down and shared was sorely needed. Legend has it that the best sportsman of the day was responsible for this achievement. Like all sporting myths, what happened was not the story that got passed down.

---

* The AFL's insistence on rules that require a lot of interpretation means these days it often appears each umpire is still using a different set of rules.

TOM WILLS

How to describe Tom Wills? He was a prototype of the Australian athlete who is a flawed genius; epic on the field, an ongoing disaster off it.

Born in Australia in 1835, Wills was sent to England when he was fourteen. At the Rugby School his sporting ability made him stand out, and he was made captain of its cricket team. A colonial being made captain of such an exclusive school's cricket team was astounding. Most English people at the time thought they were effectively barbarians (that Viking heritage, I suspect). He went on to play first-class cricket in England and, when he returned home to Australia, he captained Victoria. He was the best cricketer in the Australian colonies.

Wills lived a life normally reserved for the pages of a particularly dramatic kind of fiction. Outside sport, his life was a dumpster fire of epic proportions. That often seems to be the way. Having ridiculous talent in one area seems to always come at the cost of being below average in every other endeavour. For example, Wills' stint as MCC secretary was cut short because he never showed up to meetings, running the club so shambolically it went into debt.

His sporting ability, however, was unquestionable. He was playing cricket at the highest level as well as playing football. As well as helping to establish the rules of the game, he was involved in forming the Melbourne Football Club in 1858, serving as Melbourne's first captain.

Then, in 1861, Wills took off for Queensland with his father, Horatio, to set up a new family property. Shortly after arriving, Horatio was killed, along with eighteen others, in the largest massacre of white settlers by Indigenous people in Australia's history.

Many people would spend their time trying to get revenge, yet just five years later Wills coached the Aboriginal cricket team that toured England in 1868. Wills seemed to lack the racist animosity towards Indigenous people that many others carried so easily, an amazing fact considering his father's fate.

As his life went on, it seems Wills – the greatest Australian cricketer and footballer of his age – was struggling with his mental health and alcoholism. He became a recluse and suffered from paranoid delusions. In 1880, Wills committed suicide, stabbing himself in the heart three times with a pair of scissors.

While Wills was certainly a key figure in the early development of football, he wasn't the sole 'father of the game'. He lacked the stability to administer a sport as chaotic and fast growing as Victorian Rules, work that tended to fall to others. Tragically, he lived in times before there was any understanding of mental health, and he suffered because of it. In remembrance Victoria named a complex, unnavigable freeway interchange after him, the greatest honour Victorians can bestow.

ORGANISED CHAOS

The earliest games of football in Melbourne would be unrecognisable today; so rapid was the game's evolution, by the 1870s the sport looked nothing like the game that had emerged just twenty years before. It's often claimed that the first ever game of 'Australian Rules' took place on 7 August 1858, between Scotch College and Melbourne Grammar, in Yarra Park. That game, though, was a rough approximation of the various rules used in English schools. The goals were so far apart you couldn't see one end when standing at the other. It was just a group of eighty people tackling each other at once, and it took three hours for someone to score a goal. How exciting does that sound? The game went for five hours and ended in a draw because it got dark. After that display, it's amazing a crowd showed up for a rematch, but they did. Netflix hadn't been invented yet.

This match wasn't even the first organised game of football in

ROMANTIC THINGS TO SAY TO A SPORTS FAN

'One day I hope to make you as happy as your team does, but I also hope to not let you down as often.'

'Even though the team you barrack for isn't playing, I know this match is important to you.'

'My love for you burns as bright as this flare I just smuggled through security soon will.'

'If it clashes with the footy we should just reschedule it.'

'We should get a bigger TV.'

'Why don't we make our honeymoon a trip to England to watch the Ashes?'

'I hate the Fanatics too.'

the colony,* but what can be said is that games like that one led to a desire for football to be played with a modicum of organisation. People wanted it to look less like a pub brawl between drunk school boys (which would be entertaining but frowned upon in polite company) and more like an athletic pursuit worthy of private school lads.

FOUR MEN WALK INTO A PUB

So four men walk into a pub. Instead of the beginning of a joke, this was the beginning of THE MOST SERIOUS THING EVER. Well, for many people it was. When they left, they had the gospel of Australian Rules in their hands, a document that in the coming years would be tinkered with almost as much as the actual gospels and spread with equal fervour.

---

* It's not surprising that a contest between two private schools was considered the first game even though it wasn't. This was Melbourne, where school ties are weirdly important and when you meet someone often the first question you get asked is, 'What school did you go to?' Imagine being a full-grown adult and still caring what school you went to. It's like meeting another 40-year-old and feeling a deep kinship because you both liked He-Man as kids.

The pub was the Parade Hotel in East Melbourne, where publican James 'Jerry' Bryant had let it be known that players could borrow a football from his establishment. This was common practice in England, to encourage players to have a drink afterwards.

The four men were James Bogue Thompson, Tom Wills, William Hammersley and Thomas Henry Smith, committee members of the Melbourne Football Club. In a clear case of putting the cart before the horse, three days earlier they had founded a club for a sport that didn't have rules yet. There is nothing more typically male than starting something before you've figured out how to do it. It's the 'she'll be right' approach that, surprisingly, works out more often than you'd think.

It was the equivalent of building something from IKEA by just glancing at the front of the instructions. In this case, though, there were no instructions to ignore so they just made it up entirely, which is how I do IKEA too. The couch I bought last week has developed into a wonderful wardrobe.

Some claim the impetus for all this rule-making was a letter Tom Wills wrote in 1958 to *Bell's Life in Victoria and Sporting Chronicle*:

> Now that cricket has been put aside for some few months to come, and cricketers have assumed somewhat of the chrysalis nature (for a time only 'tis true), but at length will again burst forth in all their varied hues, rather than allow this state of torpor to creep over them, and stifle their new supple limbs, why can they not, I say, form a foot-ball club, and form a committee of three or more to draw up a code of laws?

For a start, the idea that football would keep cricketers fit is amusing, because let's face it, most cricketers would need to actually *get* fit first. Still, the letter highlights one thing: people wrote a lot better back then.

This letter has now generally been discounted as a significant moment in Australian Rules history. It seems Wills just wrote to the papers a lot and, in this case, was summing up what a lot of the people who were playing these embryonic games were already thinking and doing. In essence, Wills was probably one of those characters who just summarise other people's hard work, state the bleeding obvious and talk about it as if it was their idea. You would have worked with a Wills at some point in your life.

The task of the newly formed committee was to develop a set of rules so the pick-up games being played would stop turning into rolling messes punctuated by arguments about the rules (not that different from the current game, some would say). Part of the problem was there were no clear rules to build on. There were certainly some simple rules from England, such as those from Rugby, Eton, Harrow and Winchester, and these were all considered. It was decided to try to take the best bits from each and form a code that suited the committee. It's often said that Australian Rules is not as 'tough' as rugby, but that was a conscious decision made by the founders. The rugby rules resulted in a lot of injuries and this was a concern for working men. There was no sick leave and missing weeks of work was a risk many couldn't take. For that reason 'hacking', the old kicking in the shins, was not allowed.

What the rules did allow was the captains deciding the length of the field. It was also agreed there'd be two goal posts at each end and a 'mark' when the ball was caught, allowing the player to then kick the ball without interference.

It took them less than two months to start tinkering with these rules, a proud practice that continues to this day. The first rule change was to outlaw tripping. Again, working men getting injured was the reason.

Other tweaks followed, aiming to make the sport more fun to play and watch. James Thompson, one of the four rule-makers, was keen to promote the game as entertainment and also wanted to encourage women to come along. Not as players of course! That would be madness, what with their delicate bones and constant fainting from excitement. This desire to attract spectators turned the game into less of a sport and more a proselytising religion.

RAPID GROWTH

In the early days of Australian Rules, spectators wandering onto the field seemed to be a rather alarming issue. It was often complained about by administrators, the players and the media. These weren't angry or excited fans trying to get close to their heroes, it was couples going for a stroll or someone walking their dog. Organised sport wasn't really a thing yet so people just saw a bunch of blokes taking up a lot of space in the local park.

These interruptions showed that while the sport was gaining popularity, it was still seen as a leisure pursuit. But growth was quick. By the early 1860s, the sport was gaining broader appeal. The Melbourne Football Club had been formed in 1858 and the Geelong Football Club in 1859 and, in the following years, clubs were established in Bendigo, Ballarat, Sydney, Adelaide, Brisbane, Williamstown and Port Adelaide, to name a few. It was an exciting time but it wasn't all good news; the Carlton Football Club was also established in this period.

Some of these football clubs were formed even before the rules were codified, but they soon adopted 'Victorian Rules', as they were known. Part of the game's early success was having different places all agree to play by the same rules. Both Geelong and South Australia agreed to get rid of their own rules and play by the rules drafted up at the Parade Hotel. This helped to avoid what had happened in England, where the various school's rules had limited their growth, since everyone wanted to keep their own rules and refused to play by any other rules. The opposite happened here, with the Victorian Rules rapidly becoming widespread. Clubs and individuals didn't insist on their own rules, so clubs could play each other from relatively early on.

Not that it was all one way; some rules from other areas had an influence. In the original Victorian Rules, you couldn't pick the ball up off the ground but instead had to kick it up to yourself. The Geelong rules had no such restriction so the Geelong players would just pick the ball up and, if you know people from Geelong, it's easier to just go along with them than argue the point.

As with other sports, the gold rush helped to spread the game beyond Melbourne, with converts travelling at first to the Victorian goldfields and then beyond, including to Western Australia in the 1890s. I can imagine them going tent to tent, saying, 'Can I speak to you about the sport of Victorian Rules? I believe it has a plan for you.'

Expanding beyond Melbourne saw the game become less of a winter hobby to keep cricketers fit and more a serious and popular pursuit in itself. In 1877, the MCC finally allowed football to be played on the MCG regularly. Prior to that it had been considered too much of a risk for the surface of the ground but, with crowds increasing, the MCC saw an opportunity to make a dollar. It was a momentous decision for both football and the MCG.

An enclosed ground meant you could charge patrons, and football certainly brought in the public. It was an early glimpse of how footy, not cricket, would come to be the cash cow for many cricket grounds. For footy, playing on established cricket grounds standardised the rough shape of the field of play. It also stopped spectators wandering onto the field, a massive relief for all involved.

Having a home ground where they could charge for admission became a key difference between the rich and powerful clubs and the poor ones. From relatively early on, the game took a casual approach to player payments. At first no one talked about payment, in the same way no one talks about eating a whole tub of ice-cream even though everyone does it. Later on, it became less secretive,* with South Melbourne quite open about paying players from the 1870s onwards. The game was in essence professional, but in those days that meant getting enough money to cover your playing expenses with a bit left over for a few beers.

THE COACHING BLUES

Over the years, Carlton has often seemed less a football club and more an organisation designed to brutally sack coaches. David Parkin, Robert Walls, Alex Jesaulenko, Denis Pagan, Brett Ratten and Mick Malthouse are just some of the coaches who came to a grisly end at the hands of the Carlton board.

Robert Walls was sacked just two years after winning the 1987 Premiership, while Pagan walked into the harsh penalties of a salary cap scandal that he had nothing to do with.

Favourite son Alex Jesaulenko was asked to coach following Walls' sacking, only to be sacked himself less than two years later. To really rub the salt in the wound, Carlton would ask him to stay on in a marketing role. Jesaulenko's response is probably best not printed.

A DIVIDED KINGDOM

At about the same time the MCC was allowing football on their hallowed turf (which wasn't that hallowed at the time), the powers that be decided they needed to formalise the fact that they were The Powers That Be. So, in 1877, they established a new body to oversee football in the colony, the Victorian Football Association (VFA).

---

* The paying of players, not the ice-cream gorging, which is still shameful in many people's eyes, a stigma that needs to change.

The VFA provided a centralised body that made sure the competition was co-ordinated properly in Victoria. They determined how the premiership was awarded and set all fixtures. By the 1890s it was well established with thirteen clubs: Carlton, Collingwood, Essendon, Fitzroy, Footscray, Geelong, Melbourne, North Melbourne, Port Melbourne, Richmond, St Kilda, South Melbourne and Williamstown.

The strength of the VFA was that it provided a competition with standardised rules, clear fixturing and clubs that could generate revenue. This centralised power, however, was resented by some clubs, exposing the standard fault line that runs through Australian sport: clubs versus administration.

POLITICS AND SPORT

During the late 1990s, then Victorian premier and future Hawthorn president Jeff Kennett had the rather dubious idea of getting former Geelong footballer Billy Brownless to run for the Liberal Party in North Geelong.

Following a meeting with Kennett, the media confronted Brownless in the following exchange:

> Mark Willacy (MW): What are the big issues in North Geelong, literacy with school children, drug abuse? What are the big issues in North Geelong?
>
> Billy Brownless (BB): Yeah, all those.
>
> MW: What's your position on the independence of the auditor-general?
>
> BB: Yeah . . .
>
> Unidentified: He does a very good job.
>
> BB: . . . he does a very good job.
>
> MW: What about the separation of powers, do you endorse that at all, or . . .
>
> BB: Oh, yeah, yeah.

Brownless's political career was over before it started.

Victorians have always had a survival of the fittest mentality when it comes to footy and, during the 1890s, some of the richer clubs were wondering why they were supporting the weaker clubs while also letting the VFA tell them what to do. At the same time, the VFA were worrying about the professionalisation of some clubs and the gap it created between the rich and poor. It's not that different from the equalisation arguments of today.

Things erupted when the VFA announced it wanted to equalise the competition by putting all gate revenue into a central fund and then distributing it equally between the clubs. This sort of communist thinking was not welcomed by the powerful clubs, who had grown fond of their money and the on-field success it could buy.

In response Carlton, Collingwood, Essendon, Fitzroy, Geelong, Melbourne, South Melbourne and St Kilda stormed out in a huff and started the Victorian Football League, the most ruthless organisation to ever exist in Australian sports history. Overnight they'd become the most powerful Australian Rules competition in the land, leaving the VFA to fight for relevance.

In 1908, Richmond left the VFA, and University joined the VFL too, from the Metropolitan Football Association. University only lasted in the competition until 1914, the university students apparently struggling to play football and study, proving once and for all that education and football players rarely mix.

In 1925, Footscray, Hawthorn and North Melbourne also left for the greener pastures of the VFL, further weakening the VFA. The VFA kept going, though, and introduced innovative ideas that often caught on. They reduced the number of men on the field from twenty to eighteen, a rule that remains to this day. Another VFA rule allowed players to throw the ball if it was underarm, which was popular with fans but eventually phased out because no other competitions allowed it.

The animosity between the two competitions would ebb and flow over the decades, like two frenemies sharing a long-distance car ride. They were stuck in the same state and had to find ways to coexist. At times it appeared the two bodies would find a way to merge back together but it never quite got over the line, mainly because no one wanted to give up their power on the respective boards. Luckily today's footy boards aren't dominated by men with huge egos.

The VFA managed to find new ways to remain relevant. It started playing on Sundays and that soon became their day (the VFL got Saturdays) and it introduced two divisions with a promotion/relegation model. Yet by the eighties, the VFA was in decline. It had neither the money nor the public support to compete at the level of the VFL, which would soon become the AFL.

By the early nineties the VFA was in discussions about becoming the Victorian feeder competition for the AFL. In 1994 the VFA was formally disbanded, a sad end to a proud and at times innovative competition. It lives on today as the VFL, with many of the participating clubs directly aligned with AFL clubs.

SOUTH AUSTRALIA – VICTORIA'S BIG RIVAL

South Australia has a long and proud Australian Rules history, going back almost as far as Victoria's. They added innovations to the game and produced some of the greatest players to have ever played, including Barrie Robran, Russell Ebert, Malcolm Blight, Craig Bradley, John Platten, Stephen Kernahan and Neil Kerley, to name but a few.

South Australians still take a lot of pride in their impressive state league, the SANFL. In 2016, the competition introduced a new logo and a new slogan, 'We love footy', which sums up the South Australian people. It's also lucky for the SANFL administration – you don't want to oversee a competition you're at best indifferent too. 'We tolerate footy' would have sent the wrong message, I believe.

South Australians, like Victorians, were quick to start playing a variety of versions of football from the 1850s, a mishmash of English school rules and an emerging set of their own rules. These chaotic games, where each team played by different rules, would sometimes result in both sides thinking they had won, much like the games young people play today where everyone is a winner! Strangely, this lack of co-ordination didn't stop people wanting to play, but it did lead to a lot of fights. Fighting, depending on what rules they were applying, may or may not have been allowed.

On 30 April 1877 twelve clubs met at the Prince Alfred Hotel in King William Street to straighten things out. They formed a governing body, the South Australian Football Association (SAFA) and agreed on some rules that were very similar to Victorian Rules. This meant the SAFA beat the VFA into existence, adding to the short list of things South Australians brag about. Those things are: quince paste, Grange, the Central Market, Haigh's Chocolates and the phrase 'heaps good'.

The inaugural season saw South Park, Willunga, Port Adelaide, Adelaide, North Adelaide, Gawler, Bankers, Woodville, South Adelaide and Victorian go at it. The following year Norwood joined, which was a mistake by the founding teams because Norwood won the next six premierships.

The SAFA struggled, however. Nine clubs left within a decade, seeing the competition reduced to just four clubs. Clubs continued to come and go in the following decades. In 1901, the SAFA changed its name to the South Australian Football League and, in 1927, they added 'National' to the name on account of being affiliated with the national body, the Australian National Football Council, which some other states also did. Now, people think the SANFL is called that because the South Australians have some delusion of grandeur, thinking they're a national comp, but that shows a lack of understanding of history. The reason South Australia has kept 'National' in is (a) it's been like that for a very long time and (b) it annoys Victorians, which is reason enough to do anything.

The league managed to weather the two world wars, with some seasons missed, before going from strength to strength after World War II. Port Adelaide dominated the competition in the 1950s under Fos Williams, winning seven premierships, including six in a row from 1954 to 1959. This period built the foundation of the elitism Port Adelaide fans feel about their club, which mystifies all others. Fos's son, Mark 'Choco' Williams, would go on to coach Port Adelaide to their first AFL premiership in 2004.

While Port dominated the fifties, Sturt won five straight premierships from 1966 to 1970. The seventies, however, saw many of the best South Australian players go to the VFL as the two leagues increasingly competed with each other for talent. Victoria, with its larger population and stronger clubs, was always going to win that one just for financial reasons. The more players left, the weaker the SANFL became. If South Australians needed more reasons to hate Victorians, this period certainly provided them.

The SANFL was learning that, when it came to the national game, the VFL was only interested in a version they controlled. This wasn't just a feeling; the VFL had decided in the late seventies that other competitions were the enemy. Keeping other leagues weak was a key part of the VFL's push for supremacy. In 1981, they rejected the idea of a combined SANFL team playing in the VFL. Admitting the SANFL would have been a lifeline and the Victorians weren't interested in letting in a league that was still very strong. Five years later, they gave Western Australia and Brisbane a licence instead.

This meant the SANFL began to struggle with attendances. The lure of the VFL – soon to become the AFL – had sucked in all the top talent from around the country. The SANFL clubs had other issues too, the main one being they couldn't agree amongst themselves about what to do next. Port Adelaide knew what to do though: stab everyone else in the back. They entered secret negotiations with the AFL about joining the competition and the AFL, always happy to destabilise another competition, signed a non-binding agreement with them in 1990.

Being sport, 'secret' negotiations can only remain secret for about seven minutes. When the SANFL found out about Port Adelaide's little affair they exploded. SANFL president Max Basheer called Port's move an 'act of betrayal' and they sought an injunction from the Supreme Court to stop Port Adelaide negotiating with the AFL.

The SANFL then quickly pulled together a new bid for their league to join the AFL. No other club in South Australia had a fanbase as big as Port, but the SANFL had an even bigger asset: a huge fanbase that really hated Port. On top of that the SANFL owned Adelaide's Football Park and their bid gave the AFL access to that, as well as the might of the whole SANFL competition. The timing was now right for the AFL. The SANFL was no longer the threat it had been back in 1981. The AFL approved the SANFL bid, leading to the formation of the Adelaide Crows, who joined the national competition 1991. Port was left on the sidelines and would not join the comp until 1997.

Today, the SANFL acts as a feeder competition for the AFL but retains its own strong following. The two Adelaide AFL clubs, the Power and the Crows, have had great success and contributed many iconic moments, like when players from both teams punched on at the Ramsgate Hotel the night after a game in 2002.

TASMANIA – THE LITTLE ISLAND THAT COULDN'T

For a small state, Tasmania sure does have a lot of divisions. Where other states have interstate rivalries, Tasmanians spend a lot of that energy fighting amongst themselves. Trying to get your head around the politics of Tasmanian football is like trying to untangle the mess in the Middle East, except I don't think we'll ever be able to sort things out in Tasmania.

Tasmania was an early starter, football of the Victorian kind rapidly took over the colony in the 1860s. With lots of small towns and no one big city like Melbourne or Adelaide, Tasmania's footy tended to be town based, with regional leagues eventually put in place. Three key competitions emerged: the Tasmanian Football League (TFL) in 1879, based around Hobart, followed by the Northern Tasmanian Football Association (NTFA) in 1886, based around Launceston, and in 1910 the North West Football Union (NWFU), based around – you guessed it – the north-west of the state.

These leagues disliked each other with an intensity usually reserved for extended family, which, being Tasmania, they probably were. The parochialism in the different parts of the state made a statewide competition harder to organise than a trip to the moon. In fact, in the time it took to organise one, we actually did organise a few trips to the moon and also sent a probe to Pluto.

It was only in 1986 that a real statewide league was put in place, when a bunch of clubs from the northern leagues left to join the TFL. The exodus of teams from their competitions meant the NTFA and the NWFU had to merge, forming the Northern Tasmanian Football League, the NTFL.[*]

The new statewide TFL lasted until 2000 and, in that time, both it and the newly merged NTFL found money hard to come by. When almost no one showed up to their 2000 Grand Final, the TFL decided that was enough of that and their clubs returned to the NTFL, as well as the new Southern Football League (SFL). By this stage, even the Tasmanians were confused.

---

[*] Don't worry, there's not a test on all these acronyms later on; although there is if you want to become a Tasmanian citizen.

In 2009, it was decided a statewide competition should be given another go and the TFL was brought back. It remains in place.

Tasmania has in recent years hosted more and more games for Hawthorn and North Melbourne, but the state still has no traction on a bid to get their own AFL team. In part this is because the AFL has preferred to focus on heartland areas like Greater Western Sydney, where as many as six people will turn up to a game. The AFL has long said a team in Tasmania makes no financial sense but, upon his retirement as AFL Chairman in 2017, Mike Fitzpatrick said it was really the fault of the Tasmanians for being too fractured. He really annoyed people in the TFL, NTFL, SFL, NTF and NWFU with those comments, let me tell you.

Despite all this infighting, Tasmania sure does churn out top level players. Even though they're an island of about four people, they've produced Darrel Baldock, Ian Stewart, Royce Hart, Peter Hudson and more recently Matthew Richardson and Alastair Lynch.

WESTERN AUSTRALIA – ACRONYM ANARCHY
Western Australia doesn't just churn out iron ore, crazy billionaires and secession bids. No, it also produces terrific footballers like Barry Cable, the wonderfully named Merv McIntosh, Dean Cox, Graham 'Polly' Farmer, Ben Cousins,* Guy McKenna, Ross Glendinning and the Krakouer brothers.

Western Australia has a proud Australian Rules history, yet this wasn't a certainty early on; by the time Australian Rules got to the west, mainly on the back of the gold rush, rugby was already established, denying the Victorian code the relatively clear run it had in South Australia and Tasmania.

This began to change as people entered the state from Victoria and South Australia. In 1885, the Fremantle Rugby Club decided

---

*   Just . . . I mean . . . just one big asterisk on this one. But see page 91 for some of it.

to switch from rugby to 'the Victorian game'. This wasn't as hard a decision as it sounds, because the club was only a few years old. You can't really break up with someone if you've only gone on a couple of dates. Plus, the Victorian game they were switching too wasn't anywhere near as different as rugby and Australian Rules are now. Switching was seen as a way to better integrate with the South Australian and Victorian colonies. On top of all this, the missionaries for Victorian Rules were keen to attract anyone and everyone; rugby was only interested in attracting the landed gentry.

After the switch by Fremantle, other clubs followed. They weren't any more wedded to rugby and were equally eager to play a sport that seemed to be on the ascendency. This sudden change of heart by the sportsmen of Western Australia meant a new association needed to be formed so in 1885 they rushed into place the West Australian Football Association (WAFA).

The early days of the competition were more unstable than the modern-day Australian Senate, with clubs coming and going like it was a bad suburban party. As more people came to Western Australia in search of gold, the powerful Goldfields Football League began and was arguably as strong as the WAFA for a long time.

The WAFA changed its name to the West Australian Football League (WAFL) in 1908, which is hardly surprising. Back then, football leagues seemed to change their names like they were in witness protection. They did it again in 1932, becoming the Western Australian National Football League (WANFL). All I can think about is the money they must have wasted on changing the stationery. These days, of course, a new logo costs millions of dollars and that might be the reason they've all slowed down on the name changes.

By 1934, the Whatever It Was Currently Being Called (WIWCBC) had settled on its core eight clubs, which are all still around: Claremont, East Fremantle, East Perth, Perth, South Fremantle, Subiaco, Swan Districts and West Perth. This stability would lead to success. In the post-war period, footy was booming in the west, and booms always end up going great for WA. This boom saw the talent level rise and that meant the VFL started to get interested. As had happened in South Australia, the top players started to head to Victoria to find fame and fortune.

At first this wasn't a huge problem but over time it became obvious that the west's best were not in the WANFL but in the VFL. The league reacted the only way it knew how: in 1980 it changed its name back to the WAFL, dropping the 'National' bit and switching 'Western' back to 'West'. Just think, there were probably dozens of marketing meetings where they discussed the significance of this change and how it would create a 'focal point to launch a cohesive narrative for the brand story' or some such nonsense that normal people roll their eyes at.

The writing was on the wall.* The VFL was now the elite league and the Western Australians decided that if you can't beat them, you'd better join them and then beat them.

The West Coast Eagles were given the green light by the VFL, entering the league in 1987. The Eagles were not a huge success right away and, before the eighties were over, there was talk of them being wound up. This proved to be a bit of an overreaction, which is kind of an AFL thing. The club recruited Mick Malthouse as coach and, in 1992, they were the first non-Victorian team to win a VFL or AFL premiership. In Victoria, a period of mourning was declared that's still going if you listen to Victorians complain about all the advantages the interstate teams have. Oh, they do go on. It was a terrific Eagles side that year, featuring players like John Worsfold, Guy McKenna and Glen Jakovich.

So popular were the Eagles by this point that a second team from Western Australia was now inevitable. Fremantle was the clear

---

* Probably written with all those letters they kept discarding.

choice, a place with one of the proudest Australian Rules pedigrees in the country, with the Dockers entering the league in 1995.

The success of these two teams meant the WAFL was by now very much a second-tier competition. It was still popular though, and played at a very high standard. It also maintained its inscrutable obsession with changing its own name, becoming the Western Australian State Football League (WASFL) in 1990 before making a fun reversal the very next year, back to WAFL, just to make sure people were paying attention.

You'd think that would be about the end of it but true champions always find another gear and in 1997 they renamed the WAFL the 'Westar Rules'. Was this as bad an idea as it sounds? Yes, yes it was. It wasn't the only change. West Perth decided to join in with the name changing fun and became Joondalup. That went over so well they had to change back after the ninth round. Nine rounds!

This enthusiasm for new ideas resulted in an expansion team being admitted, the Peel Thunder. This took the number of teams to nine, meaning the league had to introduce a bye. The great thing about that was it really annoyed all the other clubs and now every team hates the Thunder.

Finally, in 2001, the decision was made to change the name back to the WAFL, which it is currently called, just one bad marketing meeting away from being changed again.

NEW SOUTH WALES – ALMOST BUT NOT QUITE

In New South Wales, the Victorian game came very close to becoming the sport of the working class in the late nineteenth century.* Rugby, though, made it difficult for the code to gain access to enclosed grounds, where they could charge gate fees. That made it hard for Victorian Rules to exercise its greatest strength over rugby:

---

* If you're from NSW and have only flicked to this section because you recognised the name of your own state, well done, and you'll find the Rugby League chapter on page 199.

the ability to pay players. This advantage was further eroded with the formation of Rugby League, which also paid players, and by the start of the twentieth century the Victorian game was still only played on a small and amateur basis in NSW.

Despite this, NSW has contributed a surprising amount of talent to the code and many key people. For example, both Tom Wills and his cousin H. C. A. Harrison (who was an early driving force in the sport) came from New South Wales, as did a pair of the greatest coaches of all time, Jock McHale and Allan Jeans. The list of top players from New South Wales is surprisingly long: Haydn Bunton Sr., the Daniher brothers, Taylor Walker, John Longmire, Mark Maclure, Billy Brownless, Paul Kelly, Shane Crawford and arguably the greatest player of all time, Wayne Carey.*

There are some early moments in its history that suggest NSW was surprisingly close to becoming an Australian Rules state. For instance, in 1877, the Carlton Football Club travelled up to Sydney to play the Waratah Rugby Club at both rugby and Victorian Rules. This trip resulted in Waratah switching codes and then the formation of the NSW Football Association three years later, in 1880. But that body struggled, and a new league was founded in 1903 called the NSW Football League. Some of the clubs that were part of that league still exist today: North Shore, East Sydney (now UNSW-Eastern Suburbs Bulldogs) and Balmain.

The emergence of professional rugby in the form of League is often pointed to as the final blow for the fledgling code in NSW. I think Victorian Rules also struggled because in 1927 the NSWAFL inserted 'National' in its name to become the ludicrous NSWNAFL. That lasted until 1973 and in those years several people went insane trying to pronounce the name. It added hours to administration meetings and likely curtailed any interest in the sport's growth.

---

* Carey was only the greatest on the field. His exploits off it are another matter entirely. See page 93.

Surprisingly there were a few attempts to merge Rugby League with Australian Rules, creating a 'universal game' that could be played across Australia. Some of these discussions got quite far. Rules were drawn up and secret practice matches were played, but it never quite got there. The last attempt was in 1933 and since then the two codes have seen themselves as direct competitors.

While Sydney was almost dead to Australian Rules for a long time, other parts of NSW were more interested, usually the further south you travelled. The Riverina area produced a lot of talent, so much so that Melbourne clubs complained heavily when the GWS Giants were given access to area as a recruiting zone.

While the code lay dormant for most of the twentieth century in NSW, developments in Victoria reinvigorated the VFL's desire to grow the game up north. Government legislation had confined the VFL to being played on Saturdays, with the VFA playing on Sundays. This move had worked well for the VFA, and the VFL was desperate to play on Sundays, both to boost their competition and to weaken the VFA's. The government wouldn't budge, however, so the VFL came up with the cunning plan of playing games on a Sunday in Sydney and having Channel Seven broadcast them back into Melbourne.

The success of this scheme and the VFL's desire to become a national competition made Sydney an interesting target. The sport's failure up there was actually a blessing; there was no SANFL or WAFL to get upset or stand in their way.

In 1982, the cash-strapped South Melbourne Football Club decided to relocate, becoming the Sydney Swans. It was a decision borne purely out of financial distress. The VFL, who in fact contributed to South's financial problems by limiting their opportunities to improve their home ground, were only too happy to approve the move. The emotional outpouring from fans was intense and a 'Keep South at South' campaign was launched. The VFL had a difficult decision to make: whether to put its business strategy first or the interests of football fans. Just kidding, it wasn't a difficult decision for them at all and the Swans moved.

In the early years after the move, the Swans had the joy of playing in a city that was not just indifferent to them but outright hostile. They were welcomed like someone who brought peanuts to a children's party. Before long the club was in enormous difficulty again.

Enter Dr Geoffrey Edelsten. The colourful businessman bought the Swans licence for just over $6 million and set about trying to add some of that famous NSW pizazz to the enterprise. This included him driving a pink Lamborghini, introducing cheerleaders, the 'Swanettes', and spending a fortune on top players like Greg 'Diesel' Williams, Gerard Healy and Merv Neagle.

Forward Warwick Capper added to this sense of showmanship too. With his blonde mullet and shorts so small they challenged public indecency laws, Capper certainly raised the profile of the game north of the Barassi Line.* He also released a single, 'I Only Take What's Mine', in 1985, a song that at best could be described as 'awful'.**

Edelsten's spending led to better performances on the field but within twelve months he was gone due to further financial difficulties. Who would have thought the first VFL side in Sydney would struggle financially? The VFL bought back the licence for $10. At first sight not a bad deal for them, given they'd just sold it for $6 million, but they were still buying a financial disaster. A new group of financial backers was found, including TV personality Mike Willesee.

---

* The Barassi Line was proposed by historian Ian Turner and is the line that geographically divides where Australian Rules is the top sport from where League dominates. Turner believed it to start where the Victoria/NSW border meets the coast, running in a straight line up to where the NT/Queensland border meets the Gulf. The Barassi Line gets its name from Australian Rules superstar player and coach Ron Barassi. Since being coined by Turner in 1978, both codes have started teams on the opposing side of the Barassi Line, however in the main it remains true that each code dominates its respective side.

** In 2017, Capper made headlines again for getting trapped in a stairwell at a Perth Hotel for over an hour. Anyone who has met Capper was not surprised by this turn of events.

AFL SLANG

Ball: Short for 'holding the ball', which is illegal if you're tackled. The crowd yells 'Ball!' whenever an opposition player is tackled, in the hope of influencing the umpire to award a free kick. The crowd is not interested in being correct.

Clanger: An error. Kicking the ball to an opponent or out of bounds on the full would be classed as a clanger. I like the term so much I refer to many of the mistakes I've made in my life as clangers.

Jumper punch: Until very recently, players could avoid serious penalty by grabbing a handful of an opponent's jumper and then using that same hand to hit them. For some reason, the AFL judiciary believed that holding the jumper meant it wasn't a real punch. This view was not shared by my previous employer, who sacked me and reported me to the police.

Tagger: A player whose sole purpose is to stop an opponent from doing anything positive. In that regard, they are like Karen at work.

They started to cut costs but it was to no avail and, by 1992, the Swans were in real danger of folding or being relocated again.

What was by then the AFL was forced to step in. They spent a lot of money to fix things. Ron Barassi was brought in as coach (meaning he had to cross his own line) and the club turned things around, managing a grand final appearance in 1996. This success has more or less continued since and, in 2005, the Swans broke their 72-year premiership drought (if you include the South Melbourne years).

The Swans are now one of the best run and most successful clubs in the AFL, a fact that drives a lot of Victorians crazy. The AFL now has a very strong foothold in Sydney and it's only taken them thirty-odd years to do it. In 2012 they added a second AFL club, the Greater Western Sydney Giants, and, keen to avoid the mistakes of the early days of the Swans, poured hundreds of millions of dollars into them and gave them so many draft picks that the Giants don't even know what to do with them all.

On top of that, the AFL is spending money on junior programs and local leagues in the state, as do the Swans. The AFL's aim is clear: they want their sport to take over the most populous state in Australia.

QUEENSLAND – THE ONE THAT GOT AWAY

Queensland is the state that got away from Australian Rules. In the early colonial days, the sport was at least as popular as rugby. The reasons this didn't develop are many and varied, but they include the distance between Queensland and New South Wales, rugby making smart choices and most of all that up there the code was run terribly for a long time.

The first Queensland-based club, Brisbane, was formed in 1866. More clubs were founded in the 1870s and in 1880 the Queensland Football Association (QFA) was formed. By then many schools had chosen the Victorian game over rugby and the code was the dominant sport in the colony.

The rise was fast and the decline was just as rapid. By 1885, the QFA was broke. In 1887 a group of headmasters voted on what code should be played in schools; it was close, but rugby won by a single vote. It was a momentous decision that excluded Victorian Rules from Queensland schools. The subsequent formation of the Northern Rugby Union ensured rugby was the best-organised and financially strongest code in the state, until the arrival of Rugby League in 1909.

Not that the acolytes of the Victorian game gave up completely. In 1903, the Queensland Football League (QFL) became the basis of an ongoing amateur league that kept the game alive despite being overshadowed by League and Union. Of course in 1927 it added an N for 'National', to become the QANFL. It quietly went about spreading the game to the south-east and north-east of the state.

By the sixties, what was now the Queensland Australian

Football League (QAFL) was overseeing a small but devoted collection of leagues that kept spreading. This amateur competition has produced a lot of talent, such as Michael Voss, Jason Dunstall, Jason Akermanis, Simon Black, Gavin Crosisca, Nick Riewoldt and Dayne Zorko.

In the seventies Victoria looked at Queensland with fresh eyes. The state started sending thousands of sleeper agents north in the guise of 'Victorian retirees', who pretended to want a break from Melbourne's cold winters but were really a fifth column, undermining and destabilising League and Union.

The VFL was ready to expand into Queensland by the mid-eighties, to grow the game but also because they needed the cash and selling licences for expansion teams seemed like a good idea at the time. In 1986 a licence for a Brisbane team was awarded to a group headed by actor Paul Cronin. Being an actor based in Australia, Cronin had no money, but Christopher Skase did (at least on paper) and he put up the $4 million fee for the licence. Picking Christopher Skase and Geoffrey Edelsten as business partners is a great illustration of the VFL's business expertise at the time.

The new team was named the Brisbane Bears, and there were early signs of how bad that club would be. The first clue was that their mascot, a koala, was not actually a bear. The second was that calling it a Brisbane team was false advertising, with the club playing its games at Carrara Oval on the Gold Coast, an hour's drive from Brisbane.

It was no surprise that things did not go well, either on the field or off it and, in 1989, Skase's businesses collapsed. He fled to Spain to avoid some legal unpleasantness. The AFL got the licence back and promptly sold it again, to Gold Coast businessman Reuben Pelerman, who held it for two years but discovered he also didn't enjoy losing both games and money. He handed the licence back to the AFL, which makes me think that selling club licences and getting them back for free seems to have been a key part of the VFL/AFL revenue model in the eighties and nineties.

In 1993 a move to playing at the Gabba in Brisbane provided a much-needed shot in the arm for the club. With the AFL starting to get some traction, the QAFL was suffering, as the Bears were taking a lot of the limelight. A new governing body was introduced, the Queensland Australian Football Council (QAFC), which oversaw a new competition, the Queensland State Football League (QSFL).

While the game in Queensland now had a pulse, it was by no means thriving. But a clever move by the chair of the Brisbane Bears led them to unimaginable heights.

THE BERMUDA TRIANGLE OF AUSTRALIAN SPORT

The AFL's struggles to establish a team on the Gold Coast are hardly unique. The Gold Coast is a mirage in the sporting landscape. All codes tell themselves it's one of the fastest-growing regions in Australia, but there's no evidence the people living there want to watch sport. Establishing a team on the Gold Coast is like invading Russia in the winter.

The Gold Coast Titans currently play in the NRL, but before that there's been the Gold Coast–Tweed Giants, who became the Gold Coast Seagulls, who became the Gold Coast Gladiators, who became the Gold Coast Chargers, who then folded.

In the NBL, the Gold Coast Cougars began in 1990, changed their name to the Gold Coast Rollers, and then folded within six years. A decade later the Gold Coast Blaze were admitted to the league, but lasted just five seasons.

Gold Coast United FC made it just three A-League seasons, with owner Clive Palmer losing $18 million. A lot of this was Palmer's fault, for instance he limited the crowd to 5000 people to save on rent. Palmer had his licence revoked and announced he would start a competitor league. Guess what? He hasn't.

The decline of Melbourne's Fitzroy Lions had been protracted and involved a lot of debt. The club had constantly attempted to spend its way out of trouble, only to find itself on the wrong side of demographics and long-term trends. In 1996, merger talks between Fitzroy and North Melbourne seemed to be progressing well, but Fitzroy had earlier taken a loan from the government of Nauru that they couldn't pay back, which meant administrator Michael Brennan was in control of what would happen to the Lions, rather than the club itself. And at the time North was doing well on the field, so the other Victorian clubs weren't so hot on them suddenly getting their pick of the best Lions players. They decided to block the merger.

Brisbane president Noel Gordon saw an opportunity. He had an awful team that was no threat to anyone, what about merging Fitzroy with them instead? Well, the Victorian teams (bar North) fell over themselves to sign off on this option. It's not as though the Lions would turn into some sort of super team up in Brisbane. Merging two basket cases seemed like a sensible option.

Brisbane offered to pay back Nauru's loan at 90 cents in the dollar, which was accepted, because anyone who lent money to Fitzroy usually got zero cents back on the dollar. Also, while we're at it, add Nauru to the list of the VFL's shady business partners.

So the Brisbane Lions were formed and Fitzroy supporters were left to deal with the death of their club, which is easily the worst thing that can happen to a person.* The Lions won premierships in 2001, 2002, 2003 and just fell short winning in 2004. Fair to say it didn't work out quite the way the Victorian clubs would have liked. And while some former Fitzroy supporters were heartened by the success, there are many who believe that the club ceased to exist the day it was merged.

---

* Of course, there are worse things. Just recently the fried chicken shop near me shut down, despite my heroic, single-handed effort to fund it.

Footy in Queensland hasn't been all smooth sailing in the last few decades. In 1999, the QSFL went into voluntary liquidation, and a new organisation, AFL Queensland (AFLQ), was set up. The Lions, after their amazing success, have declined almost every year since and crowd numbers have plummeted, requiring the AFL to provide substantial support. On top of that, the AFL tried to chase the unicorn that is the Gold Coast sporting market, launching a second Queensland team, the Gold Coast Suns, in 2011. They have been a bitter disappointment, failing spectacularly on and off the field despite their wealth of talent, and even accidentally recruited Rodney Eade as coach.

The AFL sits behind the rugby codes in popularity in the state, but has significantly grown its junior participation numbers. It will be a long haul in Queensland to bring the game back up to where it was in the early 2000s, or in 1880 for that matter.

NORTHERN TERRITORY – NORTHERN EXPOSURE

Australian Rules really got going in Darwin during World War I, when many people were located there for the war effort. Like a lot of things in the Northern Territory, Australian Rules has been a case study in racial tension.

Some of this tension can be seen in the comments of Dr Cecil Cook, the Chief Protector of Aborigines from 1927 to 1939, who vowed to 'breed the colour out' of Australia. Surprisingly, this didn't sit well with the Indigenous population. I suppose having someone appointed to 'protect' you is patronising enough, but when that 'protector' announces they want to breed you out of existence, you have to wonder if they have the right title. It's a bit like giant corporations announcing they have a 'Head of Innovation'.

By 1917, thanks to an influx of people from South Australia, the game had grown to the point where the Northern Territory Football League (NTFL) was established. The league soon ran into trouble when Katherine, a team mainly made up of Indigenous and Chinese players, complained about the umpiring being biased against them. Things got heated and the Katherine team abandoned the game.

A week later a meeting was held and, sports administrators never being the type to overreact, the league was disbanded and a new one was formed with a constitution that only allowed white people to play. The new white-only North Australian Football League (NAFL) remained in place for three years before the clubs involved got over themselves and lifted the ban, but the competition continued to decline and in the 1934/35 season the league folded.* They again tried to form an all-white league, the Darwin Football League (DFL), but it didn't last. What a shame!

The original NTFL was now back and found itself once again the major league in the Northern Territory. It only looked good in comparison to the white-only NAFL; the only NTFL team that took 'full blooded' Indigenous players was the Wanderers Football Club.

In 1952 St Mary's entered the league with a team made up of Tiwi Islanders who were working for the Air Force and the Army. St Mary's became one of the most successful clubs in Australia and has produced some of the greatest players of the game, players like Maurice Rioli, Michael Long, Peter Burgoyne and Cyril Rioli. This is hardly surprising. The Tiwi Islanders' love of Australian Rules makes Victorians seem indifferent. It's often observed that Tiwi Islander players seem to have a natural affinity for the game, but it should be noted that about 35 per cent of the population play the game. That's insane. If you applied those participation rates across the country the standard of play would go through the roof. For comparison, the Northern Territory has a participation rate of 7 per cent, and that's the highest on the mainland.

While the success of St Mary's has hardly eradicated racism from

---

* Footy is played in summer in the Northern Territory so you don't drown while playing in the wet season.

the game, it has highlighted the foolishness of excluding a group of people on the basis of skin colour. That's the thing about sport: the results are so immediate. If a team finds better players it wins, and the other teams have to react. In wider society, the impact is never felt that immediately. People can drift along, oblivious to the harm they are doing by excluding certain groups.

Will the Northern Territory ever get an AFL team? It's unlikely. The AFL likes money and, quite simply, there's not enough of it in the Territory to get them interested. But in terms of places that love the game, it's hard to top.

AUSTRALIAN CAPITAL TERRITORY – INTENTIONALLY LEFT BLANK

Canberra didn't exist until the 1910s but unfortunately it does now and we're stuck with it. The sport of Australian Rules was popular from early on and the well-named Federal Territory Australian Rules Football League (FTARFL) was up and running by 1924. Of course within three years it was changed to the Canberra Australian National Football League (CANFL). The sport at large, however, neglected Canberra. League and Union both have ACT-based teams in their top competitions, but the VFL showed no interest.

Canberra hasn't been thrilled with being neglected and AFL has declined in popularity over the years. In response the AFL decided Greater Western Sydney would play some of their home games in the ACT. I guess the ACT is sort of part of Greater Western Sydney, if you have no idea how directions and distances work.

Over the years Canberra has produced some big football names, including Alex Jesaulenko, official Legend of the Australian Football Hall of Fame. Jesaulenko's marking skill is best remembered by his iconic mark over Collingwood's Graeme Jenkin in the 1970 Grand Final. Commentator Mike Williamson's cry of 'Jesaulenko, you beauty!' is still repeated across school yards and parks as people recreate the feat.

The capital also produced James Hird, one of the best readers of the play on the field and one of the worst off it. Hird was a worthy champion as a player but his time as coach of Essendon tarnished his legacy because of his role in the supplements saga that rocked the club and the sport. He would prove as good at losing court cases as he was at winning footy games.

A NATIONAL COMPETITION

Back in the People's Republic of Victoria, the VFA's decline was hardly accidental. From its early days, the VFL was keen to grow their competition and compete head-on with the VFA. It was increasingly clear that in the fight for sponsorship dollars and TV rights, it was a zero-sum game.

The VFL started to become a lot more professional in the sixties, and no event encapsulated this trend more than when Melbourne's star player Ron Barassi crossed to Carlton in 1965. It was a move that tore the heart out of the Melbourne Football Club and still makes me tear up when I think about it. *Why, Ron, why?*

Fans were not used to players changing clubs, especially not the top stars. It was something they were going to have to get used to in decades to come. By the seventies, the VFL was sucking in the best players from around the country like a black hole. As TV become more important, the VFL started to think about the future. There were overtures from the WAFL and the SANFL to create a national competition but the VFL, like that kid you hated in kindergarten, wasn't interested in sharing. They wanted their league to be the national one and if the other state leagues wanted to be part of it, they'd need to pay them a lot of money.

In 1978, a new strategy was developed. It was the year after the first *Star Wars* was released and it's possible the VFL just lifted their strategy wholesale from the Empire: crush all opposition. There were some clear commercial reasons for this, as well as reading the tea leaves about where the sporting landscape was heading. Cheap flights, sponsorship and television meant a national competition was not only possible, any non-national league would be relegated to being a second-rate competition.

The National Football League (NFL), a representative body, had been working closely with the VFA, SANFL and WAFL to develop programming for Channel Ten. The VFL, with its Channel Seven alliance, was not keen on this at all. Clearly, the two bodies were in direct competition. The VFL, representing the largest clubs in Australia, could be cowed by the NFL and the other leagues – or it could attempt to take over. Being Victorians, showing humility and playing well with others obviously was not an option.

Their strategy was both simple and brutal. They went head to head with the NFL's attempt at a national competition, including getting Channel Seven to pay for floodlights at VFL Park* so it could host night games. The VFL played games in Sydney to televise back into Melbourne on a Sunday, the VFA no longer owning that day.

The VFL's strategy also looked inward. The league identified early that the old suburban grounds would eventually need to go, to be replaced with modern grounds with proper seating and innovative new things like toilets. It also recognised that it had too many teams in Melbourne and needed a team in Sydney.

Looking back, they really followed through on their strategy and then some, and they caused the NFL to go close to collapse. In the resulting bloodletting, Allen Aylett became president of the NFL. He also happened to be the head of the VFL. He moved quickly to disallow the VFA re-affiliating with the NFL, confining the NFL to the outskirts of power.

---

* VFL Park was affectionately known as Arctic Park for its bracing winds. While it may have been famously cold, its real claim to fame was how long it took to exit the stadium car park after a game. Even though the last AFL game there was played in 1999, between Hawthorn and Sydney, people are to this day still waiting to get out of the car park.

With the NFL's attempt to create a national competition neutralised and the VFA facing tougher times now that its Sunday monopoly was over, the VFL stepped up for the real fight: against its own clubs. The idea of getting rid of the suburban grounds and rationalising the number of clubs in Melbourne was met with outright hostility from VFL clubs, who voted against such moves. The league didn't let that stop them, though. Since they didn't have permission to shut suburban grounds or relocate clubs, they just shut off the money to the weaker clubs. Simple.

The clubs with the lowest attendances, South Melbourne, North Melbourne and Fitzroy, stopped getting the money they needed for ground maintenance. The message was clear: if you don't agree to close the grounds, we'll just let them fall down around you. It was no surprise that, soon after, South Melbourne agreed to be relocated to Sydney, the VFL accomplishing two of its aims in one move.

DID YOU KNOW?

For every dollar the AFL invests in its Integrity Unit, it gives three to its Cover-Up Unit.

Not that all of this was just driven by the VFL being ruthless. It was teetering on bankruptcy itself. Six of the league's twelve teams were in fact technically bankrupt. They needed cash desperately. It was decided licences would be sold to interstate bidders for $4 million a pop. The club presidents were quick to approve a Brisbane bid, as they were not considered a strong contender. It was money for jam. They were less keen on a team from Western Australia. Those Western Australians actually knew what they were doing when it came to footy, and a team based there might even be good. While the Brisbane team had been approved unanimously, the Western Australian team faced trouble. Only the WAFL agreeing to put up for the cost of the licence fee got the bid over the line, meaning WA basically paid off the Victorian teams to get in.

The new AFL was now keen to improve its governance. Some money was starting to flow in, and money means responsibility. The AFL hired Mr Sports Reports, David Crawford, who recommended an AFL Commission, independent from the clubs. It was the final step towards complete centralisation of all power in the AFL's hands.

Even the improved financial position didn't stop many of the Victorian clubs being in trouble. It meant mergers were the topic of regular discussion, with talks between Footscray and Fitzroy, North and Brisbane, and Melbourne and Hawthorn.

The first of those was stopped by the anger of Footscray supporters, almost leading to the breakdown of society in Victoria. The second one fell over and Brisbane swooped in to pick at the bones of the once proud Fitzroy. The last one saw Melbourne members vote 'Yes' to the merger, only for Hawthorn members to vote 'No', like when you swipe right on Tinder only to hear nothing back.

Hawthorn has gone on to be the premier club of the competition, winning flags in 2008, 2013, 2014 and 2015. Melbourne has gone on to become a major embarrassment, suffering some of the biggest losses in VFL/AFL history and at times barely being able to field a competitive team, plus the AFL has had to bail them out financially. Clearly it's worked out for both clubs.

With teams in Brisbane, Sydney and Perth, the competition looked like a national one but with a rather large South Australia–sized hole in it. As the second strongest competition in the country, the SANFL didn't want to come under the AFL heel, and could afford to hold out for longer. But when Port Adelaide went behind its back and started negotiations for entry to the national competition, the SANFL lost any leverage it had. In response the SANFL put forward its own bid, and the Adelaide Crows were born. The national competition was now in place, with more teams from Western Australia and South Australia added before long. The strategy envisaged in 1978 had been implemented with great success.

One consequence of the new national competition was the end of State of Origin in Australian Rules. Once popular, the nineties saw a rapid decline in interest, with 1999 seeing the last Origin game involving AFL footballers. In their heyday, interstate games were massive events, with people like Ted Whitten, Neil Kerley and Mal Brown all promoting the game with a lot of passion. After Victoria defeated Western Australia in 1990, Ted Whitten famously screamed on camera, 'We stuck it right up 'em. That's what you did. We stuck it right up 'em!' Other promotions included South Australia's 'Kick a Vic' campaign, which Kerley and Whitten came up with to promote the rivalry. But professionalism and a national competition meant clubs didn't want to risk their players getting injured in what were essentially exhibition matches.

While State of Origin was gone, in 2000, the payoff for the national competition arrived in the form of a $500 million TV rights deal with Channel Nine, Ten and Foxtel. It was so much cash the AFL executives put it all in a room and just splashed around in it for three weeks straight. Suddenly, all this talk of clubs going broke went out the window. The AFL came out and said they had no plans for any more mergers and they weren't even lying. The money gave the AFL confidence to step up its push into League territory, announcing new teams in the Gold Coast and Greater Western Sydney. Both are long-term, inter-generational efforts to make Australian Rules the dominant sport across the continent. If the AFL thought $500 million was a lot back in 2000, the current TV deal is $2.5 billion over six years. Real money.

The AFL still has problems though. The Essendon saga damaged its brand and the slog to keep the game going in Queensland and New South Wales is a long one. But right now, the AFL is like the Borg from *Star Trek*, assimilating all before it.

RUGBY LEAGUE

A LEAGUE FOR POOR PEOPLE

Is there anything tougher than playing Rugby League? Maybe child-birth, but I've had no direct experience of that. Stepping on Lego is pretty tough. League, however, is a brutal sport. It's a stripped-back version of Union that says 'we just want big blokes to run into each other at speed'.

The story that always reminds me of how tough League players are is that of South Sydney's John Sattler, who, in the 1970 NSWRFL Grand Final, was punched by a Manly player, resulting in a double fracture to his jaw. Sattler insisted his teammates hold him up after the punch so the Manly players wouldn't see that he was hurt. He then went on to play the rest of the game, refusing treatment at half-time and warning his teammates not to protect him. He only went to hospital after they'd won the game and he'd given the victory speech. Sure, no one could understand the speech, but that's seri-ously tough, especially to me, a man who once called in sick due to a hangnail.

Actually, there is one thing tougher than playing League. It's called 'administering Rugby League'.

The code's ability to stumble from crisis to crisis means that it seems to spends more time in crisis than not. Being in the middle of a crisis is the game's resting state. I actually get a bit twitchy when it's trucking along nicely – that's like when the children go quiet in another room; you just know something *really* bad is going down.

To put this into perspective, here's a list of things that have had fewer scandals than Rugby League:

- Every single thing in history

For as long as I can remember, the experts have predicted League to be on the verge of collapse, ready to be overwhelmed by the AFL or soccer or the arts. Okay, maybe not the arts. It never does collapse, though. Like the Terminator or door-to-door electricity salespeople, it keeps coming. Despite the scandals, the falling outs and the alarming number of dog-related incidents, League maintains its position as the predominant winter sport in both NSW and Queensland.

Perhaps the secret to its enduring success lies in the fact that League was formed in crisis, built along a familiar fault line: who gets the money, the players or the administrators?

THE SCHISM

'Football' was a term that covered a broad assortment of games when the colony of New South Wales was founded. League emerged from the split between rugby and association football (soccer), and it all came down to who wanted to regularly kick another blokes' shins. In the early colonial days of Australia it seemed kicking shins was exactly what a lot of blokes wanted to do and so rugby was the dominant winter sport. Before 1895 there was neither Union nor League, there was only rugby.

Rugby's growing popularity would be a significant factor in the sport breaking into two versions. When players in England started to notice large amounts of paying fans at games, they asked the obvious question: where is all that money going?

You can't understand League without talking about class. Of course there's no such thing as class in Australia. Instead we have filthy rich people (inherited money), fairly rich people, the middle class (which everyone thinks they are), battlers (good poor people, often living in rural areas), bogans (not salt of the earth poor people, sometimes with money, always with bad clothes) and dole bludgers (the worst thing an Australian can be). It's more like India's caste system than a class system.

Rugby originated in the public schools and universities of England, which explains a lot of the class issues that led to the split. Those running the upper-class sport struggled to understand the working class that was increasingly playing it. In England, this started coming to a head in the late nineteenth century; the clubs based in poorer areas weren't looking to give players salaries, but they did want to compensate them for their travel costs and time.

Much like the debates around politician's salaries these days, the view was that not compensating the working-class players was effectively excluding them. A lot of people running rugby at the time didn't see this as a bad thing; in fact, they thought it was one of the great features of amateurism. It kept the poor people out and simultaneously made you feel like you were doing something noble – the same function served by TED talks today.

England's Rugby Football Union even said at the time 'if they can't afford to play, then they shouldn't play at all'. Bless them.

In 1895, clubs in England's industrial north split off from the Rugby Football Union to form the Northern Rugby Football Union. Players had been looked upon with disdain and it turns out people don't like being treated badly, in fact they will take drastic measures if it goes on for long enough. This is a recurring theme in sport* and it's something the human race seems to have to constantly relearn.

---

* These themes emerged again in World Series Cricket decades later, for instance.

Apart from anything else, it turned out that the working class produced a lot of good players. It took the RFU eighteen years to regain the international championship after the split. Rich people just aren't hungry enough.

This split in England would be a pivotal moment for Australian sport too, although it would take over a decade for its effects to be felt here. Suddenly, Rugby had a version – soon to be called 'League' – that could compensate players. Rugby Union would remain an amateur sport for another century.

League was soon confronted by the challenge of attracting paying spectators in order to pay players. This changed the dynamics of the way the sport was run. The game had to appeal to the public, so they made the sport as fast-paced and exciting as possible, and the rules needed to be relatively easy to understand, to attract newcomers. These weren't the sort of things Union worried

RUGBY LEAGUE TERMS

Biff: Slang for fighting. League has always had a love-love relationship with fighting, seeing it as both entertaining and a way to self-regulate cheap shots. If you take a cheap shot in League, you know you'll get belted. Unfortunately, sponsors aren't fond of fighting, so League has over time toughened the laws around it, causing League fans and commentators to often plead to 'bring back the biff'.

Grapple tackle: A move where the tackler applies a choke hold on the ball carrier. It's illegal but hard to spot for the referee, plus, it's all in good fun.

Hooker: Used in Union too and not in the way you think. A hooker is a position and was named for the player who used to hook the ball out of the scrum. Given scrums in League aren't contested, it's now just confusing for outsiders, who wonder why the commentator keeps calling a particular player a hooker all the time.

Sin bin: Where players are sent for ten minutes if they commit a particularly egregious penalty. It is, unfortunately, not an actual bin but usually a plastic chair.

about; they preferred to make the game more like an elaborate secret handshake.

By the time the game arrived on Australian shores in 1907, League had moved to teams of thirteen players rather than fifteen, made a deliberate knock-on a penalty, introduced playing the ball backwards with the heel rather than a messy ruck, eliminated the lineout and made goals worth only 2 points instead of 3.

Union fought hard in England, banning League from the best grounds, affecting their ability to raise revenue. But in Australia League found a lot of early success, as Union wasn't in the ascendency as it was in England, partially due to the success of Australian Rules.

A MEETING IN A PUB

Surprisingly, given the dominance of Union there now, it was New Zealand that brought League to the colonies of Australasia. The All Blacks toured England in 1905 and saw for themselves the large crowds that were heading off to see the Northern League's games. One of the All Blacks, George Smith, mentioned the popularity of the Northern game to an Australian, James J. Giltinan, upon his return from the tour. A mad sports fan, Giltinan was quick to turn his mind to professionalising the game in New South Wales, and lo, so it came to be.

Fate would have it that he was not the only person thinking this way. In New Zealand, rugby player Albert Baskerville was attempting to pull together his own money-making venture in the form of a rugby tour of the United Kingdom. George Smith, who had also discussed professionalisation with Giltinan, became involved and mentioned to the Australian that the New Zealand team would be stopping in Australia on its way to England.

Giltinan was keen to underwrite the tour and he involved legendary Australian cricketer Victor Trumper, who provided funds and much needed cache. Joining them was Henry Hoyle, later to be a state minister, and the three of them began to work out how to get Australian players to take on the New Zealanders.

Rugby in Australia was controlled by administrators affiliated with the English RFU and it seemed they shared the RFU's disdain for anyone who didn't have a large amount of money. I mean, look, we all get it, people with money are just better, but did they have to be so rude about it? Apparently they did. In fact, the authorities in New South Wales were wonderful recruiters for Giltinan and Trumper, alienating very large numbers of players and clubs.

In Sydney, the elitism that was so prevalent in England did not go over well at all. The importance of 'mateship' meant that a game that was run by the rich for the rich was always going to struggle. Australia was, after all, the land of the fair go.[*]

Rugby League's birthplace in Australia was the Bateman's Hotel in George Street. The pub was an easy place to meet because back then you were still allowed to go out after dark in Sydney. Now living in Sydney is like living in the town from *Footloose* before Kevin Bacon arrived and made things right. This is probably the first time someone's mentioned *Footloose* and Rugby League in the same paragraph but let's hope it's not the last.

It made a lot of sense to convene this particular meeting in a pub because getting someone drunk before asking them to take a leap of faith is how every single relationship gets started. I mean, I've heard couples say they hooked up when they were sober, but only ever when they're both really good looking.

This secret meeting was held on 8 August 1907. Giltinan, Trumper and Hoyle organised about fifty rugby players to be there, including the captains of about half a dozen teams. The message was straightforward: they wanted to establish a professional version

---

[*] The old 'fair go' is increasingly subject to a lot of terms and conditions these days.

of the code, based on the Northern League in England, with players needed almost immediately to play a professional New Zealand side.

It was a tempting proposal. It presented a way of getting paid other than turning to Victorian Rules, which was the alternative at the time but a bit too, you know, Victorian. The main appeal, though, was that it enabled working-class players to get some of their playing expenses covered. Plus it would really annoy the administrators who treated them like second-class citizens.

The meeting established the New South Wales Rugby Football League, with Giltinan elected treasurer, Trumper secretary and Hoyle president. An all-NSW team would be selected to take on the professional New Zealand team and the new club competition would begin the following year.

The newly formed League administration had about five seconds before it was plunged into its first crisis. The doorman they had hired to stop people getting into the secret meeting was a contributor to the *Sydney Morning Herald* and he leaked the details of the gathering. It was front-page news the next day, beginning League's proud tradition of everything being leaked to the media almost immediately.

SHOW ME THE MONEY

While the New Zealander's tour and the anger towards rugby's administrators were key factors in so many players switching to the new code, it was Dally Messenger's involvement that gave the fledgling endeavour legitimacy with the players and raised its profile with the public. Messenger was the best player Australian rugby had, so he was a drawcard for crowds. In general play he was a creative genius and his goal kicking was spoken about as supernatural. He could slot them from anywhere. He was a teetotaller and a non-smoker but he was so good they let him play anyway. Part of me suspects he wasn't that brilliant a player, it was just all the other players were drunk. It's a controversial theory and I have no proof, but proof is unnecessary these days if a theory makes you feel good.

Just having Messenger at the meeting was a huge achievement and, along with Victor Trumper, an international sports star, it was clear to people that this was a serious enterprise. Messenger's decision to switch to League is arguably the most pivotal decision made by an individual in the history of Australian sport. It would change the fortunes of three codes, possibly more.

Without Messenger, League probably would have had a very short life, if it had even managed to get off the ground. His signing brought with it publicity, crowds (and more importantly their money) and he convinced other players to join. League's relatively fast rise meant Union was soon pushed into the private school system, no longer the biggest code in New South Wales or Queensland. It also meant that Australian Rules lost its biggest edge over rugby: money. The ascent of League knocked the Victorian import on the head in New South Wales and assisted with its eventual decline in Queensland.

The move of a single player drew the geographic and demographic lines around Australian Rules, Union and League that are only now being erased, over a century later. What can't be known is what impact the move had on soccer, just then having a big surge of popularity in England and eventually around the world. League's rise meant it found its way into Australia at a time when the southern states already had a professional game in Victorian Rules and the northern states had League. It was relegated to the sidelines for a very long time, unable to get any purchase. If League had never started, soccer and Australian Rules might have been the ones fighting it out for the working class. Then again, who knows, perhaps badminton, the sleeping giant of Australian sports, would have swooped in and conquered them all.

What we do know for sure is that Messenger was a clever bugger and ensured he got paid a lot to cross over. He pretended the switch was a last-minute thing on the eve of the first game against the New Zealand touring side, who had been christened the 'All Golds' on account of them being paid. Messenger even said his mum was the one who made the decision for him, not the last time an Australian superstar would blame his mother for something. In truth, Messenger was not a last-minute inclusion but the lynchpin that held this rather ambitious plan together.

The three-match series in 1907 between the All Golds and the New South Wales All Blues was played using Union rules as the League rules weren't available yet. Weird setting up a whole new sport when you don't know the rules, but it was a different time, I guess. The story goes that Messenger dazzled the All Golds so much, he was asked to join them on their tour of England, something many suspected was actually part of the deal to have him convert in the first place.

> **DID YOU KNOW?**
>
> Jarryd Hayne's short NFL career and return to the NRL has taught us to never follow our dreams, as you pretty much end up back in the same place.

The series in Australia was a success and the money raised helped see the new NSWRFL through its first tumultuous season. Rugby Union responded by wiping all mention of Messenger from their official records, only reinstating his playing record in 2007. They sure know how to hold a grudge in rugby.

EARLY TROUBLE

On Easter Monday, 20 April 1908, the first season of League in Australia kicked off under the Northern Union Rules. Thanks to the Rugby Union administrators' efforts to alienate every player who didn't have a university degree, 138 players jumped across to League for its first season and eight sides contested the first year. They were: Glebe, Newtown, Western Suburbs, South Sydney, North Sydney, Balmain, Eastern Suburbs, Newcastle and Cumberland.

The first season was not the huge success its founders had hoped it would be. Union was working hard to tarnish the new competition and blocked them from grounds such as the SCG. At times the crowds were worryingly small. Things were dire and the money from the All Golds tour was all that stopped the NSWRFL from going completely broke. They say it's always darkest before the dawn but unfortunately for the young competition that dawn was still a while away and things were about to get a whole lot darker.

The financial challenges of the first season meant that a lot of the money that should have flowed to the players was instead being used to shore up the administration. This was not a good look, given the whole reason the players jumped codes was to get paid. The players were angry about their conditions. The League's first major off-field drama was about to unfold.

A meeting was held where the game's founders, Giltinan, Trumper and Hoyle, were all accused of financial impropriety – namely holding moneys in bank accounts for themselves. They were booted out of the game. With small crowds, low gate receipts, its founders gone, one team (Cumberland) leaving and a national team tour of England that was a financial disaster, a second season looked questionable.

It appeared Rugby Union was poised to reassert its position in New South Wales as the premier code. However, one bold move led to the reinvigoration of League and Union being confined to runner-up for the next hundred plus years.

SECOND RAID

In many ways, 1909, the second season of the NSWRFL, was one of its most shambolic, but the seeds of success were sown that year.

With its founders gone, thoughts turned to capturing the public's imagination and boosting attendance. With crowds down and leadership lacking, something drastic needed to happen. Into the void stepped Joynton Smith. Smith had come to Australia from England, via New Zealand, and made his money as a hotelier, and as a racecourse and newspaper owner. He saw an opportunity in League; his vision was so bold that many thought it was just too risky.

His plan was simple. For League to flourish, it needed the best players. Messenger had given the game its first star but he couldn't play in every single game. So Smith did what Kerry Packer would do in cricket almost seventy years later – he bought all the best players. In fact, Smith bought the Wallabies, who were returning from a highly successful tour of Britain, where they had won the gold medal at the London Olympics.

Smith managed to land fourteen of them. He organised a series between these 'Wallabies' and the Rugby League national side, the Kangaroos. The proceeds went to the South Sydney Hospital, of which he was the founder and a director. The genius of this move was that it simultaneously boosted League while decimating Union. The Union authorities reacted predictably, banning for life the fourteen Wallabies who had made the move, meaning that even after the series those players would be forced to keep playing League. To have your best players raided not once but twice in two years is a bit careless, and you'd have to say, for all their better breeding, the Union hierarchy got played by their working-class opponents.

The move was met with some rancour, including from the players who had already joined the NSWRFL the year before. They had seen very little money since moving across and now these new players were receiving huge signing-on bonuses.

The series between the Wallabies and the Kangaroos was not a huge success either. The public didn't seem that interested and, in a bid to boost interest and cover costs, organisers decided to play the final game of the series on the day of the NSWRFL grand final, with that decider relegated to being the curtain raiser for the Wallabies–Kangaroos match.

The two teams in the final, South Sydney and Balmain, were not thrilled about being downgraded. In a move that created lasting animosity, Balmain refused to take the field in protest, claiming Souths had agreed to do the same. To their surprise, Souths took the field, kicked off and scored a try, securing them the premiership. Souths maintained that there was no agreement between the two clubs.

It meant League's second full season ended in a farce but, with the fourteen Wallabies all joining NSWRFL clubs, by 1910 the pendulum had well and truly swung in League's favour. That season saw the NSWRFL eclipse Union for attendance, assuming the crown of NSW's major code. Union's revenues plummeted over the next few years, making amateurism more a result of financial necessity than a cherished principle. Without money the control of Sydney's major grounds slipped from Union's grasp. The battle had been brutal and short and was now over.

Joynton Smith would go on to be president of the NSWRFL from 1910 until 1928. He continued as its patron until 1943 (when he died), and he also ended up Lord Mayor of Sydney from 1917/18. Sport administration proved the perfect grounding for local government; both require dealing with a lot of passionate but stupid people.

A CHANGE UP NORTH

The dissatisfaction of rugby players in New South Wales was shared in Queensland. The Queensland Rugby Union, following the lead from England, was equally keen to enforce amateurism. By 1908, the Queensland Association was formed by seven players and they moved quickly to organise a League side to take on the All Golds, who were on their way home after their tour of England.

By 1909, club rugby was underway in the state, with the first game played at the Gabba. League had an additional advantage in Queensland because Victorian Rules, while popular, was run in such a shambolic fashion that they essentially banished themselves to Victoria until 1987, when the equally shambolic Brisbane Bears arrived.

League's growth in Queensland was rapid, partly due to a strong rivalry with New South Wales, a rivalry that would not be fully capitalised on for the next seventy years or so. As well as conquering Queensland, the code would establish itself outside Sydney with the formation of the Newcastle Rugby League in 1910, the Illawarra Rugby League in 1911 and leagues in Bathurst, Dubbo, Nowra and Tamworth in 1913.

A CIVIL WAR

With Union vanquished and Victorian Rules quarantined down south, New South Wales and Queensland thought about forming a harmonious partnership for about five minutes before deciding to fight each other instead. While the rivalry on the field was fierce, it was nothing compared to the rivalry off it.

At first and for good measure, Queenslanders decided to fight amongst themselves. The Queensland Rugby League had a rather substantial falling out with the lower-grade Brisbane Rugby League. The NSWRFL, always eager to help, stepped in and sided with the BRL. That didn't exactly lead to a flowering of goodwill. The formation of the Australian Rugby League Board of Control in 1924, to oversee Kangaroos tours and eventually the entire code, was another pain point, with NSWRFL representatives dominating the positions on the board and thereby gaining the power to appoint the chairman. This sort of Sydney-centric approach is obviously something that would be unheard of in any industry these days.

The NSWRFL's control of the national body was seen by Queenslanders as a dark influence that constantly worked to weaken League north of the border and strengthen it on the southern side. Of course, that's exactly what it was. New South Wales' dominance of the game's administration was a major contributor to the bitter rivalry that exists today. The relationship between administrators remained tense and the Australian Rugby League was not incorporated as a separate entity from the NSWRFL until 1984. You could be forgiven for believing this story of suffering, betrayal and oppressive regimes is the basis for George Orwell's *1984,* as I did until recently.

Yet, despite New South Wales dominance of the sport's administration, it was a different but familiar force that tipped the scales towards the NSWRFL becoming the dominant league in the country: money. Sums of money beyond everyone's wildest dreams were about to flood the New South Wales clubs, all thanks to legislation that ushered in a little something called 'pokies' in NSW.

TRUCKLOADS OF CASH

In 1956, the state government of New South Wales decided it would be great if people could go somewhere to just throw away their money, but with the government then getting some of it. Now, just throwing money in the bin isn't a terribly exciting proposition, so instead they decided the bins should have flashing lights and things that spun around and a little lever you could pull so you felt like you were not throwing your money away but rather flushing it away. It was then decided that, very occasionally, these 'pokies' would give some of the money back to people, but never more than they took.

The voters of NSW are a suspicious lot and wised up to the fact that they were basically being robbed, even with all the shiny bells and whistles. So the government decided community clubs would also get some of the huge quantities of money being taken away from people. That way, the clubs got to spend some of that money on their communities, albeit less than if they had just kept it in the first place.

The impact on Rugby League was seismic. The teams that had a social club with poker machines suddenly had a revenue source that was like someone installing a fire hose in your house that just sprays out money. Straight away, New South Wales clubs could pay players an amount that stopped them leaving for England, where the salaries had previously been higher. Even after that there was still money left over to pinch all of Queensland's best players, and then the few good ones still playing Union. In fact there was more money than they actually needed but, thankfully, graft and corruption took care of any excess money lying around.

For Queensland, this was a disaster. They just couldn't compete financially and any talent was sucked down south. It would take until 1992 for the Queensland government to legalise pokies in their state.

Pokies revenue made the NSWRFL very strong financially, providing clubs with quantities of money that weren't surpassed until TV revenue entered the game in a big way. The gambling money wasn't welcomed by everyone though. The questionable morality of the machines has often been seen as at odds with the working class, community ethos of the sport. Legislative attacks on their profitability has sometimes turned Rugby League clubs and the governing body itself into lobbyists for the gambling industry, a move that strikes some as a bad look. In response, the NRL has pointed out that morals have no place in Rugby League.

A DECADE OF DOMINANCE

The influx of pokies cash had a huge impact on well-run clubs, who used the money to attract and retain great players. While all clubs tried to do this, St George towered above the others. In the same year that pokies were legalised, 1956, the Dragons won the first of eleven premierships in a row, stretching all the way to 1966. It was a run of dominance never seen before or since in any sport around the world.

In that period, they would unearth two of the greatest players of all time, Reg Gasnier and Johnny Raper. Gasnier was truly something, the clear successor to Clive Churchill as the best player in the game.* He was a creative genius, unpredictable and exciting to watch. Yet for all the attacking brilliance, St George's success was based on brutal defence, and in Johnny Raper they found a man who tackled for fun.

These were the days of unlimited tackles. In today's game there's a limited number of tackles before a team hands over the ball to the other side, but back then a team could hold the ball until they scored or turned it over. Being able to defend for long periods of time was essential. St George's solution was to try something radical: they got fit. They introduced interval training at a time when most thought that meant pausing for a smoke.

For Johnny Raper even this training was not enough and he did extra weight training and running on his own. That meant he could tackle someone into next week, get up, and tackle the next person into the week after that. On top of that, playing as a lock forward, he worked extensively on his ball-handling skills, making him a force in attack too.

St George were so dominant that something had to be done to stop them. The answer was to change the rules of the game.

THERE ARE LIMITS

In 1967, League made one of the biggest changes to the game ever, right up there with playing the ball instead of forming a ruck.

---

* Churchill won five premierships with South Sydney and then coached them to three more, confirming his status as an all-time great of the game. The man of the match medal in the grand final is called the Clive Churchill Medal. He once broke his arm in a game but just put cardboard around it and played on, scoring the winning try. I'm not sure the medical community are as pro-cardboard these days.

It introduced a rule that meant teams could only keep possession of the ball for four tackles and then the other team got a turn at attacking, like two toddlers being made to share a toy.

Nowadays they'll tell you that the move from unlimited- to limited-tackle footy was to make the game more appealing to play and watch, stopping teams from just holding onto the ball for as long as possible. The real reason was the NSWRFL clubs had a massive tantrum about the fact that St George wouldn't share the premiership. Ask any St George supporter and they'll agree with me, and we all know how sensible they are.

Others will argue that there had been concerns about the game becoming stale in the UK too, as a result of unlimited tackles. Rugby, and the sports that have evolved from its earliest incarnation, have always struggled with one thing: what to do when someone is tackled. Early forms of the game involved large groups of men all trying to get hold of the ball, but instead they all grabbed the guy with the ball and tried to push the pack that formed around him in one direction or the other. This meant games often went for an entire day but with no score.

Funnily enough, this did not prove particularly popular with either the participants or the spectators. Various solutions were proposed, such as the player with the ball having to release it if tackled, which occurs in both Union and Australian Rules albeit in slightly different ways. In American football they fixed the problem by ruling the play dead after a tackle and then starting again from set formations. It sorted out the problem but also made an hour of gameplay take about ten hours of real time.

League got rid of the rucks that were a feature of Union, deeming them ugly, and replaced them with playing the ball after a tackle. While spectators certainly responded to this cleaner version of the game, it made it a lot easier to keep the ball for longer as there was no contest whenever a tackle occurred. Play often involved a team just trying to hold onto the ball for as long as possible with no meaningful attacking.

This was never a major problem for anyone until the Dragons racked up eleven premierships in a row, which is just showing off really. Not only could the Dragons hold onto the ball for a long time due to their great skills, they could defend for longer because of their superior fitness. Obviously the other teams could have gotten fitter themselves but that takes a lot of effort and time spent in gyms, which are awful places.

In 1967 the NSWRFL decided that if you can't beat them, you change the rules so that you can. They announced the four-tackle rule,* which seemed to work – the last of St George's eleven-premiership run was in 1966, although some believe they were declining anyway.

Following the introduction of the new rule, it turned out attacking became very difficult, with four tackles giving a team little time to create a real offensive opportunity. Instead teams acted like it was a giant game of hot potato, flinging the ball around in such a rush that it quickly became obvious that playing the game this way was almost as bad as St George winning all the time.

In 1971, the tackle rule was changed to six, where it remains. It was a massive step that further differentiated League from Union, demonstrating the younger code's ability to innovate in order to stay relevant. It can't be overstated how much this one change rejuvenated League, turning it into a fast-paced, attacking sport, and one that was perfect for television.

---

* Under this rule teams get to possess the ball until they've been tackled four times, at which point they have to hand over possession to the opposition at the spot on the field where the final tackle was made. It's like a 'taking turns' approach but for adults. Of course, knowing they'd have to hand possession over on the fourth tackle meant that after the third tackle, teams kicked the ball far down the field for territory.

ONE ROTTEN APPLE SPOILS IT FOR ALL THE OTHER ROTTEN APPLES

Power, money and gambling always carry a high price tag. NSWRFL had gone from strength to strength thanks to the financial might that came from the pokies, but they were about to pay heavily for that privilege.

Chronic gambling is often a vital source of funds for sports codes, but they find it less fun when the person doing it is their executive chairman. In many ways, Kevin Humphreys was a visionary sports administrator. Appointed president of the NSWRFL and chairman of the Australian Rugby League in 1973, he oversaw the introduction of the wildly successful State of Origin concept, sponsorship naming rights for the competition, sponsors on jumpers and negotiated their first TV rights deal.

However, Humphreys was also the secretary-manager of the Balmain Leagues Club, one of several clubs that poured money into NSWRFL teams. In this position, Humphreys had access to a lot of cash and, from 1974, he began taking money from the cash float to fund his gambling habit. This meant the proceeds of gambling were now going to a chronic gambler, in a rather circular arrangement.

It took a little while but, in 1976, an auditor noticed a discrepancy of $30 579 in the club's finances. Humphreys would tell the auditor that he made a loan to a friend who was in trouble and it would be paid back within the month. In fact, he had actually taken just over $50 000 out of the float in less than two years, which takes some doing.

Here's what happened next: Humphreys, in a panic, managed to borrow $52 000 from some League powerbrokers and paid back the money he'd taken. He wasn't punished. In fact, he was appointed to a further ten-year contract as NSWRFL president. Ever notice how rich people seem to be treated a bit differently when caught stealing than poor people? There aren't many pickpockets who are just allowed to hand the money back and then all is forgotten. On top of that, some on the NSWRFL executive committee were aware of his 'borrowing' of funds but they still agreed to give him a loan of $36 000 from the NSWRFL.*

Eventually there was a police investigation into Humphreys' creative approach to club finances. Humphreys tried to use his considerable clout to get the investigation stopped but the NSW Police – playing against type – decided to do the right thing and take the matter to court. The great thing about corruption, though, is that there's almost always someone else to lean on. If pressuring the police fails, I always like to go after the judiciary. Humphreys found a friend in Chief Stipendiary Magistrate Murray Farquhar, who made sure the case wouldn't stand up. Farquhar, on behalf of Humphreys, told his subordinate magistrate, Kevin Jones, that finding Humphreys guilty would be a bad career move. On 12 August 1977, Jones dismissed the charges.

That really should have been the end of it, and would have been if it wasn't for those pesky journalists. Six years later, on ABC's *Four Corners* program, reporter Chris Masters described widespread corruption in the NSWRFL, with the Humphreys case the main part of the story. Masters outlined the cover-up, including a claim that NSW Premier Neville Wran had also intervened to get Humphreys off. All hell broke loose and the NSW attorney-general announced a royal commission. Wran stood aside as premier until the commission made its findings, and sued the ABC for defamation.

Shortly after the *Four Corners* program aired, it was revealed that Humphreys had only paid off $7000 of the $36 000 loan he'd received from the NSWRL seven years before; he still owed $29 000.

The Royal Commission found Chief Justice Murray Farquhar did influence the committal hearing, and he was sentenced to

---

* This seems to be a strange way of doing business but this was New South Wales in the seventies and this probably wasn't even in the top thousand dodgiest things done that year.

POLITICS AND SPORT

Mal Meninga

In 2001, Rugby League hall-of-famer Mal Meninga set the record for the shortest political career. It will probably never be beaten. Meninga had announced he was running for a seat in the ACT parliament, and 28 seconds into his first interview, with ABC's Chris Uhlmann, after several soft warm-up questions he was asked why he was standing for election:

> Mal Meninga (MM): I was . . . I'm buggered. I'm sorry.
>
> Chris Uhlmann (CU): That's all right.
>
> MM: I have to resign.
>
> CU: Okay. So Mal Meninga is leaving the studio. And he says that he can't do it.

Even though it was embarrassing, Meninga probably made the best decision of his life.

four years in jail. Humphreys resigned from all his positions in Rugby League and admitted in the royal commission that he'd used the money for gambling. He was convicted of the original offence and fined $4000.

Premier Wran was cleared of wrongdoing by the royal commission and his defamation case against the ABC was settled out of court, so that was a bit awkward for the ABC. The whole mess would shake up the governance of League and, if you don't count the numerous corruption cases since, there have been no more problems.

STATE OF ORIGIN

In typical League style, the seeds of future success were planted at the same time as crisis enveloped the sport. League is like many Australian plants: it needs a good bushfire every few years to help it grow. Introducing State of Origin was a huge success both financially and with fans, and it also gave Queensland a platform to exact revenge for all the years of humiliation they'd suffered at the hands of the NSWRFL.

By the seventies, interstate competition in League was dying a slow, painful death. At its root was a simple fact: New South Wales had stacked the decks in their favour. The rules of selection were based on where players were playing their football, not their home state. With the NSW clubs luring all of Queensland's best players with their pokies loot, this made for very one-sided affairs.

The president of the Queensland Rugby League, Senator Ron McAuliffe, decided that they'd had enough of this nonsense. He promoted the idea of players being selected on the basis of their state of origin (the state in which they had first played first-grade football). Naturally, the New South Wales clubs reacted to this idea like someone suggesting you should be given a venereal disease.[*]

However, McAuliffe found an unlikely ally in the not-yet-disgraced Kevin Humphreys. Humphreys saw that, if it continued in its current form, the interstate series was likely to die; change was the only way to save the whole thing. Humphreys may have stolen a lot of money from his employer and then acted corruptly to try to get away with it, but he did have vision for the sport.

A compromised deal was finally struck that, as a trial, a State of Origin game would be played if the third game of the interstate series was a dead rubber. That was big of those New South Wales guys, letting Queensland have their players but only if the game meant nothing. I bet New South Wales wishes that rule still applied.

The first test of this new arrangement took place in 1980. Queensland were belted 35–3 in the first game and lost the second 17–7. The third game would be a dead rubber; the stage was set.

---

[*] Something the club presidents were probably familiar with.

Excitement north of the border was high. Finally their players would be able to represent them. Arthur Beetson was a star and the first Indigenous Australian to have captained his country in any sport. Beetson had the honour of captaining this first Queensland State of Origin team, which was right up there with his other career highlights. And he had plenty to choose from; for example, in 1973, he ate eleven hot dogs before a gala dinner for the Australian team. I don't know about you, but I think that's amazing.

The game attracted a sell-out crowd of 33 210, dwarfing many of the recent crowds at interstate games and surprising all those who had been sceptical. Queensland won convincingly too, 20–10; from then the State of Origin concept was taken a bit more seriously. The next year, New South Wales again won the first two games under the old selection rules and then Queensland won the third game under State of Origin rules.

By that point the genie was out of the bottle. State of Origin had unleashed the passion of both New South Wales fans and Queenslanders. This was a real rivalry and years of feeling like second-class citizens had made Queenslanders embrace the concept with a fanatical edge that remains genuinely scary. Talk to a Queenslander about Origin and they get a mad look in their eye, even madder than usual – like Mel Gibson in *Braveheart* or on a night out. Blues fans, in turn, give a genuinely pained look, given Queensland's recent dominance. Like all great sporting rivalries, this one delivers pure ecstasy when you win and it really hurts to lose.

In 1982, the series moved to a full State of Origin concept. The New South Wales powerbrokers had come around thanks to the oldest persuader in history: the promise of untold riches. Its still massively successful in the current day, both financially and as a promotion for the sport. The nation, especially New South Wales and Queensland, goes a little loopy while it's on. Even in federal parliament, politicians from either state will wear maroon or blue in a desperate and futile attempt to make themselves seem vaguely human.

NO ONE LIKES CHANGE

I dislike change so much that I don't even like it if it makes things better. Give me inertia any day. Unfortunately, life is all about change. By the late seventies, this was becoming apparent in Rugby League; State of Origin was only the first step along a path that saw League break out of its Sydney confines and expand nationally.

Up until the seventies, sports administrations had settled for being based in just one state, or even one city. Once the code wars of the early twentieth century were settled, League didn't really compete with Australian Rules anymore. Everyone just kept to their own patch, like teenage gangs. Yet the ease and lower cost of air travel, combined with television's reach, meant previous geographical constraints were disappearing.

In the seventies, TV stations were also beginning to realise that sport could provide relatively cheap programming that would fill up hours of their schedules. While the eye-watering broadcast deals that would later make sports obscenely rich were yet to appear, it was clear that TV could at least help to grow the games and get more money out of sponsors.

Sensing an opportunity, in 1974 promotor Colin McLennan pulled together a made-for-TV midweek knockout competition for Channel Ten. Building on the six-tackle rule, the Amco Cup consisted of 20-minute quarters and a penalty countback to decide the winner in the event of a draw. It aired Wednesday nights, at a time when night-time sport was a rarity, and featured teams from a range of divisions including the NSW and Brisbane leagues. Seeing teams from a lower division take on the big clubs proved very popular, and the competition expanded to include New Zealand teams and even a team from Port Moresby. Running until 1989, the Amco Cup showed the benefits of League expanding beyond the borders of New South Wales, televised content allowing the sport to find (and capitalise on) fans outside Sydney.

After decades of sucking in every good player with pokies money, the heady mix of television and sponsorship money had NSWRFL administrators thinking more and more about how to develop 'content' and 'properties' for sponsorship. In 1980, it was decided the Illawarra Steelers and the Canberra Raiders would be awarded licences, with both entering the competition in 1982. Then, after years of decimating Queensland League, in 1988 the NSWRL finally decided they would allow them to have a couple of teams in the competition! What great guys they were.

The Brisbane Broncos and the Gold Coast–Tweed Giants entered the league, as did the Newcastle Knights. The Broncos and Knights would go on to be great successes (the Giants would not) and the league started to think about further expansion. In 1995 the Auckland Warriors, the North Queensland Cowboys, the South Queensland Crushers and the Western Reds (Perth) all joined what was now the Australian Rugby League. This rapid expansion took what was basically a Sydney-based competition and turned it into a twenty-team, nation-spanning enterprise in the space of just thirteen years. It had not been without pain; in 1983 the Newtown Jets, a foundation club, was booted out of the competition due to enormous financial problems.

GREAT NICKNAMES

✑

Glenn 'The Brick with Eyes' Lazarus: Roy and H.G. Nelson bestowed this one during one of their famous State of Origin calls. Lazarus certainly looked like a brick and later agreed to join the Palmer United Party.

It was the canary in the coalmine that showed the competition's new emphasis on finances. Overall Rugby League was flying high. It was now a national competition that was in good shape financially, drawing good crowds and ratings, with TV rights deals just starting to become big. State of Origin was also flying; in 1994 a then record crowd of 87161 turned up to see a game at the MCG. An amazing number in a town that only usually cares about origin when it comes to their coffee.

The transition to a national competition was completed in 1995, when the NSWRL handed control of the Winfield Cup to the ARL. Sitting there at ARL headquarters in the early nineties, you could have seen League not only challenging Australian Rules as the national winter code but having a real shot at being number one. Yet the game that was formed through crisis was about to have its biggest crisis ever.

WAR IN OUR TIME

The ARL's successful expansion hid the fact it had too many teams, especially in Sydney. While new clubs such as Newcastle and Brisbane could command large areas of support, the suburban Sydney teams were often locked into small catchment areas. These once acted like castles but were now becoming more like prisons.

The ARL had already made significant noise about clubs that couldn't attract at least 10000 people to home games; they'd been warned that they might not remain in the league. In the early nineties, by that criteria, a host of Sydney teams were on the chopping block. On top of this the Brisbane Broncos, riding a wave of success on and off the field, felt that despite all the recent changes, New South Wales still held too much influence in the ARL. The Broncos were open to changing the way the competition was being run.

It was against this backdrop that Rupert Murdoch kicked off the Super League war, a battle for TV rights. When a couple has a fight, a bit of pressure opens up all the fault lines in the relationship. The fight that appears to be happening on the surface is not always the whole story. That was very much the case with the Super League war; many clubs did not make it out the other side.

By 1995, the ARL had signed with Kerry Packer's Nine Network and his pay TV enterprise, Optus Vision. It left Rupert Murdoch's Foxtel without a major sporting code to attract subscribers in New South Wales and Queensland. You don't become a billionaire by accepting the status quo, so in a move that echoed Packer's reaction to missing out on the TV rights to cricket in the seventies, Murdoch decided the best thing to do was to create his own competition and pinch as many teams and players from the ARL as he could. But unlike the World Series Cricket war, Murdoch wasn't up against amateur administrators who had no idea what hit them. This was a street fight, if a street fight can involve billionaires and highly paid lawyers, which in Sydney they often do.

Murdoch's News Limited planned to build a new competition unencumbered by the financially weaker Sydney clubs. To make the whole enterprise stack up financially, it needed to be the sole premier competition, so News first made the ARL some of the worst offers in the history of capitalism.

News proposed to the ARL that their existing twenty-team competition could become a feeder competition to a twelve-team 'Super League'. Under the deal Kerry Packer would keep the rights to the twenty-team competition and would have been eligible to bid for the free-to-air broadcast rights to the new Super League. Packer was not exactly keen on the twenty-team competition being downgraded to a feeder comp; he had already won the rights to the top level and wasn't interested in having to re-bid for them in another form. He threatened to sue any club that left the ARL for another competition.

News's problem was that they were trying to force their way into the existing ARL framework with the threat of an alternative competition, but no one believed they would actually set one up. Packer, having seen this all before and knowing how hard it was to set up an alternative competition, basically called their bluff and used some old-fashioned intimidation to keep clubs in the ARL.

Murdoch realised that Plan A had failed. Without an actual rebel competition, the ARL could just legally threaten the clubs and they would have nowhere to go. Plan B was hastily drawn up: form a new competition and target the best players. Salaries would be doubled. News would challenge any legal agreements that said clubs could not leave the ARL. At almost every turn, Murdoch was taking a leaf out of Packer's World Series Cricket playbook. And like Packer, ultimately he wanted TV rights, not to run a sport. His preference was to have the ARL accept him and if they wouldn't do it willingly, he would force them to.

The first step, and it was a clever one, was to target the coaches. By getting the coaches on board, usually with the tacit approval of the clubs, they stood a great chance of convincing players to come across. The coaches from Auckland, Canberra, Canterbury-Bankstown, Cronulla-Sutherland and the Western Reds were all quick to sign on. Soon meetings were being held with the players. The salaries on offer were huge and sign-on bonuses went as high as $100 000. That's a lot of avocado on toast, the official currency of Australia.

Soon enough, Super League had secured the Auckland Warriors, Brisbane Broncos, Canberra Raiders, Canterbury Bulldogs, Cronulla Sharks, North Queensland Cowboys, Penrith Panthers and Western Reds.

This secretive approach infuriated the ARL. Ken Arthurson, the ARL chairman, confronted News's Paul Cowley about a promise that News would always come through the front door if they were to challenge the ARL. Cowley replied, 'We thought that after we had bought your players that it would have such an effect on you that we would be better able to negotiate with you and come through the front door.'

The ARL hit back, using a war chest of Optus Vision's money to sign and retain players. The bidding war was on. With Rugby Union finally turning professional in 1995, it wasn't an ideal time.

Despite the ARL's best efforts, Super League recruited 307 players and ten coaches. And News wasn't done. It quickly signed up TV rights for the UK's Rugby Football League and the New Zealand Rugby League, which prevented those countries from playing against non–Super League aligned players in international games, effectively isolating the ARL internationally. Super League was basically ready. They had eight teams originally in the ARL, players, international control and they announced two new sides, the Adelaide Rams and the Hunter Mariners, the latter designed to hurt the ARL-loyal Newcastle Knights.

For their part, the ARL had managed to retain Souths, Norths, Balmain, Easts, West, St George, Manly, Newcastle, Illawarra, Gold Coast, Parramatta and South Queensland.

With two League competitions effectively ready to go, the ARL launched a barrage of legal challenges to stop Super League beginning in 1996. On 23 February 1996 the Federal Court ruled that the ARL owned all the club colours, names, logos and other associated intellectual property. On top of that, Justice James Burchett said News had acted with 'dishonesty' and 'duplicity'.

The 1996 start date was dead in the water but News appealed immediately, making the lawyers happy and ensuring storm clouds continued to hang over the sport. In October 1996, the appeal was successful, effectively reversing the decision and paving the way for Super League to begin in 1997.

In a sign that money trumps loyalty, Packer's Channel Nine quickly secured the free-to-air rights for Super League, meaning it would show both competitions in 1997. An odd position for them to take, to say the least.

That year saw two competitions being played, each featuring

twenty-two teams. That's a lot of League, even for League fanatics. The bitterness that had built up left many rusted-on fans disillusioned. Many Super League team's crowds were poor, while the ARL found that its financial position was only worsening with sponsorship dollars and audiences spread so thin. The ARL posted a $9.5 million loss in 1996 and it wasn't a cheap exercise for News either, the *Australian Financial Review* estimating Super League cost them up to $560 million.

Peace talks began and, in December 1997, the ARL teams voted to accept News's peace offering. As a result, the National Rugby League was formed, a joint venture between News and the ARL, kicking off in 1998. Murdoch had achieved his aim. He was now a part owner in the peak League competition in the country and Foxtel held the pay TV rights, severely weakening its rival, Optus Vision. Packer acquired the free-to-air rights to the NRL for $13 million a year and purchased a quarter of Foxtel from News for $160 million.

The Super League war had been brutal and expensive, and it signified that in the future it would be media companies that shaped sports. As for the sport itself, the peace agreement tore the soul of the League community apart.

THE TERRIBLE PEACE

While a unified competition was welcome, the peace treaty prescribed a cure for the problem of too many teams that, unfortunately, was the equivalent of shock therapy: by 2000 the new competition was to be reduced from twenty to fourteen teams.

Even before the first NRL season started in 1998, News wound down the South Queensland Crushers, the Hunter Mariners and the Western Reds. The Reds had somehow managed to get themselves into $10 million of debt in the space of five years. That would be hard to achieve if you were doing it deliberately. However, the ARL did form a new team, the Melbourne Storm, and they joined the inaugural season.

At the end of 1998, the Adelaide Rams and the Gold Coast Chargers were also shut down. These were relatively painless decisions; the teams were relatively new and had never been enormous successes. But there were still eighteen teams left, meaning four would not be around in a couple of years. To try to encourage some clubs to merge, the NRL offered a lot of money and a guaranteed position in the 2000 competition to any teams that did. St George and Illawarra were the first take up the offer, followed by Balmain and Wests, then Manly and North Sydney.

All those teams merged because of the threat of being excluded from the top flight from 2000 onwards. These shotgun marriages were bitter outcomes for teams that had stayed loyal to the ARL during the war. In each merger there were varying degrees of equality.

The most controversial was the Manly and North Sydney merger. It was more of a takeover by Manly, with the new 'Northern Eagles' retaining Manly's name and colours. In fact, it was impossible to see any link at all to the North Sydney Bears, a foundation club of the NSWRL dating back to 1908. The merger was short lived – by 2003 Manly were back to being a stand-alone club in the NRL and the Bears were out of the national competition. It was a move that drove many fans away from the game.

These mergers meant that as the 2000 deadline approached, like a game of musical chairs, there was just one club left that didn't meet the criteria established by the NRL, the South Sydney Rabbitohs. The NRL announced that one of their most popular teams, and a foundation club, was out.

Looking back now, what stands out is how brutal these forced mergers and expulsions were. In many cases the history, loyalty, passion and financial support of rusted-on League fans was killed off overnight. These long-standing clubs' debts would be seen as negligible nowadays, given the TV dollars rolling in. The year 2000 marked a turning point; League was clearly no longer a community-based sport. It was a business, run as brutally as any corporation in the country.

Yet the long arm of tradition would reach out and curtail some of the NRL's PowerPoint-driven vision of the future. The fans of Souths would not go quietly; they turned to the courts to save their club. It was a long battle, powered by marching in the streets and lawyers – so many lawyers. The club argued their exclusion breached the Trade Practices Act. They were at first rebuffed by the courts but following an appeal to the Federal Court, the Rabbitohs were ordered back into the league. It was a true victory for grassroots fans over the people running the sport, but it couldn't mask the fact that the period left many disillusioned with the code.

> **DID YOU KNOW?**
>
> Rugby league player Mark Gasnier's teammates spent seven hours coming up with his nickname: 'Gaz'.

Soon enough, though, fans returned in big numbers, and the sport went back to churning out scandals at a regular pace. The shiny new NRL delivered a significant crisis as the Canterbury Bulldogs were found to be in breach of the salary cap in 2001 and 2002, followed by Melbourne Storm going one better in 2009 and getting caught running two sets of books.*

INDEPENDENCE DAY

Looking back at the Super League war, the clubs had little power over a lot of the decisions being made. But the ARL was falling behind its main competitor code, the AFL, which was an

---

* See page 70.

independent commission that could make tough calls for the good of the entire game, not factions within it or individual clubs.

In 2012 an independent ARL commission was formed to take control of the whole sport in Australia. It was a bold step forward for the code. After the chaos of the Super League war, the sport was back on its feet and looking to move towards a better governed and more successful future.

But the clubs and state associations are already pushing back against the commission, with demands for representative seats at the decision-making table. It's possible they don't know what 'independent commission' means but more likely they understand perfectly well and just don't like it. Either way, it's provided more off-field drama at the highest levels.

This comes at a time when the AFL is free of these issues and is pouring a lot of money into the northern states. League, though, has shown it's a lot stronger than people give it credit for. If anything, the battle over the independent commission is a sign that the game is still alive and continuing as it always has, lurching from crisis to crisis, a bit like a prop forward running through a defensive line. League will always have that major strength: people just love watching big blokes running into each other.

SOCCER

THE WORLD GAME

Soccer. Even the name is controversial. In Australia, calling it 'soccer' makes you an instant enemy of 'football' according to many. It's amazing watching men argue about this (it's always men). I mean, who really cares? Most men go through life not knowing the difference between a dress and a skirt. They just use the words interchangeably, even when it's pointed out to them that a skirt and a dress are not the same thing. They just shrug and move on with life.

In this case soccer and football *are* the same thing, yet people get upset and start yelling at each other, and then Derek takes it too far and the barman asks him to leave the pub, meaning we all have to leave, and just when I was getting along so well with the woman in the blue dress or skirt or whatever the hell it was she was wearing.

I've used the term soccer* throughout this book just because it's easier** and I am a lazy, path-of-least-resistance type of person. This doesn't mean I hate soccer, I'm actually a big fan and a rare Australian sports writer who doesn't think every person who goes

---

* The term 'soccer' is derived from association football, which was the early term used to differentiate it from rugby. Association football was first played in 1863. Like all sports England invented, the English aren't very good at it.

** I was going to call it 'soccer football', just to annoy all groups, but I'm confident I'll do that anyway.

232

to a game is a flare-throwing anarchist who should be deported. I only think that about Western Sydney Wanderers fans.

My love of soccer began early. I went to a National Soccer League (NSL) game and not only made it out alive, I enjoyed the experience. Watching the Socceroos fail to qualify for the World Cup again and again just added to my interest, which probably speaks to some deep-seated psychological problems. When the Australians finally did qualify, the feeling was pure joy, the dam bursting after a lot of pent up frustration. That's the appeal of soccer: it frustrates you, but the highs are more addictive than Tim Tams.

One thing's for certain, whatever it's called, it has been the 'sleeping giant' of Australian sport for as long as I can remember, although it's becoming clear it's a very sound sleeper. For those who fear it, soccer is the greatest threat to Australian society since communism. In their minds, it's only a matter of time until it rises up and sweeps aside AFL, NRL and everything Australian. The reality, however, is that it's been less of a sleeping giant and more an accident-prone sleepwalker.

A SLOW START

Soccer has a long history in Australia and it's this history that explains why it has failed to match the success of sports like League and Australian Rules here, or indeed the sport's popularity elsewhere in the world. The game's major problem was timing. British association football became popular late in the nineteenth century. While there were games played in Australia as early as 1880, and possibly earlier, it wasn't until after rugby's split in 1895 that the game really took off in England.

This meant that by the time it started being played here with any seriousness (in the early twentieth century), Victorian Rules and the rugby codes were already duking it out for control of stadiums and players. In England, players being paid made soccer very popular with the working class and gave the game a real point of difference to the originally more popular rugby. After rugby split into two codes, professional rugby was only played in northern England, giving association football a great opportunity to grow – which it did.

Australia offered a much tougher environment. By 1908 Victorian Rules was dominant in the southern states and Rugby League was on its way to dominating the northern ones. They could use their popularity to control grounds, attract and retain players and, like soccer, they both offered money to the best athletes. Back then there was no sense that soccer was some sort of foreign plague that would wipe everyone out, it was very British and people still liked British things, it was just bad timing.

If soccer had arrived earlier, when the other codes weren't as established, we could now all be watching Manly United take on Collingwood Rangers and we would hate both teams.

John Walter Fletcher is widely considered the first person to seriously try to introduce the game to the Australian colonies. In 1880 he was behind a match involving Wanderers FC* and the King School rugby team, in what was for a long time thought to be the first soccer game played in Australia, although earlier games have since been discovered. In 1882 Fletcher founded the New South Wales English Football Association, which of course meant the other colonies started their own associations soon after.

By 1911 the Commonwealth Football Association had been formed, a national body that was then replaced by the Australian Soccer Association in 1921. Australia's isolation from the rest of the world meant we played New Zealand and South Africa a lot in

---

* The current Wanderers in the A-League are not the same team, but they are named after them to honour the soccer history in that area. They only started in 2012, after Clive Palmer's Gold Coast United fell into trouble and had their licence revoked. I know, who could have seen that coming?

THE OFFSIDE RULE

People make a big deal about the offside rule being hard to understand but it's not. As an attacking player, an indirect free kick is given against you if you receive the ball in the attacking half of the field and the ball was played by a teammate at a time when there were fewer than two defending players between you and the goal line, typically but not necessarily the goalkeeper and a defender, unless you were behind the ball or the ball was being played sideways or backwards (including from a corner kick), except from a throw-in or a goal kick, in which case you are onside even if the ball does go forward, however even if you don't touch the ball at all but a teammate who was not offside gets the ball or it goes in the goal, for an indeterminate amount of time, if you were interfering with play, for instance by obstructing the goalkeeper's vision or appearing to go for the ball and drawing a defender to you, you are still offside. See? Simple.

the first half of the nineteenth century. When we faced stiffer opposition we often struggled, like on 30 June 1951 when we lost 17–0 to a touring England side.

THOSE NEW AUSTRALIANS

After World War II, especially from the fifties onwards, Australia started to let in some people who weren't quite as white as before – basically people with good suntans. These 'New Australians' hailed from a range of European countries, notably Italy and Greece, and brought with them a love of the beautiful game. However, most established soccer clubs in Australia weren't so keen on having them join. As a result, these immigrant communities were forced to form their own clubs, often built around one ethnicity.* The fact that they

---

* These were teams like Sydney Croatia and South Melbourne Hellas, or the more optimistically named Adelaide Juventus and, my favourite, Green Gully Ajax. The nineties saw attempts to be more inclusive, read 'less ethnic', and resulted in abominations like Northern Spirit and Canberra Cosmos. Not to be outdone, the Kiwis topped the lot with Auckland's Football Kingz FC.

did this would later be thrown back at them: they were accused of preventing soccer from growing by making 'normal' Aussies feel left out. Amazing. We should be able to see past race and judge people solely on who they barrack for.

The predominance of these groups started to shift the view other Australians had of the game. They went from thinking about soccer as a British sport to considering it a 'foreign' game, full of 'un-Australian values' or other such nonsense. There has always been a racist element to the commentary around soccer in this country, as well as the racism between various ethnic groups. One of the wonderful features of a truly international sport is different groups coming together to fear and dislike each other for no reason.

On the positive side, post-war immigration provided the code with a significant boost to players and supporters, marking one of the turning points for the sport in this country.

NATIONAL AND INTERNATIONAL DEVELOPMENT

By the fifties the sport was growing into the international giant it is today and Australia was taking small steps to join the rest of the world. In 1956, Australia joined the Fédération Internationale de Football Association (FIFA)* but within four years was suspended for recruiting players from European clubs without paying transfer fees. So stealing, basically. It was an early indicator that the administration of the code in Australia would leave a lot to be desired.

By 1961, a whole new governing body was formed, the Australian Soccer Federation (ASF), looking to claw Australia's way back into FIFA's good books. An outstanding fine was paid and Australia

---

* Is FIFA the most corrupt organisation on the planet? It's a tough call as there's a lot of competition – all those crime gangs and authoritarian governments. But even they blush at what FIFA have gotten up to. For example, FIFA's idea of the best places to hold a World Cup? Russia in 2018 and Qatar in 2022. That's all the proof you'll ever need that corruption is involved. If you do want more proof, google 'FIFA corruption' and set aside several years of your life to read everything.

agreed to stop stealing players from elsewhere. Despite being in FIFA, there was no doubt Australia was merely on the fringes of the sport; its application for membership of the Asian Football Confederation (AFC) was knocked back, forcing it to become a founding member of the Oceania Football Confederation (OFC) in 1966, a strong body featuring traditional powerhouses of world football like New Caledonia, the Cook Islands, Tuvalu and Niue.

Australia spent the next forty years desperately trying to get out of the Oceania Confederation. In 1970 the ASF resigned from the OFC and tried to join the AFC again, only to be denied, again (seems like something they should have sorted out before leaving Oceania). It was getting embar-

> **DID YOU KNOW?**
>
> A-League fans are so committed to marine safety that at games they will often hold free demonstrations of proper flare use.

rassing and Australia was coming across as a bit of stalker. Eight years later, Australia returned to the Oceania Confederation, like a terrible ex-boyfriend who'd realised no one else wanted him. The OFC took them back, convinced things would be different this time. Oh OFC, why do you do this to yourself? Australia hadn't changed and, in 2006, was finally admitted to the AFC, presumably after the right bribes were paid to the right people.

OUR FIRST WORLD CUP (FOLLOWED BY A LOT OF LOSING)

Australia's international record for most of the twentieth century was poor at best. Attempts to make the FIFA World Cup in 1966 and 1970 failed, as we lost qualifying playoffs to North Korea in 1966 and Israel in 1970. You know things are bad when North Korea are beating you in real life and not just in North Korean media reports.

Then came the breakthrough. In 1974, the newly coined 'Socceroos' qualified for the World Cup in West Germany, prompting the majority of Australians to ask, 'What's the World Cup?' The excitement of qualification was somewhat tempered by the fact that Australia were put in a group with East Germany, West Germany and Chile, making Australia more sacrificial lamb than competitor.

In their first game, against the evil Germany, the Socceroos played well in the first half, but after the break they gave the East Germans an own goal and then conceded a late second.

The next game, against the good Germany, was a 3–0 loss. While not as accomplished a performance as the first game, the fact that they weren't destroyed by the host nation was impressive. After all, the Socceroos were basically amateurs up against professionals – professionals who had their entire nation invested in their success. In sharp contrast, the Socceroos had plenty of people back home who were indifferent or actively hated the sport.

The last game against Chile was a nil-all draw played in torrential rain, the only highlight being a protest by some students against the Chilean government. It had been a rough tournament, but the Socceroos had achieved their key goal: they had not completely embarrassed themselves. Despite that, they didn't actually score any goals in the tournament. Still, it had been a good experience, and surely they would be back in four years' time.

One major outcome of this period was the emergence of Johnny Warren. A player in the 1974 squad, Warren preached the doctrine of soccer across Australia, often in tandem with Les Murray, Australia's most prominent soccer presenter.* Warren championed the underappreciated code, believing it was being kept from emerging as the force it deserved to be by a range of prejudice. His 2002

---

* Les Murray's ability to pronounce non-Anglo-Saxon names astonished Australians for decades; pronouncing names with no vowels was equivalent to wizardry. Hearing Murray once rattle off the Hungarian starting eleven was the best thing that happened to me in the entire eighties.

book *Sheilas, Wogs and Poofters* didn't make it hard to guess what he felt most Australians thought of the game he loved.

Despite this, Warren never doubted the sport would overcome these issues. As the code began growing in popularity, he famously coined the phrase 'I told you so' in his last years. He passed away in 2004 and received a state funeral.

THE REVOLVING DOOR THAT WAS THE NSL

The improvement of the Socceroos and the game's growth in the seventies saw the sport form a national competition ahead of the more dominant codes. The National Soccer League (NSL) was formed in 1977. Over its 28-season history, a slide ruler and a spreadsheet were necessary to keep up with the competition's format and the teams in it. By the end of the NSL's time, forty-two different teams had played in the league. It was no wonder it struggled to win over a broad audience.

The most momentous change came in the 1989/90 season, which was moved from winter to summer, where the sport remains to this day. This move was made to avoid going directly up against Australian Rules and Rugby, the AFL and NRL at that time beginning to broaden their competitions nationally.

The late eighties and early nineties saw attempts to make more Australians feel comfortable with soccer, including the removal of some ethnic club names and logos. A lot of clubs and their supporters resisted this. Incredibly, they believed their culture and heritage were something to be proud of. What they failed to understand was that Australians find other cultures confusing and threatening. I mean, Australians considered focaccia exotic until the late nineties. In Adelaide they still do. It's why Australians have avoided developing a culture at all.

For all the turmoil, the depth of the competition afforded opportunities to young players that laid the groundwork for future

AUSTRALIAN SOCCER PLAYERS YOU MAY HAVE HEARD OF

Joe Marston: Marston's story reads like a movie. He was a paintbrush maker who played for Leichhardt-Annandale in Sydney, hardly the centre of the footballing universe. In 1949, he got word that an English scout had seen him play and Preston North End wanted him to try out for them. Marston not only passed the trial, he played 185 league appearances for them, including being the first Australian ever to play in an FA Cup final, where Preston lost to West Bromwich Albion.

Craig Johnston: Born in South Africa to Australian parents, Johnston played at Lake Macquarie City FC in Newcastle. At fourteen he wrote to several English clubs asking for a trial, with Middlesbrough telling him to pop over. After playing a few seasons there, he ended up joining the dominant Liverpool side of the eighties, winning five league titles with them. In the eighties, he was the only soccer player most Australians were aware existed.

Mark Bosnich: As a goalkeeper, Bosnich played for Manchester United, Aston Villa and Chelsea, picking up a Premier League winner's medal along the way. He was described by legendary manager Alex Ferguson as a 'terrible professional'. Bosnich's career was dogged by cocaine addiction, and he ended up bankrupt in 2008.

Mark Schwarzer: Schwarzer replaced the out-of-favour Bosnich as the Socceroos goalkeeper and carved out a terrific career in the English top flight, playing over 500 games, mainly for Middlesbrough and Fulham. Schwarzer made two crucial penalty saves in the shootout that got Australia into the 2006 World Cup, making him one of the greatest Australians that ever lived.

Harry Kewell: Apart from being injured a lot, Kewell is best known as Australia's greatest footballer. As a winger, Kewell was a skilful, exciting player who, when not injured, terrorised defenders while playing at Leeds and Liverpool. Before his retirement he returned to Australia to play in the A-League, occasionally overcoming injury to show glimpses of his undeniable class.

Tim Cahill: Cahill currently plays for Melbourne City, but don't let that fool you, he was once a really good player. Cahill played for Millwall and Everton in England, as well as having stints in America and China. Because of his incredible leaping ability, the roof must remain open whenever he plays at Docklands stadium. He is Australia's all-time top goal-scorer, saving the Socceroos from embarrassment more times than I care to remember.

success. Players including Mark Schwarzer, Mark Viduka and Brett Emerton made their debut in the league as teenagers, with others like Harry Kewell and Tim Cahill moving to Europe directly from NSL clubs' youth teams.

On the opposite end of the scale, international 'guest players' including George Best, Bobby Charlton and Ian Rush played a handful of games for NSL teams, beginning the long tradition of throwing money at players who are well past it in the hopes they'll somehow fix everything. They didn't. Money was a constant problem for the league and, despite these attempts to reach mainstream Australia with big names and the whitewashing of ethnic club histories, attendances remained patchy. Perth Glory, a newer club, was successful, but they were more the exception than the rule.

With limited TV coverage, declining sponsorship and many clubs in the red, the NSL played its last game on 4 April 2004. The game was now in a parlous state.

LOST IN THE WILDERNESS

While the domestic competition was lurching along, the Socceroos were building up an impressive resumé of inventing new ways to miss World Cups. The 1974 World Cup proved to be a false dawn, with Australia embarking on a 32-year journey through the wilderness of world football, failing to qualify for a single World Cup. Australia developed a real knack for falling at the final hurdle, losing qualifying playoffs in 1985 to Scotland, 1993 to Argentina, 1997 to Iran and 2001 to Uruguay. It was brutal, heartbreaking stuff.

Still, Australians were showing more interest in the sport than ever before, with increased broadcasting of the English Premier League and tireless coverage of the whole sport by SBS.

Outside of World Cup qualification, the Socceroos were producing better results, but this only made missing the big stage all the more painful. Part of the Socceroos' problem was the fact that they had to qualify for the decisive playoff game through Oceania, which meant lots of games against poor competition before facing a top side from another conference, often from South America. Playing the Solomon Islands was hardly good preparation for taking on Uruguay. Or, for instance, taking on Argentina in 1993, in Argentina, with Diego Maradona in their side – a fair step-up in class from the Cook Islands. Maradona has since claimed the Argentinians cheated in that game, able to run more because they'd been given 'speedy coffee', which seems especially unfair given they were so much better anyway.

The 1998 World Cup qualifying playoff game was probably the most brutal moment in Australian soccer history. The Socceroos were leading Iran 2–0 with only 20 minutes to go when infamous serial public pest Peter Hore ran onto the MCG and pulled down the goal net, causing a significant delay. The break enabled the Iranians to regroup and they came storming home to equalise the game, qualifying on the away goals rule at Australia's expense. I was at the MCG that night and it's hard to convey the feeling of an entire stadium going from elation to despair within a 20-minute period. On a personal level, it was a bit like my love life condensed into a 20-minute block. To this day I wish only bad things for Peter Hore.

The 2002 qualifying campaign was another one marked by uncompetitive matches in Oceania, a 31–0 game against American Samoa underlining the pointlessness of the games.[*] After winning Oceania relatively easily, the Socceroos fell to Uruguay, who scored two late goals. Once again the Socceroos had come up short, but this time the government would get involved, as they always do in Australia when not enough winning is occurring.

---

[*] One thing this game did produce is the world record for the most goals scored by a player in a single game, with Archie Thompson scoring 13 of Australia's 31 goals. That FIFA record still stands today. Thompson also notably scored 5 goals in the 2007 A-League Grand Final against Adelaide United, although many maintain the 2002 American Samoa team were a better side than Adelaide.

EVERYTHING HITS THE FAN

Throughout its history, soccer in Australia has suffered from the disease that infects all codes from time to time: terrible administration. By the start of the twenty-first century, Australian soccer had a raging case of it, so bad it threatened the code's existence at the top level. Terrible administrators can range from the idiotic, to the inept, to the outright corrupt. Soccer managed to collect the whole set and then some.

The federal government decided enough was enough. Everyone was sick of the constant media reports of corruption in the game and the fact that the sport was broke. The national team's failure to qualify for the 2002 World Cup was the last straw. The government established the Independent Soccer Review Committee to conduct an inquiry. Let me tell you, it's never good to have a committee set up to look into you – it never happens for good reasons. Take for example the various reviews that sprung up after the 2012 London Olympics.*

In a tactical misstep, many powerbrokers in Australian soccer attacked the inquiry and announced they wouldn't accept the findings before it had even started, which just screams innocence if you ask me.

The government appointed Mr Sports Reports, David Crawford, as chair of the committee. In 2003 the committee produced a report that confirmed that soccer suffered from financial problems, reduced staffing levels, political infighting, a lack of strategic direction and planning, and mixed results on the field in the international arena. The report didn't hold back, saying within soccer existed 'a plethora of problems that can generally be defined as mistrust and disharmony, loss of focus, inappropriate behaviour, and concentration on local or factional issues rather than broad whole-of-sport

---

*   See page 49.

development and "bigger picture" issues.' In other words, soccer was stuffed.

The Crawford Report, as it became known, made fifty-three recommendations, including a complete overhaul of the sport and its governance structure. It basically called for independent management and the destruction of the mini fiefdoms that controlled parts of the game. The report annoyed a lot of people, who vowed to fight the recommendations, and the whole board of Soccer Australia* resigned in protest. This was a bad move, because the government was pretty thrilled to see them gone. In my experience, threats work best when people don't want them to happen. Further resistance to the reforms magically disappeared when the Australian Sports Commission threatened to cut all funding to Soccer Australia.

To replace the board, a new body was put in place, Football Federation Australia (FFA), headed by Frank Lowy.** Lowy had decided that Soccer Australia was beyond saving and there was no one left there to argue with him. Lowy brought an iron fist to the running of the game, at a time when it really needed it. The FFA was quick to establish the A-League, bringing on board sponsors and securing new TV deals for the code, with the competition kicking off in August 2005, just over a year after the end of the NSL.

The A-League was established with more of Franky Lowy's iron-handed approach, with almost all former NSL clubs told they would have no chance of entering the league. Instead there was a call for new clubs to be launched, free of ethnic legacies. This was resisted by some but the collapse of the NSL, government pressure and the Crawford Report gave the FFA the power to pretty much

---

* The Australian Soccer Federation changed its name to Soccer Australia in 1995. Why? Well, like all boards, if they have no idea what they're doing but want to give the appearance of a plan, they rebrand.

** Frank Lowy is the third richest Australian and chairman of the Westfield Corporation. He is assessed to be worth $8.26 billion, which can get you a nice one-bedroom apartment in Sydney these days.

do whatever it wanted. It has to be said that the A-League has worked, overall, and it's been a superior product to the NSL. Not that there hasn't been the odd misstep, such as giving Clive Palmer a franchise.

The FFA soon had sponsors lined up and relatively competent people running it, so started to turn its mind to qualifying for the 2006 World Cup. This would again demonstrate the new ruling body's ruthless streak, as it sacked Socceroos coach Frank Farina in 2005 after failure at the FIFA Confederations Cup. The FFA were going to take this World Cup qualifying thing seriously.

When highly respected international coach Guus Hiddink was announced as Farina's replacement, it seemed things might finally be moving in the right direction, with a time-honoured seven-goal drubbing of the Solomon Islands rebuilding some of the Socceroos' confidence.

Australia was still in the Oceania Confederation at this stage, so to qualify they had to beat their old rivals Uruguay. Hiddink was a veteran of these kind of matches. He knew the Uruguayans would play funny buggers in the away leg in Montevideo (past antics included setting off firecrackers outside the team hotel all night so the Australians got no sleep ahead of the game) so he set up camp in Buenos Aires and arrived in Uruguay at the last minute.

The Socceroos lost 1–0, which meant they needed to win the return leg in Sydney. Again Hiddink showed his experience, booking blocks of seats on scheduled flights to Sydney to disrupt Uruguay's travel to Sydney.

The game in Sydney was tempestuous, the referee dishing out nine yellow cards as it threatened to boil over. Tony Popovic was carded for elbowing Uruguayan playmaker Álvaro Recoba in the face and, fearing a red card was on its way, the wily Hiddink substituted Popovic for Kewell after just half an hour. Four minutes later, Kewell set up a goal for Mark Bresciano, tying the game up on aggregate. With no away goals scored, the game went to extra time and then a penalty shootout, the worst way to decide a sporting event ever invented. Well, except for golf, the entirety of which is bad.

The tension was immense as Harry Kewell, Lucas Neill and Tony Vidmar scored their penalties, only for Mark Viduka to miss. It seemed the Socceroos had found yet another heartbreaking way to lose. Australians around the country were glued to their TVs; suddenly everyone cared about soccer. Step up Mark Schwarzer – with an amazing save, leaping to his left and with his right hand deflecting the ball wide.

The stadium went what we in the business call 'nuts'. I'm getting tears in my eyes just writing this. To be fair, that could be because I've been eating Barbecue Shapes and accidentally rubbed some of the seasoning in my eyes.

Schwarzer's save meant the hopes of a nation rested on John Aloisi's shoulders. If he converted his penalty, Australia were through to the World Cup for the first time in thirty-two years. Aloisi stepped up and drilled it. I mean *drilled* it. The place went nuttser. Aloisi ripped off his shirt and twirled it around his head as he ran down the ground.

It was a huge moment for Australia, up there with the America's Cup in 1983. Suddenly Australia wasn't sitting out the biggest team sporting event in the world. Soccer was no longer the bastard child of Australian sport.

THE WORLD STAGE

The 2006 World Cup, held in Germany, as it had been in 1974, was another high point for the game in Australia. The squad was replete with a golden generation of talent, who'd proven themselves in the top leagues of Europe. In the group games the Socceroos secured a win over Japan, a brave loss to Brazil and a two-all draw with

Croatia. This record meant they went through to the round of sixteen, where they played Italy.

Australia took it right up to the Italians all game and in my view outplayed them. Then, with only minutes left to go, Italy's Fabio Grosso was awarded a penalty for flopping over a challenge by Lucas Neill. IT WAS NOT A PENALTY. The Italians ran over to Grosso and embraced him as he lay on the ground, pretending to be injured. The not-penalty was converted and the Italians won. Australia was robbed.

Back home the fury towards the referee was immense. Billy Vojtek, a former Socceroo, said, 'He should get ten years at Guantanamo Bay with hard labour, that referee. He should not be allowed in this country, he should be classed as a terrorist.' In my opinion Vojtek didn't go far enough.

The big change that came from the 2006 success is that the broader Australian public now see qualifying for the World Cup as their birthright, not an impossible dream. Where once mention of the World Cup was met with blank stares, Australians now become instant experts every four years, telling their workmates things like 'Well Group C is the group of death' even though they haven't watched a single game since the previous World Cup.

Following Guus Hiddink's achievements, the FFA appointed another Dutch coach, Pim Verbeek, to lead the Socceroos. While he secured qualification for the next World Cup, Verbeek faced serious media criticism for his negative tactics, and was dismissed after three dour displays at the 2010 World Cup. Australians won't accept losing at the best of times, but if they think you're not even trying to win, that's basically treason.

German Holger Osieck took over and coached the Socceroos to the final of the 2011 Asian Cup, where they lost to rivals Japan in extra time. Under Osieck the team qualified for the 2014 World Cup, but consecutive 6–0 losses (to France and Brazil) in the lead-up to the tournament made it clear he hadn't done enough to revitalise the squad, which was still reliant on aging stars from 2006's golden generation. He was fired ahead of the tournament itself.

Both Verbeek and Osieck were criticised for not grasping the Australian character: even if you know for sure that you're going to lose, you need to charge ahead blindly with the conviction that you're going to win. Seemingly learning their lesson, the FFA chose an Australian to be the next Socceroos coach. Ange Postecoglou had made a name for himself in the A-League, his Brisbane Roar and Melbourne Victory teams playing an attacking, creative brand of soccer. His premiership-winning Brisbane Roar team still hold the record for the longest unbeaten run in any Australian football code, at thirty-six games without defeat.

With little time to prepare ahead of the 2014 World Cup, Postecoglou's overhauled Socceroos lost all three group games, to Chile, the Netherlands and Spain. But he'd clearly made his mark on the team, with the defeated Socceroos widely praised for their combative style, taking the game to their highly rated

IT'S ALL IN THE NAME

Gold Coast United FC (A-League)

Another team lost in the Bermuda Triangle of Australian sport, Gold Coast United entered the A-League in the 2009/10 season. If their location wasn't enough of a concern, the club being owned by Clive Palmer should have been a red flag.

From early on, the 'United' tag was put to the test, with Palmer seemingly at war with the fans of the club and the Queensland government. He limited the number of grandstands open at games to save money and criticised his own fans and the A-League administration. You'll be surprised to learn this didn't make things better and crowds dwindled. In 2012, the FFA revoked Palmer's licence, ending the club. Palmer went on to tackle politics with equal success.

opponents – actually trying to win the game rather than just look-ing to avoid a pantsing was a pleasant change from the previous eight years.

The FFA backed Postecoglou and his vision for the national team, and essentially the same squad that had crashed out in Brazil the year before lined up for the 2015 Asian Cup – this time on home soil. The Socceroos made it to the final in Sydney, having managed to avoid their Asian Confederation nemesis Japan in the knock-out phase of the tournament. Despite dominating South Korea in the final, the game again went to extra-time, just as it had in 2011. But this time it was an Australian, James Troisi, who came up with the winner, securing the Asian Cup, Australian soccer's first major trophy. After all those decades of awkwardly courting the confeder-ation, the Socceroos were now champions of Asia. Australian soccer had made it into the winner's circle of world soccer.

TROUBLE AHEAD?

While the game has come on in leaps and bounds since the 2003 Crawford Report, it still has some issues to resolve. Australia's failed bid to host the 2022 World Cup was a major blow for the sport, especially after it was revealed that the bid cost taxpayers $45.6 million, despite the corruption within FIFA that's been reported since.

While the 2006 World Cup was viewed as a success, subsequent World Cups have not seen any improvement on that perfor-mance. If it wasn't for Tim Cahill's goalscoring heroics rescuing the Socceroos on a regular basis, things could have been much worse. The retirement of the golden generation that went to Germany in 2006, including the imminent retirement of Cahill, presents the game with the need to develop new stars, both to perform on the pitch and to capture the broader public's imagination. It remains to be seen if the A-League and the FFA's grassroots policies are capable of producing players of that quality, and if national coach Ange Postecoglou can shape a team capable of challenging the top sides.

Off the field, Frank Lowy's authoritarian approach suited the code well for a period of renewal and consolidation, but he was increasingly resented by others who had invested their time and money in the new vision of the game. They too wanted a say in how the game was run. It also hasn't helped that when Lowy retired, his son was appointed his replacement, apparently after an 'exhaustive search'. It seems the new administration is a lot like the old administration.

The A-League today is a strong competition, but it is still financially struggling in many areas. In 2017 the league announced it was putting expansion plans on hold because it would send them broke. At the same time, there is a power struggle going on across the football community, with A-League clubs and the players' association among those wanting a greater say in the running of the game. It's gotten to the point where FIFA is intervening in the FFA's business, which is sure to lead to smooth and uncontroversial changes that leave everyone happy.

What all this reveals is that, for its many positives, soccer in Australia still suffers from having to compete in one of the most crowded sports markets in the world. Despite everything, it finds itself structurally boxed in by the AFL and NRL, a situation that hasn't changed since soccer first arrived on these shores.

PART IV

THE IRREGULAR SPORTS

The major codes of Australian Rules, League, cricket, Union and soccer dominate the daily coverage of sport in this country. They also tend to dominate the TV deals and sponsorship dollars. Yet there is a range of other sports that Australians love that are also important in different ways.

Many of them become popular in a seasonal fashion, like the cherry blossoms in Japan: tennis during the Australian Open, horseracing in the Spring Carnival, motorsports when there's a big crash and the Olympic sports once every four years.

Other sports are important for their historical importance, even if they've lost their lustre in recent decades – boxing being an obvious example – while others have delivered key moments in our history, such as the 1983 America's Cup victory.

This section doesn't attempt to cover every sport ever played in Australia; that would be tedious to read and even more tedious for me to write. I'm interested in how things got to be the way they are. Sports like baseball and badminton have long histories in Australia but couldn't be said to have shaped our current sporting environment.

If that upsets anyone, I understand. I would suggest they write a book too. My advice is to set aside time in this way: 12 per cent for research, 30 per cent for writing, 23 per cent for telling people you're working on your book and the rest for procrastinating.

Part of the problem with writing about Australian sports history is the pure volume of sports Australians not only play but are good at. In this section, we cover a lot of these, from tennis, golf and netball, to the wide array of Olympic sports.

OLYMPICS

In Australia, every single person has the ability to every four years magically become an expert on the full range of sports that are staples of the Olympics. What's really impressive is that Australians can do this even if they've never seen the sport before, let alone played it. Diving, judo, fencing, rhythmic gymnastics – for two weeks, nothing is beyond the armchair expertise of the average Australian punter.

'See what she did there? Tucked the shoulder a second too late.'

'Yeah, the Tunisian woman had the right idea.'

Outside the Olympic years (let's not oversell the Commonwealth Games here), we're completely uninterested in watching these sports. Yet once the Olympics roll around, Australians demand gold medals like it's their birthright. It means Olympic athletes toil in darkness for most of their careers, only to suddenly be thrust into the harsh glare of the public spotlight when the stakes are highest. Australians demand the reflected glory brought by Olympic medals, the assurance that we are relevant in this world. Failure is not treated kindly.

AN OLYMPIC NATION

When the French aristocrat Pierre de Coubertin decided to reboot the Olympic games in 1889, he appointed a host of delegates to the first International Olympic Committee. De Coubertin was a man who obviously knew it was easier to apologise than to ask permission, as he appointed many people to the committee without checking with them first. He announced that Leonard Albert Cuff, a New Zealander who captained the first Kiwi cricket team, would represent Australasia – both Australia and New Zealand. Cuff found out about his appointment in a letter from de Coubertin, and was given the gig based on the basis of two criteria: his previous experience of setting up athletic competitions between Australia and New Zealand, and the fact that de Coubertin didn't know many other people from Australia or New Zealand.

Cuff's appointment was significant because it means that both Australia and New Zealand have technically been members of the IOC from the very beginning. While we're proud of that now, at the time no one cared. In fact, as the first modern games approached, no one in Australia really knew they were on or that we were participating.

Unbeknown to his fellow citizens, Edwin Flack, an Australian living in London, made his way to the games in Athens. This was not an organised thing; Flack had heard about the games and taken leave from his job as an accountant, funding the trip himself. It was a far cry from the junket today's delegates go on.

Given there was no official team, Flack decided to wear his old school blazer with the Melbourne Grammar logo on it, the first in a long line of awful Australian uniforms at the Olympics. Despite this hiccup, Flack had a very successful games, winning gold in the 1500- and 800-metre track races. He also entered the doubles tennis, and managed to qualify for the semi-final when his opponents didn't show up. He lost that game, but that was still good enough for third place.* I reckon he could have won gold, but he was partnered with an Englishman.

On top of all that, he thought he'd give the marathon a go, despite the fact he'd never actually run one before. He led until the 34-kilometre mark and eventually collapsed just six kilometres from the finish line, which is a bit soft really. Back in Australia, reports of his success raised some interest in the games, but I think the fact that you could get third place simply because someone didn't show up indicates the Olympics were not quite at the standard they are today.

After Leonard Cuff's surprise appointment to the IOC (Cuff himself perhaps being the most surprised), not much had occurred to make Australians take the Olympics seriously. In 1905, Cuff retired after ten years of not really doing anything except talking about his role,** which must have been a challenge given he was bewildered as to why he was even there. He was replaced by Richard Coombes, an Englishman who had relocated to Australia and was both a journalist and passionate supporter of athletics. Coombes was the organising force that propelled Australia to sending strong and better-organised teams. Coombes was so successful he stayed on the IOC until 1932.

While Coombes raised the organisation standard of Australia's Olympic movement, it was the awarding of the 1956 games to Melbourne that turned Australia's fondness for the Olympics into a passionate love affair so intense it's usually reserved for AFL Headquarters.

THE FRIENDLY GAMES

The 1956 Melbourne Olympics were so good it wasn't until the year 2000 that another city came close to matching them. It was a chance

---

* Bronze medals were not yet being awarded for third place.
** These days, an Olympic delegate's schedule is flat out: taking bribes, going on junkets, laundering the bribes and bullying people. It's an exhausting and thankless task.

for Australians to show that not only are we the chosen people when it comes to playing sports, we are also the best at running them.

The Melbourne Games were known as the 'Friendly Games', despite the fact the world at the time was not really very friendly at all. Many countries refused to participate; China didn't come because Taiwan was going, while Liechtenstein, Spain, Switzerland and the Netherlands all withdrew in protest following the Soviet invasion of Hungary. On top of that, Lebanon and Egypt boycotted due to the Suez Crisis. All these boycotts remind me what it's like trying to host a party. People won't come because so and so is coming, even though it's your party and they're punishing *you* by not coming. Then no one shows up and you're alone on your twenty-first crying into a pillow.

While a lot of countries boycotted because of Hungary, the Hungarians themselves showed up. They were matched against the Soviets in water polo in what would become known as the 'Blood in the Water' match, a Hungarian player left bleeding as the two teams belted each other. Hungary won after the game was ended early, going on to win gold. As well as this bit of Cold War history, the Melbourne Olympics were marked by numerous defections. Australians were all for this, of course – we've always supported people fleeing oppressive regimes provided they are ridiculously good at sport.

Holding the Olympics in your own country gives you a huge advantage, and we didn't waste it. Australia sent 325 athletes to the games, dwarfing any previous team and then some. The results were impressive. Australia finished third overall in the medal tally with thirty-five medals, thirteen of them gold.

Shirley Strickland picked up two gold medals, while Betty Cuthbert, just eighteen at the time, won three. That's always the downside of being an athlete, your career highlights come at a very young age. Still, just having a highlight during your career must be nice. The closest I've had to a career highlight was when they were letting a bunch of people go at work and I missed the cut because they'd forgotten I still worked there.

While Strickland and Cuthbert were dominating the track, Murray Rose and Dawn Fraser performed similar feats in the pool. Rose won three gold medals, the 400-metre freestyle, 1500-metre freestyle and 4×200-metre freestyle. Fraser won the 100-metre free-style and the 4×100-metre freestyle. All these feats were beamed into homes around Australia through the magic of television, with cutting edge black-and-white technology, making these athletes more well-known than most before them. Even today these names stand out.

The closing ceremony was the first where all the athletes entered the stadium together in the spirit of friendship. That spirit of friend-ship was probably helped along by the fact that a lot of countries didn't show up.

The Australian obsession with the Olympics was well and truly set, as was the expectation that Australia would always per-form well. That expectation was fulfilled for a long time, until the Montreal Disaster turned our world upside down.

THE FUN GAMES

On 4 September 1993, Sydney was selected to host the 2000 Olympics, beating Beijing, Berlin, Istanbul and Manchester – all pretty rubbish cities really. The announcement was met with eupho-ria in Australia, followed by a sense of panic similar to when you realise you've just volunteered to organise the school working bee without thinking about how much work goes into it. It led to the normal fights over funding between the city of Sydney, NSW, the AOC and the federal government.

Yet when the event kicked off, it stuck the landing in every possible way. It's now considered the *Citizen Kane* of Olympics.

The opening ceremony was a triumph, despite involving Human Nature, and showcased a wonderful artistic interpretation of Australia's history with all the nasty bits taken out. It also featured a young girl by the name of Nikki Webster, the birth of a star who went on to have a long and successful showbiz career.

These games were run very efficiently and had a fantastic feel to them, something that was palpable around the country and the world. The reason they didn't completely bankrupt the city was the massive army of volunteers, who took on almost every possible job. Around 47 000 people worked for nothing at the games, almost all of them intentionally. These were fun games as well as being an amazing athletic spectacle.

The Australian team made everyone proud, picking up fifty-eight medals, sixteen of them gold, putting Australia fourth on the medal tally. There were many heroes at these games. Seventeen-year-old Ian Thorpe won five medals – three gold and two silver, including helping defeat the Americans in the 4×100-metre freestyle relay. Victory was especially gratifying because US swimmer Gary Hall Jr. had promised the Americans would 'smash them [Australia] like guitars'. Revenge was sweet; Thorpe came home strongly to win the gold and now the Americans have Donald Trump as president.

The women of the Hockeyroos won gold, shaming our men's hockey team, while in the pool Grant Hackett defeated Kieren Perkins to take gold in the 1500 metres. Our women's water polo team also won gold by defeating the Americans, while in the equestrian three-day eventing, Australia won its third consecutive gold medal.

To Australians, the biggest event without a doubt was Cathy Freeman running in the women's 400 metres. The pressure building up to it was immense. Not only was Freeman a favourite, she was a proud Indigenous athlete competing in a sport Australia had not had a lot of success in. With the eyes of the nation and the world glued to TV screens, this event took on huge significance as Freeman took to the starting blocks. Once they were away it felt like the longest 49.11 seconds, until commentator Bruce McAvaney said, 'This is a famous victory,' and we had our first individual Indigenous Olympic champion.

It was a defining moment for Australia. Well, not in terms of ushering in a new spirit of reconciliation and equality, but everyone remembers it and we got a gold medal.

By the closing ceremony, the Sydney Olympics had delivered one of the most uniting, fun and exciting few weeks in the history of this country. It was a high point of national pride and gave people a sense that anything was possible, a feeling our politicians have worked incredibly hard to get rid of.

By the end of the Sydney games, Australia was even more crazy about the Olympics, something previously not thought possible. Recent struggles have left people unhappy, reminding politicians and administrators that in this country, Olympic success is a non-negotiable part of our culture.

SYDNEY OLYMPICS FACTS

The volunteers at the games were all heroes, except for Bruce at my work, who never shuts up about having been one. It was almost twenty years ago – move on Bruce, move on.

Bruce still wears a 'Sydney 2000 volunteer' polo to work on every single casual Friday, just in case we hadn't realised what a vital role he played.

Seriously though, every single morning Bruce goes on about the time he helped some German tourists find the right train.

Worst of all, Bruce is one of those people who just puts his lunch dishes in the staffroom sink and expects someone else to deal with it.

THE OLYMPIC SPIRIT

Australia is one of only five countries to attend every Summer Olympics – along with Greece, France, Great Britain and Switzerland* – so it's worth recapping what each games meant to us and how we fared.

1896 ATHENS

The first of the modern games were a low key, amateur affair, with Australians completely oblivious to their existence. When Australians heard one of their countrymen had won some medals in a competition they'd never heard of, they said 'Is that right?' and went back to work.

1900 PARIS

The Paris Olympics were even more amateurish than the Athens version. For starters, the event ran for five months, which seems excessive. Australia had two athletes at these games, a massive 100 per cent increase from the previous games. Frederick Lane won two gold medals in swimming, an important first for a sport Australia became a world power in. Sprinter Stan Rowley won four medals at the games, three bronze and then a gold as part of the Great Britain track relay team. Back then, Australians could swap countries just like that, being judged to still be part of Great Britain.

Apart from that medal success, the Paris Olympics were a bit of a disaster. They were the only Olympics to feature live pigeons as targets in the shooting, which is both cruel and messy, and they included a range of weird events like ballooning and underwater swimming. Perhaps my favourite thing is the rule, which they have

---

* While Switzerland boycotted the Melbourne 1956 Olympics, the equestrian events were held in Sweden to get around Australia's harsh quarantine laws – laws Johnny Depp and Amber Heard would learn all about years later. As the Swiss attended the equestrian events they technically have been to all the games.

unfortunately changed, that children could be used as coxswains in rowing.

1904 ST LOUIS

The St Louis Olympics were, frankly, rubbish. They ran over four and a half months during the World's Fair, and Britain and France didn't even bother showing up. Originally it was believed only two Australians competed, neither winning medals, but later it came to light that Frank Bailey had been marked down as an American but was actually Australian, and he'd won three silver and one bronze. Bailey did become an American citizen in 1906, so let's not get too excited about him.

1908 LONDON

The 1908 Olympics saw Australia and New Zealand send a joint 'Australasia' team, composed of thirty-two Australians and three New Zealanders. It was the first serious team sent to a games. The New Zealanders won just one bronze medal and it was in the walking event, so it was hardly worth having them there. This Olympics was notable for the Australian Rugby Union team winning gold, before returning home and deserting the code almost en masse for League. Australia picked up two silvers and one bronze as well.

1912 STOCKHOLM

Another joint Australia–New Zealand team was sent, with the New Zealanders contributing another bronze. One of them was also part of the gold-medal swimming relay team, but the Australians did all the heavy lifting, of course.

Stockholm was most notable for Fanny Durack winning gold in the 100-metre freestyle. The fact she was even there was a feat in itself, as the New South Wales Ladies Amateur Swimming Association had opposed women participating in the Olympic

Games, mainly on the grounds that men would see them. Oh dear. Luckily, they changed their minds, and Fanny and her closest rival and friend Mina Wylie were allowed to go, so long as they paid for the trip themselves and took along chaperones. Remember, this was the era when women were treated like children, whereas now we treat them like teenagers. Durack went on to be the greatest female swimmer of her time, and this was when women were made to wear almost full-length costumes made of wool.

1920 ANTWERP

The 1916 games were meant to be in Berlin but the Germans went and started World War I, a global event that was even more costly and damaging than hosting the Olympics is these days. As a result, the games didn't go ahead and Antwerp was awarded the next games, due to the suffering the people of Belgium had been through during the war. While it wasn't a highly successful games for Australia, it was notable for there no longer being a joint team from Australasia. The New Zealanders had actually left the Olympic Federation of Australia and New Zealand, presumably in the pursuit of less success – an effort that was successful.

1924 PARIS

Australia sent its biggest team to date to these games: thirty-four men and no women. It was like an ASX Top 50 board meeting with that sort of ratio. In terms of medals, Australia secured three gold, one silver and two bronze medals. Andrew 'Boy' Charlton won the 1500-metre freestyle, an event that Australians dominated in the future.

1928 AMSTERDAM

With Australia suffering a financial downturn, just eighteen athletes were sent to these games, with eight of them having to fund themselves. The Australian Olympic Committee was broke. Only Bobby Pearce returned with a gold medal, in the single scull. Pearce famously stopped mid-race in the quarter-final to let a family of ducks pass. He still won the race, which shows it's possible to be an Olympic gold medallist and adorable at the same time.

1932 LOS ANGELES

The Great Depression loomed large over this Olympics. Australia only managed to send thirteen athletes, but some countries didn't send anyone, which is soft. Australia won three gold medals, with Dunc Gray winning Australia's first ever gold in cycling. Clare Dennis won the women's 200-metre breaststroke, overcoming a protest that alleged her costume exposed too much of her shoulder-blade. I don't know about you but I find a woman's shoulderblade very offensive and I'm glad someone was onto this. I once caught a glimpse of a women's shoulder blade and I still get horrifying flashbacks.

1936 BERLIN

Berlin in 1936 was not a happy place because this guy called Adolf Hitler was in charge. Hitler was literally a Nazi. Many athletes refused to attend the games. Australia sent a team of thirty-three athletes and Dunc Gray later regretted the fact that, as the flag-bearer at the opening ceremony, he showed respect by dipping the flag to Hitler as they marched past. Gray had decided not to do a Nazi salute, as some flag-bearers did. He later said he thought of impaling Hitler on the flag, an act that would surely have made him the greatest Olympian ever. In terms of athletic success, the team returned with only a single bronze to their name and, as we all know, that's not a real medal.

1948 LONDON

Thanks to Dunc Gray not turning Hitler into a human flag, the Olympics took a long hiatus during World War II. The London games became known as the 'Austerity Games' due to the world still recovering from the war. That was a terrible bit of marketing – austerity is a hard sell – but people were just happy to still be alive. Australia sent seventy-five competitors to these games and won thirteen medals, two of them gold.

1952 HELSINKI

Apart from being fun to say, the Helsinki Olympics saw an unprecedented gold rush and the emergence of the Lithgow Flash, Marjorie Jackson. Jackson won both the 100 metres and 200 metres in Helsinki, fulfilling the potential she showed when, at seventeen, she beat the Dutch Olympic champion Fanny Blankers-Koen over 100 yards and then, a week later, beat her again over 100 metres. You know someone's good when they beat the reigning gold medallist over both imperial and metric distances. Helsinki also signalled the emergence of Shirley Strickland, who won gold in the 80-metre hurdles, which boded well for the next Olympics, to be held in Melbourne.

1956 OLYMPICS

As mentioned earlier, these were the greatest games so far, and the first that saw the athletes mingle in a closing ceremony. This was the suggestion of an Australian schoolboy, John Wing. Now Olympic athletes of the world mingle so well that the IOC provided forty-two condoms per athlete at the Rio games. Forty-two! No wonder so many of them turn to doping.

1960 ROME

The Soviet Union dominated the Rome medal tally for the second Olympics in a row, as their state-sponsored doping program really

BRAVE MOMENTS

In 1960 at the Rome Olympics, Bill Roycroft was competing in the equestrian when he was thrown from his horse, resulting in a broken shoulder, a dislocated collarbone, and concussion for good measure. He was airlifted to hospital. The team still needed a rider to compete, so Roycroft checked himself out of hospital, against the doctors' orders, and competed the next day.

Rick McCosker had his jaw broken in his first innings of the 1977 Centenary Test. With the test in the balance, he came out in the second innings, his head swollen and covered in bandages, to carve out 25 runs and help the Aussies to victory.

North Melbourne footballer Jason McCartney was a victim of the 2002 Bali bombings, suffering severe second-degree burns to over 50 per cent of his body. He came back in 2003 to play one last game, wearing heavy protection, and set up the winning goal before retiring.

kicked into gear. Luckily, the Russians have stopped that malarky these days. Australia's momentum from Melbourne continued with the team bringing home twenty-two medals, eight of them gold.

Rome is best known for Herb Elliott winning the 1500 metres with a lead of 18 metres. The story goes that Elliott's coach had told him that if he was waving a white towel, it meant someone was right behind him or that the world record was close. When Elliott saw the white towel being waved he assumed someone was right behind him and he took off. But his coach was flagging that the world record was within reach, and he was right. Elliott's panic pushed him to set a new world record of 3 minutes and 35.6 seconds, which was so fast it took seven years for someone to beat it. On top of that, Elliott's time would have been good enough to win gold at Seoul in 1988, Barcelona in 1992 and Rio in 2016. Elliott did what many greats seem to do and retired young at twenty-two. I wanted to retire at twenty-two but you can't really retire from going to nightclubs and drinking; it's more that you grow out of it or, in my case, security has your photo.

1964 TOKYO

Betty Cuthbert won her fourth gold medal in Tokyo, but these Olympics belonged to Dawn Fraser and her achievements in the pool. She not only won the 100-metre freestyle for the third Olympics in a row but was also arrested for stealing a flag from the Emperor's palace. Upon realising who she was, the police let her off and gave her the flag, which is weird. Only famous people can steal things and retain the proceeds of their crimes even after they're caught. Well, bankers too, I guess.

When Fraser returned home from the games, she was suspended from swimming for ten years – a huge overreaction if ever I saw one – so she retired. With eight Olympic medals, four of them gold, she remains one of our great champions. However, since retiring she's had a slight problem with saying stupid things.

In 1997, she supported Pauline Hanson, saying, 'I wish I could be as outspoken, I suppose, as Pauline Hanson and say, "Look, I'm sick and tired of the immigrants that are coming into my country."' That seems like she has no problem at all being outspoken. More recently, Fraser said tennis players Nick Kyrgios and Bernard Tomic should 'go back to where their fathers or their parents came from [. . .] if they act like that'. Kyrgios is from Canberra, so that really is hate speech.

1968 MEXICO CITY

Australia sent 128 athletes to Mexico City, a team half the size of the one they sent to Tokyo. Funding was an issue. Personally, I would have sent a huge team, the biggest, and got the Mexicans to pay for it. While Australia did relatively well with seventeen medals, five of them gold, these Olympics are best known for a famous image:

two African-American athletes on the podium, wearing a black glove each, fists above their heads in a human rights salute, raising awareness of racism in sport and segregation in the US.

Australian track athlete Peter Norman had come second in the 200 metres, and Tommie Smith and John Carlos approached him and told him they planned to do the salute on the podium. Norman not only backed their right to do it, he wore the badge of the Olympic Project for Human Rights in support. This meant a lot to Smith and Carlos, who knew that Peter's gesture put him into the firing line.

It meant so much, in fact, that thirty-eight years later at Norman's funeral, Smith and Carlos both gave eulogies and were pallbearers. Smith said Norman was 'a man who believed right could never be wrong' and told Norman's family: 'Peter Norman's legacy is a rock. Stand on that rock. Peter shall always be my friend. The spirit shall prevail.'

1972 MUNICH

The Munich Games were overshadowed by the massacre of eleven members of the Israeli team and a police officer, killed by members of Palestinian terrorist group Black September. After a delay, the games went ahead, serving as a reminder that while many don't want sports and politics to mix, it's actually impossible to ever separate them.

For Australia, 1972 saw the spectacular arrival of Shane Gould. She was just fifteen and the year before she had broken every world record in freestyle, from the 100 to the 1500 metres. Talk about overachieving. At fifteen, I was trying to figure out how to not appear awkward all the time, something I've never truly mastered.

So impressive were Gould's feats that some of the women in the USA swim team wore t-shirts that said 'All that glitters is not Gould'. There's nothing more American sports culture than trying to intimidate a fifteen-year-old schoolgirl. This is a nation whose athletes celebrate every play like they've won the Super Bowl, making the actual celebrations when a team wins the Super Bowl rather anti-climactic.

Gould did glitter gold, winning the 200-metre individual medley, the 200-metre freestyle and the 400-metre freestyle. She retired from competitive swimming at seventeen, hating life in the public eye. She was like a reverse reality TV star: had talent, didn't want attention.

1976 MONTREAL

Montreal was the disaster we had to have, with only five medals coming home and none of them gold. The utter failure of this Olympic team galvanised the Australian government, who responded with the kind of focus and effort usually reserved for wars. Let's move on, this still upsets me and I need to go eat ice-cream.*

1980 MOSCOW

It's hard to imagine now, but in 1980 there was a lot of tension between Russia and the West. Much of it stemmed from Russia's invasion of Afghanistan, a country that has had no problems since. Due to that invasion and a host of other issues, several nations boycotted the Olympics. There was enormous pressure on Australia to not send a team, but the decision was made that sport is more important than war. The decision wasn't an easy one. The federal government placed enormous pressure on the AOC and the individual sports to boycott the Moscow games. However, the AOC, in a close vote, decided a junket was still a junket, even if it was within the evil empire, and so they went.

The decision was not a popular one and many key athletes stayed at home. Entire sports, like equestrian, sailing and hockey, withdrew teams. The reduced Australian team did not perform well, with just

---

* If you really must do it yourself, you can read about it in all its miserable detail on page 34.

nine medals returning home. Considering the United States, Japan and West Germany were all absent, that was not a great effort.

This was certainly a bad period for Australia at the Olympics and everything seemed to go wrong. The *Empire Strikes Back* period, I like to call it. Oh, Montreal is totally those awful prequels George Lucas did. Montreal was the Jar Jar Binks of Olympics for Australia.

1984 LOS ANGELES

The commies returned the favour at Los Angeles, with fourteen Eastern Bloc countries not attending. It was their loss, as Lionel Richie performed a nine-minute rendition of 'All Night Long' at the closing ceremony. No wonder communism collapsed.

Australia had their best Olympic result in a while, securing four gold medals. Dean Lukin, the South Australian tuna fisherman (Australian law requires me to mention that), won Australia's only ever Olympic gold medal in weightlifting. Armchair experts around the country were momentarily interested in weightlifting.

But while the overall team result was an improvement on recent games, New Zealand won twice as many gold medals as Australia, meaning all Australians felt a deep sense of shame that previously only Rugby Union delivered.

1988 SEOUL

In a less than ideal start, live doves were released during the opening ceremony in Seoul as a symbol of world peace only for a number of them to be burned alive by the lighting of the Olympic cauldron. This was a more realistic portrayal of geopolitical attempts at world peace.

Australians won three gold medals in Seoul, with Debbie Flintoff-King winning the 400-metre hurdles, Duncan Armstrong the 200-metre freestyle and the Hockeyroos were the first-ever

Australian women's team to win Olympic gold. With thirteen medals won in all, the Australians were hardly back to their very best, but that was all about to change.

1992 BARCELONA

In Barcelona the hard work and the investment that had followed Montreal began to pay dividends. Not only did the Australians win twenty-seven medals, seven of them gold, new stars emerged, like Kieren Perkins, who won the 1500-metre freestyle and reminded us that we are kind of good at this swimming thing. The Oarsome Foursome, the best rowing crew in the world, also emerged at these Olympics, winning the coxless four, while Kathy Watt won the women's cycling road race. Even the sleeping giant of Australian sport, canoeing, brought home gold, with Clint Robinson winning the men's K-1 1000 metres.

Australia was back at last, with their best medal haul since the 1956 Melbourne Olympics. It had only taken sixteen years and hundreds of millions of dollars to do it.

1996 ATLANTA

While the Atlanta Olympics were one of the worst Olympics ever (mainly because they were in Atlanta), Australia had one of their greatest games ever. Given that Sydney would be hosting the 2000 games, the pressure was on to perform and perform they did. Forty-one medals came home, nine of them good ones, the most medals an Australian team had ever won and enough to see Australia finish seventh on the medal tally. Kieren Perkins again won gold in the 1500 metres and the Oarsome Foursome defended their title too.

Susie O'Neill won the women's 200-metre butterfly, condemning her to a life of being called 'Madame Butterfly'. The Hockeyroos again won gold and, in the sport of shooting, Michael Diamond and Russell Mark won golds.

Perhaps most surprisingly of all, 'The Woodies', Todd Wood-bridge and Mark Woodforde, won gold in the doubles tennis, even though tennis has no place in the Olympics.

In his closing speech IOC President Juan Antonio Samaranch said, 'Well done, Atlanta' and called the games 'most exceptional'. This broke with precedent as he had previously called each iteration 'the best Olympics ever'. It was a bit like a parent telling one of their children that they liked them but didn't love them, and made people wonder if General Sherman had had the right idea.

2000 SYDNEY

Reeling from the awfulness of Atlanta, the Olympic movement desperately needed a good games. They got even more than that, with the Sydney Olympics being the greatest event humankind has ever held, just taking top spot from the Deniliquin Ute Muster.

2004 ATHENS

The Athens Olympics left Greece with a monumental financial hang-over that not even a Berocca and some hash browns from Maccas could fix. Australia's performance was one of its best ever, finishing fourth on the medal tally with fifty medals, seventeen of them gold. When you consider Russia and China were above us, we were second on the clean medal tally.

The Kookaburras, our men's hockey team, finally achieved gold, meaning they could now look the women's team in the eye. Ian Thorpe won two more gold medals, giving him five in total. Grant Hackett also got the job done in the 1500-metre freestyle. Our cyclists performed well, with Anna Meares winning Australia's first ever women's track cycling gold.

There was, however, a lowlight among all the high-fiving. In the final of the women's eight, Australia was three seconds behind the lead when Sally Robbins stopped rowing and lay back on the teammate behind her. Australia finished last. Her teammates were furious, believing she had simply given up. The Australian media labelled her 'Lay-down Sally' and a nationwide campaign of public shaming followed.

'Lay-down Sally-gate' was a reminder of the pressure elite athletes are under. Australians demand athletic excellence, even if we are one of the most obese countries in the world.

2008 BEIJING

Australia's strong performances continued in Beijing, with forty-six medals in total, fourteen of them gold. Steve Hooker surprised everyone by winning gold in the pole vault, mainly because most Australians know nothing about the pole vault. Hooker's outstanding performance, a rare gold medal in track and field for Australia, unfortunately also disproved my theory that it's bad luck to have redheads on the team. Oh well, you have to respect the data.

Matthew Mitcham surprised the Chinese by winning gold in the men's 10-metre platform, the only diving gold medal the Chinese didn't win. I was surprised they allowed him to leave the country with it.

However, these games were all about Stephanie Rice, who won three golds and set three world records. It was the sort of swimming performance Australia seems to throw up fairly regularly. And, if that wasn't enough, in 2013 Rice won season 3 of *The Celebrity Apprentice Australia*. Most people don't even get one dream that comes true in their lives.

2012 LONDON

The success of the London Olympics (thirty-five medals, eight of them gold) was marred by off-field problems and the failure of some favourites. In many ways, the Australian public had become used to success again, so any decline was seen as a crisis.

Anna Meares cemented herself as a cycling great, with a gold in the women's sprint, while Sally Pearson won the women's 100-metre hurdles in a heroic effort under a lot of pressure.

But it was the swim team that received the most coverage, and not for good reasons. Their result was Australia's worst since Barcelona in 1992, with just one gold medal and ten medals overall. Two post-games inquiries revealed that swimmers breached team rules regarding alcohol, prescription drugs, bullying and team curfews, with one report describing the team as 'culturally toxic'.

Six swimmers from the men's relay team (James Magnussen, Eamon Sullivan, Matt Targett, James Roberts, Tommaso D'Orsogna and Cameron McEvoy) had a bonding session in Manchester, where they harassed female team members by door-knocking and making prank calls. All six were accused of taking sleeping tablets, with only Roberts denying that he did. When head swimming coach Leigh Nugent was made aware of it, he did nothing, and morale plummeted. The 'Stilnox Six', as they became known, failed to perform in the pool. The fallout was so great that the top levels of Swimming Australia were cleaned out after the games.

2016 RIO

Perhaps the greatest performance by an Australian at the Rio Olympics was that of Chef de Mission Kitty Chiller, who managed to get in front of any TV camera faster than Usain Bolt. Chiller was everywhere, the very public face of the team and making a big deal of the tough line she was taking towards the athletes, basically overcorrecting for the lack of discipline in London.

That would have been fine if the team didn't then underperform, winning just twenty-nine medals, only eight of them gold. Before the games, the team had been predicted to win as many as sixteen gold medals. It was a failure that Chiller acknowledged: 'When you underperform in elite sport the blame game always follows. I'm not interested in the blame game.' Which is what the people who are to blame always say. The person who had run around spouting off about discipline and accountability was now telling everyone that they weren't interested in accountability.

The fallout from these games continued, with the head of the AOC, John Coates, and the head of the Australian Sport Commission, John Wylie, having public shouting matches as the debate rages about how to turn around Australia's Olympic malaise. Again.

On the positive side, no one got Zika virus in Rio.

PARALYMPICS

Australia has gone to every Summer Paralympics since the event began in 1960, and we've attended the Winter Paralympics since 1980. Success was high from early on, with the 1960 team of twelve athletes winning three gold, six silver and one bronze.

The Paralympic movement in Australia had no overarching body until 1990, when the Australian Paralympic Committee was established. The impetus for this was that it looked pretty bad to not have a peak body when the country was bidding for the 2000 Olympics and Paralympics.

Australia's Paralympians certainly deserve every bit of support, having done the country proud to an astounding degree; In the all-time medal tally for the Summer Paralympics, Australia is fourth, compared to eighth in the Summer Olympics. We've also produced some of the greatest Paralympians ever, such as swimmer Matthew Cowdrey, who has won thirteen Paralympic gold medals and twenty-three Paralympic medals overall. Anything over ten is just showing off I'd say.

Daphne Hilton is a personal favourite, because she won fourteen medals in five different sports. She won two in archery, five in athletics and swimming, one in table tennis and another in wheelchair fencing. That's a pretty diverse set of skills to master – I get confused between the remote for the TV and AppleTV.

The first Indigenous athlete to represent Australia at the Paralympics was Kevin Coombs, a wheelchair basketballer, who attended the inaugural Rome 1960 Paralympic Games. More recently, one Paralympian stands out above all others as perhaps our greatest ever: Louise Sauvage. Sauvage won nine gold medals in wheelchair racing, two of them at the Sydney Paralympics. As well as Paralympic success, Sauvage won four Boston Marathons. In one Boston Marathon, she came fourth despite having a tyre puncture. When you can come fourth with a blown tyre, you're probably a bit too good at your chosen sport.

Slowly, the Paralympics have built a better profile in Australia, but it still lags significantly behind the Olympics. It works best when athletes have a public profile, like Sauvage and more recently Kurt Fearnley. As well as being a multiple gold medallist, Fearnley is a great public speaker, both inspiring and funny. For sports to be followed, people have to care about the individuals involved, and for that they need to know about them. That's the path ahead for the Paralympians.

WINTER OLYMPICS

The Winter Olympics have always been a secondary consideration for us. Snow is kind of important in the Winter Olympics, and it's in limited supply in Australia. We don't win very much, which makes us feel small, so we pretend they're not that important. Luckily for us, global warming should mean the Winter Olympics won't be around much longer.

Australia first competed in the Winter Olympic Games in 1936 in Garmisch-Partenkirchen in Germany, and has competed in every games since, except the 1948 Games, which proved too difficult so soon after the war. It wasn't until 1994 that Australia won its first medal at the Winter Olympics, in the ice-skating short-track relay team, a bronze.

The breakthrough came in 2002, when Australia won its first ever gold at the winter games. It's our most famous one too, because it involved our opponents stuffing up, which often makes for the sweetest victory. Steven Bradbury delivered that precious gold, in the men's short-track 1000 meters at Salt Lake City in 2002. Easily the slowest skater in the final, Bradbury decided to hang back and wait for any chaos to occur. He was well off the pace when all four of his opponents crashed on the final corner, letting him scrape through to victory. Australians now refer to anything good that falls into their laps as 'doing a Bradbury'. In fairness to Bradbury, he was a worthy winner, having overcome countless hardships, including almost dying on the ice when an opponent's skate sliced open his thigh, causing him to lose four litres of blood. Just being in the final was an amazing accomplishment.

The Winter Olympics have certainly grown in profile in Australia, but to put it in context, in its entire history Australia has won just twelve Winter Olympic medals – five gold, three silver and four bronze.

COMMONWEALTH GAMES

The Commonwealth Games are a glimpse into a parallel universe where none of the good countries show up to the Olympics. Australian athletes have a long, proud history of dominating the Commonwealth Games and the Australian public have a long, proud history of being only vaguely interested. They're like a not-very-good movie you stumble onto on TV one night but because it's got that actor in it from another show you like, you watch it anyway.

The first Commonwealth Games were held in 1911 as part of the coronation of King George V. They were then known as the Festival of Empire. It took until 1930 for another Empire games to be held. Over the years, the name for this competition between countries that make up the Commonwealth has been changed several times, mainly because 'Empire' seemed to convey the killing and subjugation of large groups of non-white populations, which has become super awkward for people these days, especially from a branding standpoint.

Australia has hosted the Commonwealth Games four times and will host them again in 2018 on the Gold Coast, providing another reason not to go to the Gold Coast. The Commonwealth Games as a whole are under threat as the Commonwealth becomes less and less relevant. The 2022 games were awarded to Durban in South Africa because no one else wanted them, and even they have recently threatened to pull out of hosting them.

ATHLETICS

Athletics competitions, especially running, have existed in Australia for a very long time, with the Indigenous population participating in a range of athletic pursuits. The earliest record of the colonists holding races was at Hyde Park in 1810, where sprints were held. At that event a 50-metre sprint was won by the wonderfully named Dicky Dowling.

Because no equipment was needed, the ease of holding races meant 'pedestrianism', as athletics was then called, spread across the country. It made sense that this popular sport needed some co-ordination and the *Sydney Morning Herald* reported on 20 May 1887 that 'a meeting of members of amateur athletics clubs and of persons interested in the formation of an amateur athletics association' had been held, leading to the creation of the Amateur Athletic Association of NSW.

Ten years later, a national governing body, the Athletic Union of Australasia, was formed to govern the sport. It also oversaw athletics in New Zealand until 1928, when the Kiwis decided that they would focus purely on Rugby Union and adapting Tolkien novels for the screen.

The Amateur Athletics Union of Australia, as it became known, was not that excited about women doing athletic things, so in 1932, an Australian Women's Amateur Athletics Union was set up. In 1978, the two bodies were combined in what later became Athletics Australia, and in 1999 the organisation adopted a 'corporate board', with the directors independent of the various member associations.

None of this has delivered good governance, however. In thirty years there have been seven reviews of the sport. The 1989 version said it all – it was called *Change or Die*.

The Buchanan Review in 2015 reported that athletics was dysfunctional in every possible way – governance, management, high performance, competition and the coaching structure all would need major reform. A perfect score. The report recommended the ASC withhold 40 per cent of funding to force change, but the ASC didn't want to risk Australia's performance at the 2016 Rio Olympics.

One of the interesting storylines of the review was that lawyer David Grace, Athletics Australia's president at the time, was representing the Essendon players in their case against ASADA. Grace didn't last long as president and was replaced by former federal minister for sport, Mark Arbib. Arbib must have realised that the junkets in Olympic sports dwarfed those in politics and made the jump.

In his new role Arbib supported AOC President John Coates's re-election bid, despite widespread reports of bullying under Coates's leadership. Coates's right-hand man and media director Mike Tancred once rang then chief executive Fiona de Jong, after she made a complaint about him, and she claims he told her, 'Fiona, withdraw the complaint or I will bury you.' Athletics may well be more competitive off the field than on.

SWIMMING

Swimming has long been linked with Australia's love of the beach, with many of the early Australian swimming champions, like Cecil Healy, also being lifesavers. Healy won gold and silver medals at the 1912 Olympic Games in Stockholm but he also invented 'side breathing' in swimming. I guess before that most competitive swimmers either drowned or races were over very short distances. In February 1906 the first surf lifesaving club in the world was set up at Bondi Beach, and the following year the New South Wales Surf Bathing Association was founded (now Surf Life Saving Australia). To stop people drowning, you had to be a handy swimmer yourself, and Australia started to produce a lot of elite swimmers.

In the early days of swimming, there were all types of strokes. Reading up on the strange combinations makes you wonder why more people didn't drown. From this mishmash of strokes emerged the Australian Crawl, now known as freestyle. The stroke came from Alick Wickham, a Solomon Islander who visited Australia in 1898 and used a 'crawl stroke'. Members of the Cavil family, who were all pioneers in Australia's early swimming scene, saw Wickham swim and Arthur 'Tums' Cavill was credited with making some modifications to it and creating the stroke used in freestyle races today.

Early on, swimming administrators spent huge amounts of time on strange debates and rules. Like the fact that swimming in the surf in daylight hours was illegal until 1902, or the debate about whether women and men could swim at the same time. Mixed bathing was a hot-button issues in the nineteenth and early twentieth century, as was bathing attire, with men wanting women to swim in hessian sacks, before settling for neck-to-toe woollen suits. One group that wasn't controversial for administrators was Indigenous people; they were just banned outright from the many swimming baths on the NSW coast.

Swimming clubs began springing up in the 1860s and by 1909 the Amateur Swimming Union of Australia was set up to govern the sport nationally. In 1985, with Olympic athletes increasingly professional, the AMSU decide the word 'amateur' should be dropped from their name and they became Australian Swimming Incorporated. From that point on, the only amateurish stuff would be the administration's running of the sport.[*]

The biggest issue swimming has had to deal with is the Royal Commission into Institutional Responses to Child Sexual Abuse, which investigated their responses to allegations of child sexual abuse against swimming coaches Scott Volkers, Terrence Buck and Stephen Roser. The royal commission found Swimming Australia had not handled all three matters well, leading Swimming Australia president John Bertrand to issue an 'unreserved' apology to victims of sexual abuse over the past twenty years. It reflects the seriousness of sports administrations' responsibility and the huge risk factor

---

[*] In 2004, they renamed themselves Swimming Australia because someone in marketing hadn't done anything for a while and knew that just switching the order of the words would create years of work for them to do.

that all sports must now manage, especially as they seek to control the 'pathways' from junior sport to the professional level.

Swimming Australia has had other issues, the Silnox Six incident at the London Olympics being the poster child for the divisions that have rocked the senior team on a regular basis. In 2013, then president Barclay Nettlefold resigned amid allegations he made inappropriate comments in two separate incidents. In one incident, it is alleged he told staff to refer to him as 'donkey' in reference to the size of his genitals. Perhaps 'donkey' is a good descriptor, but not in the way he meant.

Following the Rio Olympics, Swimming Australia had to defend itself as the team underperformed once again, despite receiving $37.9 million to prepare. That's the problem with being the golden sport of the Australian Olympic team, the higher the highs, the lower the lows.

HORSERACING

SPORT OF KINGS AND DEGENERATE GAMBLERS

Horseracing; it's not just a way to launder money, it's also the sport of kings. Since the very start of colonisation, Australians have loved it. It's probably our favourite and least successful investment scheme.

For our population size, Australia has possibly the biggest racing industry in the world. And it's not just degenerate gamblers that follow it . . . alright, it has mostly been degenerate gamblers, but there are casual punters too. And yes, you are correct, no one would like horseracing if it wasn't for the gambling. How do we know this? I mean, it's so obvious it barely needs to be proven, but when South Australia did ban gambling on racing in 1883 their industry pretty much died overnight.

Yet despite the constant gambling, there is something magical about horseracing, especially if you can get past the awkwardness of some of the horses being horribly injured and then killed, which most Australians seem able to do pretty easily once they've got enough alcohol in them.

AND THEY'RE OFF

Horseracing is one of Australia's oldest sports and certainly its most colourful. Horses arrived with the First Fleet and were looked after better than the convicts, which is only fair considering the horses hadn't committed any crimes.

These were workhorses, but there is evidence people raced them anyway. From the late eighteenth century actual racehorses were being imported as part of the unofficial 'Turn Australia Into England' policy. By 1810, Australia had its first three-day carnival of horseracing and, in a familiar pattern, there was lots going on that had nothing to do with horseracing. It was held at Hyde Park in Sydney, with the support of the governor, and featured balls and official dinners.

Over the next few decades the sport exploded in popularity. In1825, the Sydney Turf Club (STC) was formed to organise race days and to give the wealthy colonists a club they could join to show they were better than everyone else. In a further sign that racing was growing in popularity, in 1833 the government put aside land at Randwick for a racecourse.

By 1842, the Australian Jockey Club (AJC) was formed and one of its first priorities was to make sure jockeys wore proper uniforms; men do care about fashion, but only when it relates to sport. The AJC controlled racing in New South Wales and, with an enclosed track and proper grandstands at Randwick, they could generate funds to underwrite a lot of the sport.

With New South Wales conquered very quickly, it did not take long for the practice of putting a really small person on a massive horse and making them ride it at dangerous speeds to spread across the colonies.

MONEY!

While NSW was undoubtedly the leader of the sport early on, the gold rush that supercharged Victorian Rules did the same for horseracing. Not only did the population surge in the Victorian colony, some people actually found gold. Victoria's economy boomed. The strange thing about money is that people who've fought really hard to get it then seem to go out of their way to find ways to spend it, and this is where horseracing comes into play.

Two clubs, the Victoria Turf Club and the Victoria Jockey Club, were the beneficiaries of this booming economy. They offered the most prize money in the colonies, drawing the centre of racing away from New South Wales. This

> ### DID YOU KNOW?
> ℘
> Investing in racehorses is a surefire way to make money.

also enabled the Australian industry to start importing better and better bloodstock.

It was on the back of this boom that, in 1861, the Victorian Turf Club introduced a two-mile handicap race called the Melbourne Cup. You may have heard of it.

THE MELBOURNE CUP

Melbourne's spring racing carnival is known for people getting dressed up, going to the track, falling down drunk and never seeing a single horse. Generations of Australians have gotten spectacularly drunk while sort of watching the Melbourne Cup.

The first Melbourne Cup was run on 7 November 1861. It was a handicap race, meaning the better horses carried extra weight to make the race more equal.* Four thousand people attended the first Melbourne Cup and watched Archer, a horse from New South Wales, take home the cup, the prize money and a gold watch. The fact that Archer won the first race and then backed it up by winning again the very next year considerably increased national interest in the race.

---

* Like how if you're good at your job, your boss asks you to do way more work than your idiot colleagues who stuff everything up.

By 1877, the race was so successful that the first Tuesday in November was declared a public holiday in Melbourne, perhaps the surest sign that Melburnians are mad. The public holiday turned out to be a masterstroke, swelling crowds to as many as 150 000 people. Considering the population of Melbourne at the time was 280 000, that made the Melbourne Cup a force beyond racing. It was the social event of the year and has pretty much stayed that way ever since.

From its earliest days, the Melbourne Cup was the place to be seen and to drink more than you should. No less a visitor than Mark Twain attended in 1895. Twain wrote about the Cup with great enthusiasm and captured the hold the race had on the nation:

> The Melbourne Cup is the Australasian National Day. It would be difficult to overstate its importance. It overshadows all other holidays and specialised days of whatever sort in that congeries of colonies. Overshadows them? I might almost say it blots them out [. . .] every man and woman, of high degree or low, who can afford the expense, put away their other duties and come. They begin to swarm in by ship and rail a fortnight before the day, and they swarm thicker and thicker day after day, until all the vehicles of transportation are taxed to their uttermost to meet the demands of the occasion, and all hotels and lodgings are bulging outward because of the pressure from within.

Part of the appeal of the race nationally was the development of the 'sweep'. People enter a lottery where everyone gets allocated a horse at random and the winner collects the pooled prize money. Sweeps became so popular that they now occur in homes and workplaces across the country, even where the Melbourne Cup is not a public holiday.

To win the Melbourne Cup is to enter the pantheon of great racehorses, with multiple winners becoming household names, like Archer, Phar Lap, Peter Pan, Rain Lover and Think Big. Between 2003 and 2005, Makybe Diva won three Melbourne Cups in a row, making her one of the most famous horses in global racing history.

The Melbourne Cup is a true institution, a day when every Australian can realise their birthright: to lose money punting on a racehorse.

AN INDUSTRY

By the late nineteenth century horseracing was popular enough to become an industry more than an amateur pursuit. Most colonies had organising clubs, with the South Australian Jockey Club formed in 1850, the Western Australian Turf Club in 1852 and the Queensland Turf Club in 1863. In 1864, the Victorian Jockey Club and the Victorian Turf Club merged to form the powerful Victorian Racing Club (VRC). The formation of these clubs meant racing employed more and more people, and the integration of the clubs with the elite of the colonies made them a source of political and economic power.

Therefore, by the start of the twentieth century, horseracing had gotten to the point where it needed consistency. Most racetracks had very few facilities. Often tracks did not have a fence around them and, like the early days of rugby and Australian Rules, pedestrians often wandered onto the track. Unlike unwittingly wandering onto a footy field, having a field of galloping horses bearing down on you was a more serious matter. Dogs were even worse, often running at horses and causing accidents. It was often the position of racecourses to shoot dogs on sight, with warning signs placed around the racetrack. The main problem with this was that, to my knowledge, dogs can't read.

The major race clubs got together in 1912 and accepted the Australian Rules of Racing as the supreme rules of racing in Australia, which at least gave trainers, jockeys and punters a consistent set of rules to find ways to circumvent. The major race clubs were controlled by committees and saw themselves as the upholders of a well-organised, regulated industry, focused on the purest racing with thoroughbreds. They viewed themselves as custodians of what was an industry, run by gentlemen, with the proceeds being reinvested into the industry. Others simply saw the opportunity to make money.

THE PONIES

'Proprietary tracks' were privately owned racetracks that saw the racing of 'ponies', horses 14.2-hands and smaller.* These tracks were aimed at the working class, with as many races as possible jammed into each race day to increase the amount of betting.

Controlled by individuals and with a focus on gambling, these tracks attracted all sorts of unsavoury characters and were where the terms 'colourful racing identity' and 'high profile Sydney business man' originated. Both Sydney and Melbourne had them. In Victoria there were proprietary tracks like Moonee Valley, Brighton, Sherwood Park, Oakleigh Park, Mordialloc, Mentone, Epsom, Dandenong, Melton, Wyndham and Cranbourne. In Sydney these courses emerged at places like Victoria Park, Kensington, Rosebery and Ascot. Other states had them too, but to a lesser extent.

These racetracks outraged the non-proprietary clubs like the VRC and the AJC, who felt they sullied the highbrow nature of thoroughbred racing. It was a pure clash of the elite and the lower

---

* The 'hand' unit of measurement has been standardised to be exactly 4 inches, because imperial measurement is so much more intuitive and straightforward.

classes. The ponies were a target for the thoroughbred industry and the clubs as they were seen to bring negative attention to the sport, while anti-gambling forces saw the ponies as a more vulnerable target than the well-connected clubs.

Perhaps most famously, John Wren* drew a lot of attention to the proprietary clubs, with his courses at Ascot, Richmond and Fitzroy attracting the ire of the racing fraternity, in part because of their refusal to accept the rules of the major clubs, including ignoring the VRC. The proprietary clubs didn't reinvest profits back into the industry, they just went into the owner's pocket. Since most of the people who ran clubs like the VRC were already rich, they found this practice distasteful; it's only wealthy people who find other people getting rich distasteful.

Around the country, a collection of thoroughbred racing interests and anti-gambling forces brought pressure against these clubs, with the Victorian government introducing the *Police Offences (Race Meeting) Act 1929,* which forced the closure of Richmond, Fitzroy, Aspendale and Sandown Park from 31 July 1931.

Stanley Argyle, soon to be premier, said during the parliamentary debate that a class of parasites had sprung up around proprietary clubs:

> Such people never worked, but wandered from one race meeting to another living on the confiding public. Members of the underworld were also attracted to some meetings. Employers complained that their work was upset very frequently by the number of weekday race meetings for sporting workmen very

---

* Wren was an underworld figure whose life inspired the bestselling book *Power without Glory*. His illegal gambling operations funded a variety of business, of varying legality, spread across thirty-one companies. He had his hand in all types of sports, from cycling to horseracing to Australian Rules. Perhaps his greatest crime was being a major benefactor of the Collingwood Football Club.

often neglected their work to attend meetings when
it would be better for themselves and their wives and
families if they attended to their jobs.

In Sydney the fight was similar, the AJC doing everything in its
power to weaken the position of the ponies, usually by lobbying for a decrease in the amount of days they could hold races on.
By the time of World War II, the pony races were in deep trouble and
the premier, William McKell, was determined to end them entirely.
McKell viewed the pony races as an exploitation of the working
class and used the war as a chance to push through the Sydney Turf
Club Act in 1943.

The act created the Sydney Turf Club, and put the proprietary
courses under their auspices, including the power to wind them up
or use them for thoroughbred racing. It was a huge move and if
there hadn't been a war going on it may have caused public outrage. Following the war, the racing industry in Australia was all
thoroughbred racing, controlled by non-proprietary clubs and with
close links to legislators around the country.

THE GREATEST AUSTRALIAN FROM NEW ZEALAND

Phar Lap may have been the greatest Australian that ever lived,
despite the fact he was a horse and was actually from New
Zealand – trivial details. Like a souvlaki van at 3 a.m., Phar Lap was
there when people needed him most, during the Great Depression.
He was born in 1926 and won thirty-seven of his fifty-one races,
winning a lot of people a lot of money, something that will endear
you to anyone.

Phar Lap was known to have a massive heart. In fact, it weighed
6.2 kilograms; you won't need telling that a normal horse's heart
weighs 3.2 kilograms. It's become part of the Australian vernacular to say someone has 'a heart as big as Phar Lap's' but that

would actually be concerning, with the human heart only weighing between 250 to 350 grams. If you have a heart as big as Phar Lap's you should go to hospital immediately. An enlarged heart is nothing to laugh about.

Phar Lap won on all four days of the 1930 Flemington Spring Carnival. At one stage he was up to fourteen wins in a row. It was soon decided he would be sent to Mexico to race in the Agua Caliente Handicap, at the time the richest race in the world. He died on his way there, in San Francisco, in suspicious circumstances.

There were many who believe Phar Lap was poisoned by American gangsters, who feared the champion would unleash massive losses on their betting operations. An autopsy revealed his stomach and intestines were severely inflamed, which gives the theory credence. There have been tests since that suggest he digested a large amount of arsenic in the hours before his death, but in those days a lot of horses were given arsenic in tonics as a matter of course. Making a tonic with arsenic in it seems counterintuitive but these were simpler times.

Either way, Phar Lap's death was mourned more than that of most humans and he was awarded the greatest honour a New Zealander can receive: he was claimed as an Australian.

DECLINE

Phar Lap's era was a high point for the racing industry and not long after, World War II severely disrupt horseracing across the country. After the war, crowds did not return in the same numbers. Horseracing competed more and more with other sports and forms of entertainment, and radio and the advent of television meant people were able to follow the races off track, often with punters betting illegally.*

---

* See page 60 for a full history of sports gambling in Australia. Spoiler: government and big corporations ended up using it to make heaps of money off poor people.

The race clubs tried to win back the crowds, with the VRC hosting a Fashions on the Field competition in 1962 to try to increase the sport's appeal. This was the start of a big focus on the non-racing aspects of racing, which is an odd way to promote a sport. In many ways it worked, but only for big events like the Spring Carnival. As off-track betting became legal and satellite TV bought racing to TABs around the country, people increasingly stayed away from the track itself.

The racing clubs tried to appeal more to TV audiences than the crowds at the track, holding midweek race meetings to fit into a national schedule of racing. That's not to say racing wasn't still a very successful industry, it was – if you consider it a success to provide content for people to bet on. For most of the year racing is irrelevant to most Australians, except then they all annoyingly become experts when the first Tuesday in November comes around.

As a result, many racing clubs have merged in recent years. The sport has become more consolidated around a national calendar that's driven by TV schedules and betting markets. For example, the Australian Jockey Club and the Sydney Turf Club merged in 2011 to create the Australian Turf Club (ATC).

Now racing faces an interesting future. It's so heavily linked to gambling, and the rise of online gambling has led to questions being asked about the lack of regulation around betting in all sports. On top of that, horses dying is seen as a real downer. Campaigns against the mistreatment of horses and the sport as a whole have increased. These challenges mean that, unlike human-based sports, horseracing could face an uncertain future at the hands of government regulation.

FINE COTTON AND OTHER CONTROVERSIES

Racing folk have shown a level of artistry and creativity in fixing races that matches the painters of the Renaissance. From whips with electric shocks in them to doping, from painting horses to trap-doors, there's a good reason many suspect horseracing isn't on the level: the constant evidence that it isn't on the level.

I have so many favourite racing scams that one book can contain only a fraction. One of my favourites happened in 1939, when Harry Solomon called a race in Melbourne on 3XY – after cutting the wires to the other radio stations – and in his made-up version of the race, the horse he had put money on won the race. His 'winner' was a horse called Buoyancy, which was paying 6 to 1. Solomon was investigated, after all there had been an actual race run and people saw it, but he had skipped the country. He was found about six months later in Fiji and brought home to serve six months in jail.

Another favourite was when in 1955 a long shot, Thundering Legion, saw a massive betting plunge in its favour. The chief steward confronted the jockey and snatched his whip, only to get an electronic shock. The jockey, Bill Attrill, admitted to giving electric shocks to the horses he was riding to help him win. He was kicked out of racing for ten years.

While electrocuting horses is something most people frown upon, this next scam at least showed a level of creativity you can admire. In 1903, a horse called Gentleman Jim was given huge odds due to carrying a lot of weight. The horse was owned by Jim 'The Grafter' Kingsley, one of those colourful racing identities Australia specialises in. After winning the race, Kingsley was told by the steward that the jockey was 13 kilograms light. Kingsley said this couldn't be true and stamped the floor. They weighed the jockey again and he was found to be at the correct weight. The stewards, however, decided to inspect the scales and found a trapdoor underneath that revealed a boy holding a 13-kilogram weight. Other scales were inspected where Gentleman Jim had previously raced, revealing similar set-ups. Just imagine if these people had devoted themselves to doing good.

Perhaps the most famous racing scam was the Fine Cotton affair, known mostly for its farcical execution. Fine Cotton was a horse that raced in Queensland. It wasn't particularly good. The syndicate that owned it came up with the grand plan of getting an identical horse called Dashing Solitaire, which was much better, racing it as Fine Cotton, and betting big on it winning at long odds.

Here's where things get tricky. When Dashing Solitaire was injured, the syndicate decided to buy a horse called Bold Personality to race as the ring-in instead. Bold Personality was a lot better than Fine Cotton but unfortunately it was also a completely different colour, which was not ideal for the scam. This was probably the moment to pull up stumps, but what the syndicate lacked in brains they made up for with commitment.

They decided the sensible thing to do was dye the horse's hair using off-the-shelf human hair dye. This was not a fit-for-purpose solution and the results were literally and figuratively patchy. Even worse, on the day of the race they remembered that Fine Cotton had some white markings on its rear legs and they decided a bit of white paint would sort that out.

On the day of the race, betting markets across the country began to put a lot of money on 'Fine Cotton', slightly weird for a horse racing in a minor race in Queensland, especially one that was a massive outsider. Despite suspicions, the race was run and 'Fine Cotton' won narrowly.

Immediately after the race an investigation was launched. By the time the horse was taken to be weighed, the paint was starting to run. A request for Fine Cotton's trainer to show the horse's registrations papers resulted in him fleeing the course, another subtle hint that something was up.

Not long after that 'Fine Cotton' was disqualified and the syndicate lost all the money it had put on the ring-in. The official inquiry resulted in six people being banned for life, and Bill and

Robbie Waterhouse were banned for fourteen years due to having prior knowledge of the scam.

Robbie is the husband of prominent trainer Gai Waterhouse, and his son Tom Waterhouse had an online gambling business, where Robbie was a company director before it was sold to a big British bookmaker. That's the thing about the racing industry, it's so insular that people don't even raise an eyebrow at all that.

That's the wonder of horseracing: power, money and people with questionable morals, all gilded with glamour.

TENNIS

It might be hard to imagine now, but Australia once dominated tennis. Yes, before players made it their priority to embarrass us internationally, Australians won everything, then they didn't, then they occasionally did and now we're back to winning not a lot.

Tennis came to Australia after its invention in England in the 1870s. The people of the colonies were excited to have a new sport to beat England at and took to it with relish. However, poor quality courts and equipment meant it didn't really take off in Australia until after World War I.

Early on it was a social game, perfect for having a casual hit because it required fewer people than the football codes and less space than something like golf. You can also play a decent game while holding a beer, an important consideration for Australians.

Tennis began as a sport for the well-off. Grass courts require a lot of maintenance and while I just get my staff to mow mine, I know that's not possible for poor people. Clay courts were the solution that made tennis accessible to more Australians. They were called ant bed courts in most parts of the country, except in Victoria, where they called them *en tout cas* (French for 'in any case'), further proof that Victorians lead the country in pretentiousness. While the clay court was the great equaliser and allowed tennis to spread both across the country and classes, at the top level of the game lawn remained the preferred surface.

EARLY ORGANISATION

While state-based associations sprung up towards the end of the nineteenth century, the International Lawn Tennis Challenge (which was renamed the Davis Cup quite quickly), was the catalyst for Australia getting organised. It was decided that New Zealand and Australia would send a joint team. I don't know why; I can only assume it was out of pity.

As a result, in 1904 the Australasian Lawn Tennis Association (ALTA) was formed, with a view to also conducting a national championship, similar to the opens in other parts of the world. It was another example of Australia being an early adopter of international sport despite its remoteness. It also made the ALTA one of twelve national associations that established the International Lawn Tennis Federation (ILTF). The joint Australian and New Zealand team was be incredibly successful, winning the Davis Cup in 1907, 1908, 1909, 1911, 1914 and 1919.

In 1922, the New Zealanders decided to walk away from the partnership so they could represent their own country, much like they did with the joint Olympic team. Not only were they no longer part of the Davis Cup team, they were also no longer joint hosts of the Australasian Championships, which later became the Australian Open. It was a great move for them because the New Zealand Open is such a huge event.[*]

Australia's interest in tennis was boosted by Norm Brookes winning the Wimbledon singles title in 1907. He won the Australasian Championship in 1911 and was a big part of the organisation of

---

[*] Note to self: check if there is a New Zealand Open or if they still play tennis over there.

that event, and won Wimbledon again in 1914. He was the best tennis player in the world around these times and did a lot to make the sport popular, including serving as president of the Australian Lawn Tennis Association from 1926 to 1955, shaping tennis in Australia more than any other individual.

AUSTRALIAN OPEN

As an impartial observer, the Australian Open is the greatest of all the grand slams. It is friendlier than the US Open, has fewer English people in attendance than Wimbledon and significantly benefits from not being the French Open.

Created in 1905 by the aforementioned ALTA, it was first known as the Australasian Men's Championship and was of course contested on grass. It was held in state capitals in Australia and New Zealand and struggled to attract people from other states, let alone other countries. Australia and New Zealand were just too remote.

When the New Zealanders left in 1922 it became an Australian-only event but still moved from city to city. It was renamed the Australian Championships in 1927. Women were allowed to play in the championship from 1922, tennis being seen as one of the few sports women were able to play without fainting instantly.

Major issues plagued the championship, even after air travel removed the logistical nightmare of getting to the matches. The ALTA decided hosting the tournament over the Christmas and New Year period was a really good idea, which meant many international and Australian players just boycotted the tournament. The prize money was low, so there was no real incentive to give up your Christmas break to play; basically, there were no penalty rates.

In 1969, reacting to a global sporting trend towards profession-alism, the championship decided to allow both professionals and amateurs to enter, renaming itself the Australian Open.

The ongoing move to professionalism and the cost of holding the tournament meant that in 1972 it was decided the Open should move to Melbourne permanently. Melbourne was chosen because it had always drawn the biggest crowds, Melburnians turning up to any sporting event with the enthusiasm of a herd of lemmings heading towards a cliff.

By the eighties the organisers woke up to the fact that the timing of the Open was a problem and moved it to mid-January, where it remains. The new timing might almost kill a few players each year because of the heat, but at least they show up now that they don't have to give up Christmas and New Year's for it.

The Open was played at the Kooyong Lawn Tennis Club until 1988, when the International Tennis Federation pointed out you couldn't hold a modern, international sporting event at what was basically a really big suburban tennis club. The state government responded by building Flinders Park next to the MCG. The move meant the end of grass, with a new surface, 'Rebound Ace', being

TENNIS TERMS

Ball kids: Kids who fetch balls and, if they're lucky, get to hold the players' sweaty towels. The tennis court is one of the last remaining places where child labour can be used.

Deuce: The French gave us this one. When both players are on 40, it's called 'deuce' because it is a 'deux de jeu' – two points to win the game. Those crazy French, it's like they've got a whole language of their own.

Love: In tennis scoring this means '0', and again we can thank those French. One theory is that it's from the word *l'oeuf*, which means 'the egg', as in, the shape of a zero. I told you they had all the words.

Sparring partner: Slang for hitting-practice partner, except when Bernard Tomic's father is involved, in which case it's more like a boxing sparring partner.

used. The new venue was a huge success as there was enough room for more people to attend, increasing the money going into the Open. Prize money was increased.

Rebound Ace was a popular surface, but after twenty years it was retired and replaced with a medium-pace surface called Plexicushion Prestige, which is a ridiculous name for anything except maybe an Eastern Bloc car model.

Now the Australian Open is a massive event and Australians become intensely interested in tennis for two weeks each year before going back to being indifferent. The event starts with the traditional bundling out of Sam Stosur, followed by all the Australians being knocked out, then Channel Seven fry an egg on an outside court to show how hot it is and then it's over and everyone turns their attention to their respective football season.

GOLDEN ERA

Australia dominated tennis in the fifties and sixties like no other nation. The great names are almost too many to mention but the top flight included Frank Sedgman, Lew Hoad, Ashley Cooper, Malcolm Anderson, Ken Rosewall, Margaret Court, John Newcombe, Tony Roche, Fred Stolle and Rod Laver.

Australians won so many grand slam tournaments during this period that you had to actually complete *the* grand slam, winning all four majors, to really stand out. Rod Laver managed to do this twice, in 1962 and 1969, the only person to have done so. Laver was arguably the greatest player of all time, so much so the major stadium at Melbourne Park (as Flinders Park is now known) is named after him. You often see him in the crowd during the Australian Open. Just a guy sitting in a stadium named after him.

As well as Laver dominating the men's, Margaret Court dominated women's tennis in the sixties and seventies, completing the grand slam in 1970 and compiling a list of victories that included winning the Australian Open eleven times, the French Open five times, the US Open five times and Wimbledon three times.

Since her retirement, she has become an independent Pentecostal minister who campaigns vigorously against homosexuality and marriage equality. She once got up at a prayer breakfast at Parliament House and yelled, 'Homosexuality is an abomination to the Lord! Abortion is an abomination to the Lord!' She sounds fun, doesn't she? In 2017, she announced she would avoid flying Qantas because they support marriage equality. She also said tennis is full of lesbians and said LGBT tendencies in young people were 'all the devil'.

It just goes to show that being amazing at sport doesn't make you a particularly nice or interesting person. She still has one of the main courts named after her at Melbourne Park, but then Australians also named a swimming pool after a prime minster who drowned.

DECLINE

By 1969 tennis was changing and Australia was not changing fast enough to keep up. The game was now fully professional and metal-frame rackets were being used, completely changing the game to a more power baseline style. John Newcombe was the last Australian man dominating the singles scene in the seventies, as the golden era of the fifties and sixties slipped away. In the women's, Evonne Goolagong Cawley would at least keep the torch burning a little longer, winning the Australian Open four times in a row from 1974 on, and winning the French Open once and Wimbledon twice.

But as the seventies made way for the eighties, it was clear Australia was no longer the world power it once was. It was harder for Australians to win the Australian Open because it featured professionals and had worthwhile prize money, which meant the best players attended. In fact, no Australian has won their home open since Mark Edmondson won the men's in 1976 and Goolagong

Cawley the women's in 1977. Any Australian who wins it now would be lauded as a hero, possibly even Nick Kyrgios.

Since the golden age, it's been pretty slim pickings. Pat Cash flew the flag in the eighties, winning Wimbledon, Pat Rafter won the US Open twice, in 1997 and '98, before becoming an underwear model, Lleyton Hewitt won the US Open in 2001 and Wimbledon in 2002, and Sam Stosur won the US Open in 2011. 'The Woodies' (Todd Woodbridge and Mark Woodforde) were the most successful tennis export of this whole period, winning eleven grand slams and an Olympic gold medal in their doubles career. Unfortunately doubles tennis is the poor cousin of singles tennis in most people's estimation.

Which brings us to the current miserable generation, mostly Nick Kyrgios and Bernard Tomic. Both display all the bad behaviour of John McEnroe but none of the fighting spirit, often giving up if it's too hot – like 27 degrees – or if not absolutely everything is going their way. They act like petulant children but their biggest sin, in Australians' eyes, is that they don't win. Win and Australians will forgive almost anything.

Kyrgios and Tomic have lead us to a place where Australia's favourite tennis players aren't Australian. Worse, they've left such a bad impression on the Australian public that people now think they like Lleyton Hewitt.

The decline in Australian tennis has also meant that once premier events like the Davis Cup and Federation Cup get little attention from the sporting public. That's a real shame. Once Australia strode across the tennis world like a colossus and now we are more like a group of teenage schoolboys hanging out at the train station and sniggering.

GOLF

It's been said that golf is a good walk spoiled and, when you think about it, a walk is a good lie on the couch ruined. I don't know where that leaves us but there's no doubt Australians took to golf with more positivity than that oft-quoted saying. First played in Tasmania in the 1820s – arguably the last time that state was ahead of its time – golf quickly caught on. After all, one thing Australia had at the time was plenty of space; just misplace the Indigenous population living there and you had a golf course.

There is some disagreement over where and when the first golf club was started, with Royal Melbourne Golf Club claiming to be the oldest 'without interruption', which sounds like something a marketing manager would come up with. The Australian Golf Club in Sydney also claims to be the oldest, but they had to move courses at one point and it's uncertain if they played in the years in between. Unless you are massively into golf you probably don't care which one is older, but the people involved do. In fact, they take this kind of thing very seriously, a trait that seems to be common amongst golfers.

In 1898, the Royal Melbourne Golf Club held a meeting where it was decided to set up the Australian Golf Union (AGU) to control the rules of the game, the regulations for amateur status, course ratings and handicapping across Australia. The first clubs to be members were Royal Melbourne, Royal Sydney and Royal Adelaide. Eventually other states had delegates on the AGU committee too.

Not long after that, in 1911, the Professional Golfers Association of Australia (the PGA) was founded after the Australia Open was held at Royal Sydney Golf Club. Golfers at the tournament felt they were very poorly treated and decided to form a union, but because it had rich people in it too, it called itself an association because it sounds classier.*

The women were getting organised too, because they were actually allowed to play golf back then, unlike almost every other sport. Each state formed a Ladies Golf Union but the men's Australian Golf Union (AGU) co-ordinated all national events. Of course, having men organise anything is a nightmare, so in 1921, the Australians Ladies Golf Union (ALGU) was formed as the national body (later to be named Women's Golf Australia).

The AGU and the ALGU organisations were separate for a long time but there was pressure to merge the two bodies, so that there would be a single administration responsible for co-ordinating golf in Australia. Entrenched interests kept preventing this from happening, mainly because Victoria and New South Wales refused to accept an independent board. What is it with those two? Other states must roll their eyes at meetings as if to say, 'Here we go again.'

The Australian Sports Commission had to step in and basically threaten to pull government funding for the sport if they didn't merge, pretty much what happened with Soccer Australia after the Crawford Report. This merger, in 2006, was another shotgun

---

* A women's version was formed in 1972, the Ladies Professional Golf Association of Australia (LPGAA). It was renamed the Australian Ladies Professional Golf (ALPG) in 1991 and is still the peak member organisation for women's golf.

marriage in the sporting industry. The two became the cleverly named Golf Australia, which is now recognised by the federal government as the national sporting organisation and governing body for golf. So now we have Golf Australia as the governing body, the PGA representing professional male golfers and the ALPG representing the professional women. Simple. Sort of.

The obsession Australians have with golf, the easy and relatively affordable access to courses and the well organised training and support has seen us churn out top-level golfers on a regular basis in both men's and women's competitions.

Jan Stephenson was the first Australian woman to succeed overseas, winning three majors. In 2003, she said 'Asians are killing the [LPGA] Tour', which surprisingly didn't go down well, particularly in Asia. Her problem seemed to be players from Asia were winning too often, which, in fairness to them, is the entire point of the competition. She later said she 'did not to intend to make it a racial issue'. Well of course not, another statement that could so easily be misinterpreted. Personally, whether I'm watching a white, black, Asian or Hispanic golfer, it makes no difference to me, I can nod off to sleep to any of them.

The next great Australian female golfer was Karrie Webb, who to my knowledge holds no firm public views on golfing Asians. Karrie is one of the greatest golfers of all time, at 26 becoming the youngest woman to ever win a career grand slam. On top of that she led the LPGA in prize money in her very first year in the tour. Webb was such a dominant force that she was voted into the Golf Hall of Fame while still in her twenties. I mean, what do you do after that? Most people would take up golf.

In the men's, it's hard to go past Peter Thomson and Greg Norman when you're talking about homegrown champions. Thomson was a star of the fifties, winning the Open Championship in 1954, 1955, 1956, 1958 and 1965. He also had a highly successful career on

GOLF SLANG

19th hole: The bar at the course you go to after playing the eighteen holes. Drinking in the bar afterwards is the main reason people play golf.

Golf cart: An electric cart that golfers drive around the course so they don't have to walk, aka the only fun bit of golf.

Aerosol: A player who can never aim their shots consistently, as in they 'spray' the ball.

Fore: This is what you yell if a ball is in danger of hitting someone. I once set a course record for players hit, with fourteen. Worst bit was it was at a mini-golf course.

the Senior PGA Tour, proving that if you're going to force your kid into a sport, golf is both lucrative and long lasting. Just don't expect them to still love you or to be well adjusted people after you make them hit golf balls throughout their youth rather than letting them have fun with their friends.

Thomson had great business success designing golf courses, but it was Greg Norman who combined sport and business to create a golfing and money-making success story few can match. Because he was tanned and blond, and most other golfers look like a dad picking their kid up from Saturday school sport, Norman was a huge drawcard and a marketing dream. It also helped that, on top of this, he was really good at golf. So good in fact he was number one in the world for 331 weeks. In that time he won ninety-one tournaments, twenty of them on the PGA and two majors.

Despite all this success, in Australia Norman is seen as a choker. He often failed at the very last minute in the big tournaments, when the pressure was on. This shows what harsh judges Australians are, but there is also a good body of evidence to support the claim. At the 1986 Masters, he missed a putt for par on the 18th that would have sent him into a playoff with Jack Nicklaus. In the same year, at the US Open, he failed on the final day despite leading at the start, shooting 75 and finishing six strokes behind the winner. He again led on the final day of the 1986 PGA Championship but shot 76, finishing two strokes behind the winner.

Even more heartbreak was to come. At the 1987 Masters he had a birdie putt to win the tournament but missed it, sending him into a three-way playoff, which he lost. The winner, Larry Mize, pulled a 47-yard chip shot out of nowhere to win. At the 1989 Masters he had a putt that would have got him into a playoff but missed. At the 1989 Open Championship he played a final round 64, at one point sinking six birdies in a row, only to then lose in a playoff. In 1996, Norman led the Masters by six strokes on the final day, only to shoot a 78 to lose by five strokes. Basically, Greg Norman is my love life expressed in golf.

It's sad so many Australians remember him only as a choker. It probably didn't help that he was nicknamed 'The Shark' despite his lack of killer instinct. But he only needed a few of those moments to go his way and he'd be considered an unquestionable great. It goes to show that, in sports, performing when it matters is seen as the most-prized attribute, no matter what else you do.

In business, Norman had no such problems, his Great White Shark Enterprises has businesses covering golf-course design, clothing, winemaking, real estate, sunglasses, a restaurant, a line of Wagyu steaks and a wakeboarding park.*

Today, golf in Australia is still producing first-class golfers, like Adam Scott and Jason Day, who are not only nice people but also win things. They serve as a constant reminder of how bad our tennis players are.

---

* Shark Wake Park describes itself as having 'a commitment to bringing wakeboarding to the masses'. A noble cause. Thank you for your service, Shark Wake Park.

CYCLING

It's worth remembering that cycling is not just something you do when you lose your driver's licence, it's a sport with a long and proud history in this country. Personally, though, getting dressed up in lycra and surrounding myself with a bunch of other blokes in lycra sounds like hell on earth. Let's just say I can understand why they are all taking drugs.

Despite the relatively recent craze of middle-aged men getting kitted out on a Sunday morning like they're about to cross the Alps, cycling in Australia goes back all the way to 1875, when penny-farthing bikes were imported into the colonies. Cycling became a popular sport, limited only by the cost of a bike, which was too high for widespread use.

It was the invention of the safety bike, a bike like today's models, that enabled the sport to take a huge step forward. These new bikes were cheaper and also had a chain to drive them, meaning the rider didn't have to sit up above the drive wheel. This was much safer; a penny-farthing tends to kill you if you fall off it at speed, a serious design flaw.

The Austral Wheel Race began in 1887 at the MCG and attracted great crowds. A similar race at the SCG, the Sydney Thousand, was first contested in 1903. Cycling was incredibly popular at the time and the huge interest attracted a lot of betting and a lot of corruption. In 1901, there were accusations of corruption regarding the Austral, with John Wren of horseracing fame accused of fixing the race.* In 1904, The Sydney Thousand saw seven riders disqualified from the sport for colluding to block the favourite. These and other cycling scandals were one of the key reasons sports betting was banned in Australia around this time, except on horseracing.

Regardless of the scandals, cycling remained popular. Australians created a flourishing bike manufacturing industry built around the Speedwell and Malvern Star brands until, like all manufacturing in this country, it was shipped off overseas. The Malvern Star brand did very well by attaching itself to a seventeen-year-old cyclist by the name of Hubert Opperman. 'Oppy' became one of Australia's greatest ever cyclists. He won the Bol d'Or in Paris and the Paris–Brest–Paris 1166-kilometre road race. Famous not just in Australia, he boosted both cycling and Malvern Star's fortunes.

Cycling increasingly came under the sway of the Olympics in Australia, and diversified into BMX and mountain bikes. Cadel Evans won two world championships in mountain biking, also representing Australia in the Olympics in the sport, before deciding to give road racing a try. This proved to be a rather clever move. Evans was so good he even matched it with the drug-addled riders he was competing with, despite riding clean on account of his pesky morals.

Fellow Australian Robbie McEwen had done well at the Tour de France, winning the points classification (the green jersey) three times in the 2000s, but Cadel Evans went one better by winning the general classification (the yellow jersey) in 2011. It took him 86 hours to ride the course. Imagine riding a bike for 86 hours, even over three weeks. I'm sore just thinking about it. The victory made

---

* At the time, there didn't seem to be a sport Wren wasn't fixing. In fact, while he was on the scene, all sport in Australia may have been as scripted as WWE.

Evans a household name and raised him to Australian legend status, which only winning can bring.

Today, cycling is more popular than ever, with people staying up all night in Australia to watch the Tour de France. You know the type: they act like staying up late watching TV is some testament to their character, and the next day at work they tell you a million times that they're a bit tired. Like staying up watching TV to the point you can't do your job is somehow heroic. I often stay awake all night thinking about the many regrets I have but you don't see me crowing about it the next day.

Cycling's main problem is that almost all of them are massive cheats. While doping has been rife in the sport for a long time, more recently race co-ordinators have found bikes with tiny motors in them to give the competitors a boost. It makes you wonder what the point of it all is really.

NETBALL

The story goes that netball came about because women in 1890s England struggled to play basketball while wearing long skirts, so the rules were adjusted accordingly and netball, also known as ladies' basketball, was invented. You might wonder if it wouldn't have been easier to just change what they were wearing, but men back then had a fit if they caught sight of a woman's ankle. It's not known what seeing a calf would have done but it wouldn't have been good.

Netball spread across the Commonwealth and arrived in Australia around the turn of the century. Australians called it 'women's basketball' until 1970, but it got too confusing because women were also playing actual basketball.

The game caught on here, mainly because it was one of the few team sports women were allowed to play. The fact that it was so different from men's basketball meant it slipped through relatively unnoticed by men, who usually went to great pains to prevent women playing sports. In 1927, the All Australia Women's Basketball Association* was formed to administer the game. Australia and

---

* In 1970, it changed its name to the All Australia Netball Association, and in 1993 became Netball Australia, which remains the governing body to this day.

New Zealand played the first ever international game of netball in 1938 but the sport was a mess internationally, with each country playing to slightly different rules. Australia played seven-a-side and New Zealand played nine-a-side, and they had to compromise. This was hardly ideal and in the fifties attempts were made to come up with standard rules, before the International Federation of Women's Basketball and Netball Associations was established in 1960.

It was also decided a world championship would be established, to be played every four years. This is why I like netball: Australia has won ten of the thirteen tournaments ever played, an incredible result, although I'm still not happy about the three we didn't win. In that time, the top-class Australian players have dominated the sport. Anne Sargeant, Bianca Chatfield, Liz Ellis, Sharelle McMahon and Vicki Wilson would be in anyone's top ten list of the world's greatest netballers.

Domestically, there have been numerous attempts at a national netball competition over the years, but they've struggled to gain support from TV networks and sponsors. The first attempt at a national league was in 1985, the top teams in each state playing off in the Esso Superleague. By 1997, it was decided the competition needed a significant rethink. New teams were created, with the aim of attracting new fans and sponsors, and creating a truly national competition. The Commonwealth Bank signed on as the naming rights sponsor and in 1997 the Commonwealth Bank Trophy began. It was a success overall, with more sponsors coming on board and bigger crowds, but women's sport still got little coverage so making any money was hard.

In 2008, administrators decided to move to a trans-Tasman league, the ANZ Championship. In the early stages that was a huge boost – for the first time the sport was semi-professional. But the ANZ Championship had one central flaw: the Australian teams were a lot better than the New Zealand ones. The competition was uneven and limited the number of Australian players who could get top-level games; to accommodate the New Zealanders, there were fewer Australian netball teams than the talent pool demanded.

The Australians finally decided to kick out the New Zealanders, forming the Suncorp Super League, which began in 2017. That included a new TV deal with Channel Nine that will run for five-years and includes revenue sharing, which should generate higher salaries. AFL and NRL clubs have also gotten involved, with licences awarded to the Melbourne Storm, Collingwood Football Club and Greater Western Giants. It seems that finally, netball may be close to becoming a fully professional sport – long overdue.

NETBALL TERMS

Controlling umpire: The umpire in whose half of the court play is happening; not an umpire who uses guilt to control those around them.

Mixed netball: When women and men play together. Men join in the hope of meeting women, then become competitive jerks.

Stepping: A player with the ball is not allowed to take more than 1.5 steps, meaning they must stop quickly when receiving the ball, a wonderful recipe for knee and ankle injuries.

Two-handed pass: A pass that, surprisingly, is done with two hands. Not to be confused with the one-handed pass, which involves 50 per cent fewer hands.

BOXING

Boxing arrived in Australia with the English but, in reality, it was probably already here. People throwing punches at each other seems to be a language that crosses all cultures. Seeing two blokes belting each other is hardly a rare occurrence, although it's not necessarily always in a sporting context.

In the early days, boxing was incredibly brutal, because it was bare fisted. Boxing gloves were introduced in 1884 and the sport started to be seen in a slightly better light.

A lot of boxing's history has been about trying to avoid being banned or shut down by police. The brutal nature of the sport was part of the problem, but so were a lot of the promotions surrounding it. For instance, in the twenties, a group of boys wanting to box would be put in a ring with gloves on and a bag over their heads. As soon as the bell rang they would punch away blindly, often resulting in severe knockouts as they couldn't defend themselves, all for the amusement of the crowd. Nowadays this sort of good clean fun is banned because we live in a nanny state.

Australia's first world champion was 'Young Griffo', real name Albert Griffiths, who won the world featherweight championship at the White Horse Hotel in Sydney on 2 September 1890. His boxing career took him over to America, where he spent his time drinking, fighting, then drinking again. A chronic alcoholic, Young Griffo was regularly arrested, but he would make bail and then fight again.

The boxing world really started to focus on Australia in 1908, when the world heavyweight champion, Canadian boxer Tommy Burns, was convinced to cross the 'colour line' and fight a black boxer. The interest was immense, as white boxing fans around the world predicted Burns would make short work of the challenger, African-American Jack Johnson. The fight was held in Sydney on Boxing Day 1908. A crowd of 20 000 showed up after a promotional campaign built around racist portrayals of Johnson.

The fight lasted fourteen rounds, but it was fourteen rounds of Johnson just pulverising Burns. Eventually the fight was stopped by the police. The reason given was that Burns had a broken jaw, but it seemed to also be about stopping the crowd getting out of hand while watching a white boxer cop a beating at the hands of a black man. Luckily, white boxing fans have now gotten really used to a black boxer beating up a white boxer, to the point where they don't even notice anymore, which is kind of progress, I guess. The result of the 1908 bout meant Johnson was the first black heavyweight champion of the world.

Around this time, tent boxing became popular, with troupes touring the country from town to town and staging bouts. Tent boxing was one of the few ways for Indigenous people to make a living at the time. Boxing tents would show up in a town and throw open the challenge to members of the public, with no weight divisions. There were often no ropes and the fights could be brutal.

Jimmy Sharman's Boxing Troupe was the most famous and travelled the agricultural show circuit. Tent boxing was incredibly popular and continued until 1971, when new laws meant boxers could only fight once a week, making most of the troupes economically unviable. It's amazing to think these guys were often fighting several times a week, given what we know now about concussion and its effects on the brain. In many states of Australia tent boxing has been banned, although Queensland and the Northern Territory still allow it.

Boxing was incredibly popular in Australia by the middle of the twentieth century, with big crowds and big stars. There was none bigger than Lionel Rose, an Aboriginal boxer who began his professional career at sixteen. Two years later, he was the Australian bantamweight champion. In 1968, at age twenty, Rose fought his most famous fight, against Fighting Harada, at Tokyo's Nippon Budokan hall. It was broadcast into Australia over the radio, commentator Ron Casey calling it, and the fifteen-round bout made Lionel a national hero as he became the first Indigenous Australian to hold a world title.

Boxing was so popular that 100 000 people showed up to the Melbourne Town Hall to welcome him home. This popularity didn't escape Channel 0's owner Reg Ansett, who wanted to ensure viewers had TVs that could receive the UHF signal his channel was broadcast on. He decided a Rose fight might entice them to get one and organised Rose to fight Welshman Alan Rudkin in 1969. To give you an idea of the success of this scheme: it was the highest rating

BOXING TERMS

Cutman: A person whose job it is to manage cuts in between rounds, so the boxer can keep going. I prefer having a job that doesn't require someone to patch me up every few minutes so I can keep getting hit in the head.

Rabbit Punch: An illegal punch to the back of the head, named after the way people used to kill rabbits. At least that's what HR told me when they let me go.

Palooka: An old term for a clumsy and uneducated boxer. In life, I consider myself a palooka.

sports program until the opening ceremony of the Sydney Olympics in 2000, attracting 70 per cent of the viewing audience.

While Rose was dominating the scene, another great Australian boxer, Johnny Famechon, emerged, making this truly the golden era of boxing in Australia. Famechon famously never fought as an amateur, and rose to the top of the heap in 1969 when he beat Cuban José Legrá for the world featherweight title at Albert Hall in London. The victory meant both Rose and Famechon held world titles at the same time, although Rose lost his months later.

Australians were winning world titles, but boxing was also becoming a staple of TV back home, with Channel Seven's *TV Ringside* debuting in 1966 with Ron Casey commentating. It was a big hit as the whole family could gather round and watch two blokes beat the living suitcases out of each other. It ran until 1975 but, with Rose and Famechon retired, boxing started to decline in Australia as a mainstream sport. The advent of TV had caused live audiences to decline significantly and former boxing venues like Festival Hall in Melbourne now made their money from bringing out music acts.

Boxing's disappearance from free-to-air TV led to an increased reliance on pay-per-view and pay TV. This was lucrative for some cards, but made it a fringe sport for many Australians. Governments were also paying more and more attention to boxing's health and safety issues, meaning tighter regulations. But boxing still had a large following, and Jeff Fenech kept the sport relevant in the eighties. Fenech won world titles in three weight divisions and was so famous he once received a pre-bout phone call from Prime Minister Bob Hawke to wish him luck. Fenech's popularity went through the roof when he famously said after a fight, 'I love youse all [. . .] With 12 000 of the most beautifullest people in the world cheering me on, it's hard to feel pain.'

Fenech was one of those boxers who didn't know when to walk away, fighting his long-time nemesis, Azumah Nelson, in 2008.

Fenech was forty-three and Nelson forty-nine. Fenech won, but the sight of a 43-year-old belting a 49-year-old was a good indicator of the malaise that had descended on boxing.

Post-boxing, Fenech's reputation was marred by controversy. In 2004, he was stabbed in a brawl with four men, and later that year his home was shot at. Police believed the events were linked and investigated whether some of the men who attacked Fenech had gang affiliations. Fenech also plead guilty to stealing three gold watches from a store in 2005. More recently, Fenech admitted to lending gambling identity Eddie Hayson nearly $5 million, money he was still owed at the time. Fenech said he expected to get the money back after Hayson sold the brothel Stiletto, which never eventuated.

Incidents like this have damaged the love affair Australians once had with Fenech. He has lashed out, saying, 'I hate the way we are as Australians, we are just a jealous, sick race of people who do not want to give credit when others have done something good. Jealousy is worse than cancer, jealousy is worse than AIDS, jealousy is the worst thing in the world.'

Now, I'm no doctor, but I don't think jealousy is worse than AIDS or cancer. Last I checked, jealousy hadn't killed hundreds of millions of people, and anyway we all know that the worst thing in the world is pineapple on pizza.

The decline in Australian boxing meant we had to import champions. Russian boxer Kostya Tszyu emigrated to Australia in 1992, and at twenty-three he was already an accomplished amateur boxer. Upon turning professional, he won the light welterweight title twice. He became the first person in thirty years to unify the International Boxing Federation title and the World Boxing Association belt.*

---

* Boxing has more belts and more organisations than it has regulatory issues. They all kind of blur into one for me because, like the Kardashians, telling the difference between them is neither useful nor worth the effort.

Tszyu was the last of Australia's great boxers – even if he was from the Soviet Union – and since then, boxing has fallen into an almost laughable place where Danny Green and Anthony Mundine just fight each other endlessly. No one outside the boxing fraternity cares.

The best hope is Queenslander Jeff Horn, who defeated World Boxing Organisation welterweight champion Manny Pacquiao on 23 April 2017. Horn's points-decision victory upset the American media so much they demanded an independent recount, which confirmed the original result. Defeating a boxing legend and annoying the United States makes Horn even more of a legend in Australians' eyes. Before taking up boxing, he was a school teacher. That may explain his success. Spending time looking after children would give you a lot of anger to channel.

Not only is boxing in trouble because of medical concerns about the sport, it's under threat from mixed martial arts, with the highly popular UFC now seen as the prestige contact-sports brand. There is no doubt that, in Australia, boxing is close to being out on its feet. But you can never count out the sweet science. Two blokes punching each other is still incredibly popular if Australia's late-night crime stats are anything to go by.

SAILING

Australians have an affinity with the sea, probably due to being girt by it. Most Australians just swim in it, but the rich sail yachts on it, and it's given Australians two important things: the 1983 America's Cup and the annual Sydney to Hobart race.

Today, the whole nation getting excited about a boat race seems odd, but back then they didn't have pay TV or PlayStations or even UberEATS. In fact, in those days, if something got on TV it was almost guaranteed everyone would watch it.

In 1851 the US built and crewed *America* beat fifteen English yachts in a race, with the victor's cup named in its honour and held by the New York Yacht Club. Since 1876 the cup has been decided in a duel between two yachts only, over a series of races, and is won by the Americans every single time.

In 1983, the Royal Perth Yacht Club put forward a challenger, *Australia II*, owned by businessman Alan Bond and designed by Ben Lexcen. It had a new winged keel that caused the Americans to accuse the Australians of cheating before racing even started. Yet the yacht was declared legal and allowed to race, making the final against the Americans relatively easily. The US won the first two races before the Australians won the third. The American boat

Liberty won the fourth before *Australia II* won the fifth and sixth, setting up the first ever seventh race to decide the Cup.

The final race was telecast live in Australia just before dawn on 27 September 1983, which meant everyone had to stay up drinking all night. Luckily, most of us had been practicing all our lives for just such a moment. Australians had no idea about the sport or the event itself, what they knew was that Australia were in it and we were the underdogs – our two favourite things. In a tight race, it seemed the Americans had built up an unassailable lead, but the Australians started to tactically outmanoeuvre the Americans, and *Australia II* crossed the line ahead of *Liberty*. The euphoria poured out across the country. It was a major moment in our history. We had beaten the Americans at something no one else could. It was the first time the Americans had lost the cup in 132 years; in terms of time, it had been the longest winning streak in the history of sports.

Such were the celebrations that when asked if he would declare the day a public holiday, Prime Minister Bob Hawke, dressed in a colourful Australia jacket, said, 'Any boss who sacks a worker for not turning up today is a bum.'

The victory also shot to prominence the green and gold boxing kangaroo flag, which flew on *Australia II*. The Boxing Kangaroo has become a symbol of Australian sporting prowess, even if its history is not exactly the stuff of folktales. Like the yacht, the image was owned by Alan Bond, who licensed it for merchandise and tried to make as much money from it as possible. When Bond's significant dodgy business activities emerged and he had to sell off everything he owned, he sold the licence to the Australian Olympic Committee in 1993. The AOC elevated it to the position of official mascot of the Olympic team, replacing the now long-forgotten 'Willy the Koala'.*

---

* Willy now lives in a nursing home on the Sapphire Coast. His family visit him occasionally, but more out of a sense of duty than anything else. He is a bitter mascot and, in the time I spent with him, he drank heavily and made several physical threats towards the Boxing Kangaroo.

That means Boxing Kangaroo is now controlled by marketers, who say this about 'BK', as they call him: 'BK is not a lout, nor is he aggressive or arrogant. He is, however, assertive when it comes to defending his country's glory.'

What a load of nonsense. This commercialisation of an icon was one of the reasons Roy and H. G. Nelson's alternate mascot for the Sydney 2000 games, Fatso the Fat-Arsed Wombat, the battlers' prince, was so popular.

After the glory-soaked sailing days of 1983, the Australians failed to defend the America's Cup. Interest in the event declined to the point that most Australians don't have a clue if it still exists. But that moment in 1983 is forever part of Australian culture.

While the America's Cup was a one-off, the Sydney to Hobart race has been an institution since 1945. There is nothing more Australian than briefly flicking over from the Boxing Day Test to see the start of the Sydney to Hobart race, just to see if one of those spectator boats accidentally collides with one of the competitors.

The Sydney to Hobart is one of the toughest yacht races in the world, and not just because the cost of these boats is ridiculous. Bass Strait is one of the most treacherous bits of ocean in the world, so getting in a relatively small boat and sailing all the way across it is courageous, especially as we have now invented planes and discount flights.

To compete in the Sydney to Hobart is to put your body through one of the toughest tests in the world. Sailing 1170 kilometres is not easy at the best of times, but to do it in freezing and dangerous waters is madness. In 1998, the fleet was hit by a massive storm, resulting in five boats sinking and six people dying. Only forty-four of the 115 boats that set out from Sydney made it.

Surprisingly, though, people still do it.

BASKETBALL

Basketball has the honour of being one of the worst run sports in Australia, even giving soccer a real run for its (scant) money. The sport was first played in Australia in 1897 in Adelaide, but it took thirty years for a state association to be established, which happened in Victoria in 1930. In 1939, the Australian Basketball Federation was set up but, for much of the early twentieth century, basketball was a fringe sport with little impact on the broader Australian sporting landscape.

As a completely amateur sport, it grew slowly. The sport didn't get enough traction to move beyond local leagues until 1979, when the National Basketball League (NBL) was established. The league's main purpose seemed to be changing participating teams as often as humanly possible. In its history, over thirty teams have either gone broke, merged or shut down. One franchise collapse can be explained away, thirty starts to look careless. Clubs like the Bankstown Bruins, the Coburg Giants, the Devonport Warriors, the City of Sydney Astronauts, the Launceston Casino City Tigers, the Eastside Melbourne Spectres and the West Adelaide Bearcats all came and went.

IT'S ALL IN THE NAME

Gold Coast Rollers (NBL)

This basketball team entered the league in 1990 as the Gold Coast Cougars (those native American cats are all over the Gold Coast). In just two years, they would be renamed the Rollers, slang for waves, to reflect surf culture.

That should have been a clue: the Gold Coast tends to swallow sport teams beacuse everyone prefers to be at the beach. Lo and behold, the Rollers were broke and out of the league by 1996.

The Women's National Basketball League (WNBL) was formed in 1981. Basketball certainly benefited from the fact it had no state-based baggage like the footy codes, so making the move to national competitions came easily.

In the eighties, basketball boomed in Australia, off the back of the US National Basketball Association (NBA), with stars like Larry Bird and Magic Johnson boosting the sport's profile. Michael Jordan took it to a whole new level in the nineties, and in that decade, the NBL was the fastest growing league in Australia. There were sell-out crowds, TV deals, and sponsors were coming on board. It was pitched to families, with music, mascots and cheerleaders all giving an 'entertainment' feel to the sport. Players like Andrew Gaze and Shane Heal became household names and their Olympic exploits, playing for the Boomers, further increased the sport's reach.

Yet it was all built on a lot of hype and the NBL overreached, failing to manage the sport for long-term growth. Clubs lost money, ratings started to decline and sponsors left. By 1998, the NBL competition moved to the summer., to avoid competing against the football codes. This didn't help, and by 2007 the NBL was in crisis. It was out of money and teams were collapsing at a distressing rate, even for the NBL. Strangely, this was happening at a time when junior participation was still good. In the last decade or so Australia has produced top talent like Andrew Bogut, Lauren Jackson, Patrick Mills and Matthew Dellavedova.

Domestically the sport's problem was mainly bad governance. The NBL was run badly from both a financial standpoint and in terms of managing the game's various stakeholders. Something had to change and it did. In 2015, the owner of the Melbourne franchise (now called Melbourne United), Larry Kestelman, announced he was buying the whole league for $7 million. One team owner buying the whole league was an unprecedented move in Australian sport, and not everyone was happy about it. But the other owners had no choice: they were broke and no one else was waving $7 million at them.

Since taking control, Kestelman has secured a TV rights deal, attracted new sponsors and boosted crowds. Kestelman has a clear vision – like Frank Lowy had for soccer – and he has the power to push it through. How long that remains a viable approach is yet to be seen but there's no doubt the league seems to be recovering.

Australia is still producing stars. Ben Simmons from Melbourne was drafted at number one in the 2016 NBA Draft, with Sudanese-born Australian Thon Maker picked tenth in the same draft. The question is, can the NBL stop the revolving door of teams, build a sustainable base of support and sponsors, and regain the popularity of the nineties? It's possible, but it won't be easy. The summer slot, once in decline as cricket stagnated, is now more competitive than ever, with the Big Bash League dominating, the A-League achieving a higher profile than the NSL ever did, and other new arrivals like the netball Super League and the AFLW.

MOTORSPORTS

A motorsport is less a sport and more an addiction – an addiction to speed (and not the sort of speed I used to write this entire book in a mere 37 hours). You have to be a bit addicted to go around a track at crazy speeds and risk life and limb on a regular basis.

Consider motorcycle champion Mick Doohan. In 1992, he had a crash that resulted in spiral fractures of both his tibia and fibula, followed by a botched operation that cut the blood supply to his leg, leading to gangrene. It was only when he left that hospital to seek treatment elsewhere that his leg was saved. Now, if that were me, I'd have moved on to a safer sport like 'never leaving the house again'. Not our Mick though. He came back in the same season in an attempt to maintain his lead in the world championship. It didn't work, but just getting back on the bike was an act of super-human mental strength. His next season ended early too, when he broke his collarbone. I would have taken this as a second sign the universe did not want me to race motorcycles. But these athletes are addicted and Doohan returned the following season, winning the 1994 championship. He won five championships in a row.*

---

* As well as hosting the Australian MotoGP, we churn out top riders at a high rate and Doohan became part of a proud tradition of motorcycle racing in Australia. Casey Stoner won the MotoGP championship twice and Wayne Gardner won the world championship in 1987.

Australian motorsport has a long history, going back to the turn of the twentieth century. Early on, only the very wealthy could afford to own a car, let alone race one. The first recorded race was held in 1904 at Sandown in Victoria and featured a top speed of 41.8 km/h, meaning the race could have been held in a school speed zone.

Motorsport grew alongside the expanding automobile industry and, after World War I, it really took off. The first Australian Grand Prix was held on Phillip Island in 1928 and has been run every year since, except for 1936 and during World War II. In 1985, the race became part of the Formula One world championship, and was held in Adelaide for a decade before the Victorians pinched it. South Australians are used to things fleeing to other states but usually it's just their young people, and they took this personally.

Two Australians have won the Formula One drivers' championship: Jack Brabham, who won it three times, and Alan Jones. Brabham was a true legend of motorsport who, as well as being a champion driver, was a great engineer, designing and building race cars. Early on, Brabham just built cars, saying he thought the drivers 'were all lunatics'. However, once he started, he was addicted. He is not just the greatest driver Australia has produced but arguably one of the best the world has ever seen.

Since Brabham, fourteen Australians have raced in Formula One. Jones is the only other driver to win the championship, while Mark Webber has competed in the most F1 races. Currently, Daniel Ricciardo is the only Australian in the F1 championship.

While Formula One is the peak of motorsport, in Australia the crown jewel is the Bathurst 1000. It's held on Mount Panorama, the holiest site in Australia for motorsport fans. Technically it's a street circuit but, being on a mountain, it presents significant challenges – there's a 174 metre difference between the track's highest and lowest point. Cars reach 300 km/h on the downhill Conrod straight, which is significantly more than you can do in a school speed zone.

The steepness of the track and the bends make the 1000-kilometre endurance race one of the toughest in the world. It started in 1960 on Phillip Island before moving to Bathurst in 1963. Local manufacturers started to get involved in the race during the sixties, leading to the Ford, Holden and Chrysler battles that would define motor racing in Australia. Petrolheads dreamt of cars like the Falcon GT, the Monaro, the Torana and the Charger for years to come. Even when I see one in the street today, my testosterone peaks and I start grunting appreciatively. At that point, someone usually calls the police.

In 1969, a young driver by the name of Peter Brock tried his hand at defeating Mount Panorama. It was the beginning of a stunning career; Brock won the Bathurst 1000 nine times. How good was Brock? Well, Australians bestowed on him not one but three nicknames, the highest honour imaginable. On top of the regulation 'Brocky', he was also called 'Peter Perfect' and 'The King of the Mountain'.

After retiring from full-time professional racing, Brock continued to race in various forms. He tragically passed away following a crash in the Targa West rally in 2006, in Western Australia. It was a dark day, the death of a true icon of Australian sport.

In 1973, Chrysler left racing, leaving the rivalry to Holden and Ford. You were one or the other, you couldn't like both. I mean you could, but it was like going around telling everyone you were Judas.

As well as being tribal, motorsports fans can be brutal. In the 1992 Bathurst 1000, the race was ended early due to heavy rain. Jim Richards and co-driver Mark Skaife were awarded first place despite crashing out – the race result having been wound back to before everyone started crashing, when they were in the lead. The crowd booed Richards and Skaife on the podium. Richards gave a famous speech: 'I'm just really stunned for words, I can't believe the reception. I thought Australian race fans had a lot more to go than this, this is bloody disgraceful. I'll keep racing but I tell you what, this is going to remain with me for a long time, you're a pack of arseholes.' Calling them 'a pack of arseholes' seemed to endear Richards to racing fans again, which in turn shows that they really are a different breed.

The Bathurst 1000 is now part of the Supercars Championship, the premium touring car series in Australia, which is a hundred-million-dollar business. It's now a tradition for people to sit down and watch the entire Bathurst 1000, the long race being a great excuse to do nothing. Of course, it's exciting viewing in itself, but it's even more fun to see how Channel Seven can cram 15 hours of ads into a race that goes for less than seven.

Between the MotoGP, the Formula One Grand Prix and the Supercars Championship, Australia is paradise on earth for the motoring enthusiast.

THE FINAL SIREN

This book is hardly meant to cover every single event in Australian sporting history. I've probably underrepresented that game you play on the beach with a tennis ball and velcro paddles, for example. It's not trying to paint Australian sport as pure, either. I mean, that section on racism was a real downer, wasn't it?

What I hope it demonstrates is how sport has shaped whole industries, our media, our dynamic, bloodsucking gambling industry, and where a large amount of taxpayer dollars go. And because of that, you should appreciate that sport is important – gloriously stupid, but important. As well as giving us something to watch on our big flat-screen TVs, it's helped our nation take some tentative steps towards having a culture. It has been the thread that unites us, cutting across race, gender, economic status and even star signs.

Sport has helped shape our national culture, both the one we like to think we have and the one we actually have. For every tale of mateship, there is one of gross administrative incompetence, salary cap cheating and supplements programs. For every inspiring story of resilience, there are several hundred tales of public urination. And for a country that likes to think we don't take ourselves too seriously, it's a bit bizarre that we're deadly serious about being the best at chasing a ball or running really fast. Sport is important to us simply because we all believe it's important, despite the fact that at its core it's just about playing basic games.

So why does Australia punch above its weight in the sporting arena? If there's one thing this book proves, it's because we are better than other countries. Resting in the heart of every underdog-loving Australian is Rod Laver's grace, Cathy Freeman's poise, Don Bradman's focus and Greg Norman's ability to choke at the worst moment.

In the end, sport captures the whole spectrum of human behaviour, from the steely determination of Mick Doohan to the slapstick ineptitude of the Fine Cotton scandal. And how can you not like something that makes a group of grown men think that painting a horse to rig a race is a great idea?

FURTHER READING

Behrent, Sue. *History of the Socceroos*. Melbourne, Penguin Books, 2011.

Bloomfield, John. *Australia's sporting success: the inside story*. Sydney, UNSW Press, 2004.

Bluestone Edge. *The Bluestone Review: A review of culture and leadership in Australian Olympic Swimming*. 2013.

Cashman, Richard, et al. (eds.). *Australian sport through time: the history of sport in Australia*. Sydney, Random House, 1997.

Chesterton, Ray. *100 years of Rugby League: a celebration of the greatest game of all*. Sydney, Hachette, 2007.

Haigh, Gideon. *The Cricket War: The inside story of Kerry Packer's World Series Cricket*. Melbourne University Press, 2007.

— *On Warne*. Melbourne, Penguin Books, 2012.

Headon, David John. *The best ever Australian sports writing: a 200-year collection*. Melbourne, Black Inc., 2001.

Jones, Alan, and Andrew Clarke. *AJ: How Alan Jones Climbed to the Top of Formula One*. Sydney, Random House, 2017.

Lomas, Gordon. *Kings of the Mountain*. Melbourne, Penguin Random House, 2017.

Mallett, Ashley. *Bradman's Band*. Brisbane, UQP, 2000.

—— *The black lords of summer: the story of the 1868 Aboriginal tour of England and beyond.* Brisbane, UQP, 2002.

—— *Thommo Speaks Out: The Authorised Biography of Jeff Thomson.* Sydney, Allen & Unwin, 2009.

Newsome, David. *Godliness and Good Learning.* London, John Murray, 1961.

Peacock, Adam. *That night: a decade on, the story of Australian football's greatest night.* Sydney, Random House, 2015.

Perry, Roland. *Miller's Luck: the life and loves of Keith Miller, Australia's greatest all-rounder.* Sydney, Random House, 2006.

Piesse, Ken. *The Ashes: an illustrated history of cricket's greatest rivalry.* Australia, Penguin Books, 2007.

Poke, Robin, and Kevin Berry. *Olympic gold: our greatest individual Olympians since 1896.* Sydney, Murdoch Books, 2012.

Ryan, Greg. *The Changing Face of Rugby: the union game and professionalism since 1995.* Newcastle (England), Cambridge Scholars Publishing, 2008.

Slattery, Geoff. *The Australian game of football: since 1858.* Melbourne, Geoff Slattery Publishing for the Australian Football League, 2008.

Twain, Mark. *The wayward tourist: Mark Twain's adventures in Australia.* Melbourne University Press, 2006.

Warren, Johnny. *Sheilas, wogs & poofters: an incomplete biography of Johnny Warren and soccer in Australia.* Sydney, Random House, 2003.

ACKNOWLEDGEMENTS

Writing a book is hard but not as hard as having an actual job.

Obviously I couldn't have written this book without the support of whiskey, but some people also helped.

Even more supportive than whiskey were Cressida, Antigone and Cillian Wall, who upon learning I was writing a book said they thought it 'wouldn't be a complete disaster' and vaguely promised to one day read it.

I must thank the Twomey family, who supported me even when all signs pointed to it being a fool's errand.

Andrea McNamara deserves a lot of credit for editing this book. She had to spend a lot of time talking to me, never a task anyone undertakes without financial compensation. Andrea has been the editor on some of the best Australian sports books ever written but for some reason she also did this one.

The team at Penguin Random House have been a delight to work with, although they often make me feel small due to their constant displays of professionalism. Nikki Christer, Ali Watts, Louise Ryan, Jake Davies, Johannes Jakob, Alex Ross, Louisa Maggio, Jackie Money and Kate Foley have not only put up with me, but pretended it wasn't a deeply unpleasant chore.

Lastly, I'd like to thank everyone who's read my stuff over the years. To discover there was an audience for these insane ramblings has been a constant source of delight.

Titus

A NOTE ON THE FRONT COVER IMAGE

The cover image is by the famed Hamburg printer Adolph Friedländer (1851–1904) who was well known for circus and lithographic sideshow posters featuring spectacle sports like lion wrestling and kangaroo boxing.

It goes to the heart of the Australian psyche that we have always loved sports so much that we tried to get our native animals involved. Later on we frowned on this sort of animal cruelty, but I've long argued you haven't lived unless you've been in hand-to-hand combat with a kangaroo.